POINT WELL MADE

Persuasive Oral Advocacy

SECOND EDITION

Praise for the Second Edition of Point Well Made

"There will be more justice in this world if lawyers and judges follow the Gospel according to Vaidik and Diaz-Bonilla. Congratulations on this terrific contribution to fine lawyering."

— Randall Shepard, former Chief Justice of the Indiana Supreme Court and former President of the National Conference of Chief Justices

"The new edition of *Point Well Made*: Persuasive Oral Advocacy is chock full of oral argument advice that will be useful to all, regardless of their level of experience, whether arguing to a trial court or on appeal. And the advice could not be more current, concluding with a section on the 'new normal' of remote oral advocacy. It took me many years of observing and presenting oral arguments to learn the valuable lessons that this book offers to its readers."

— Howard J. Bashman, Law Offices of Howard J. Bashman and author of the "*How Appealing*" blog

"The newly updated *Point Well Made's* fresh look at the age-old profession of advocacy is as entertaining as it is instructive. Written in a colorful, approachable style, it offers memorable maxims and contrasting examples of effective and ineffective presentations—both historic and recent—to illustrate the 'science' and 'art' of persuasion. Particularly timely and helpful are the concrete, practical tips regarding the new normal of remote arguments. The pointers about managing technology, staging, body language, dress, tone, and responsiveness should be in the back pocket of every remote litigator looking to win."

— Margaret D. McGaughey, former Appellate Chief of the United States Attorney's Office for the District of Maine

"*Point Well Made* provides, in an easy and fun read, the tools and insights for effective advocacy that will benefit the novice to the most experienced and proficient advocate. Judge Vaidik and Ms. Diaz-Bonilla provide a unique combination of remarkable skills that empower the advocate through a step-by-step 'how to' to deliver the best argument the advocate is capable of providing. I only wish that I had had the benefit of their wisdom years ago as I began to learn effective advocacy by experience. This is truly a must-read for anyone advocating for their client's position in an oral presentation."

— Garrard R. Beeney, Partner and Co-Head, Intellectual Property and Technology Group, Sullivan & Cromwell LLP

"*Point Well Made* should be required reading from cover to cover at the start of a case—it encourages the reader to remember to look for, and at, the entire picture that will come through in a case, and to start thinking about the strengths and weaknesses of a case early in the process. It stresses the importance of the listener—a factor oft forgotten by practitioners—and gives real life examples and tools to have judges 'hear better' what you are arguing. It can be used as a section-by-section refresher to address the immediate hurdle one is facing—be it 'how-to' prepare when you expect the court to be hostile to an argument you must make, or 'how-to' search for middle ground before diverse appellate jurists. Suffice to say, everyone on my team will be more than encouraged to have their own copy of it."

— Mark Litvack, Intellectual Property Partner, Pillsbury Winthrop Shaw Pittman, LLP

"The authors of *Point Well Made* are outstanding teachers of advocacy. Even the most experienced litigator will benefit from the tips and strategies in this insightful practice guide."

— John Hall, Partner and Chair of Global Litigation Department, Covington & Burling, LLP

"*Point Well Made* is a remarkable resource for every courtroom advocate presenting arguments to the bench. It offers tremendous practical advice, addressing challenges lawyers frequently encounter and offering specific tips and language choices. How I wish every attorney would study this volume before entering my courtroom."

— Hon. Patricia M. Lucas, Judge and former presiding Judge, California Superior Court, Santa Clara County

"Any lawyer who wants to be an effective oral advocate needs to read, digest, and apply the principles set forth in this latest edition of *Point Well Made*. The authors describe in detail how to convince a court by understanding the judge's concerns, marshalling the facts and the law, incorporating a theme and public policy, and crafting answers to the court's questions. With this second edition's deeper exploration of appellate advocacy and new tips for remote advocacy, you will be well-equipped for motion hearings and appellate arguments alike, in whatever court you appear."

— Carl Chamberlain, Lead Appellate Counsel, California Court of Appeals and Adjunct Professor, UC Hastings Law

"*Point Well Made* is a must-read for all those who wish to improve and sharpen their oral advocacy skills. For appellate judges, well-prepared oral arguments can make a meaningful impact on our decisions. *Point Well Made* provides many practical tips—including road maps, examples, and exercises—that will ensure the delivery of a concise, organized, and compelling oral argument. I applaud the authors on providing such an educational and enjoyable resource in the realm of oral advocacy."

— Hon. Frankie J. Moore, Judge and former Chief Judge,
Nebraska Court of Appeals

"With its one-of-a-kind emphasis on 'unpacking' judges for those who need to persuade them, *Point Well Made* goes way beyond its useful catalog of practical and specific techniques and tips for preparing and presenting arguments to provide advocates with both the framework and content necessary to tailor advocacy, whether oral or written, to the all-important audiences they must persuade to get the desired results for their clients."

— Sandra Johnson, North Carolina lawyer
and legendary NITA faculty member

"*Point Well Made* is accessible and poignant. There's some irony that lawyers are in the profession of persuading and yet so much of our day-to-day work feels divorced from that. This refocuses that—whether a jury, a court, an opposing counsel, or a client—everything lawyers do distills into the moment when we seek to convince another person of something. I would (and will) keep this as a desk reference (right next to Mauet's *Trial Techniques*)."

— Chase Johnson, Associate, Covington & Burling, LLP

"Among the points most lawyers probably never learned in law school are those that are made in *Point Well Made*. It is a primer on navigating the politics and psychology of the courtroom with extremely practical advice, taught in the authors' easy-to-digest style. Read it; think about it; study it."

— Reuben Guttman, Founding Member of Guttman, Buschner &
Brooks PLLC and Senior Fellow and Adjunct Professor
at the Emory University School of Law

"*Point Well Made* gives lawyers a clear blueprint for how to prepare for an oral argument. Unlike most books on advocacy, the authors explicitly acknowledge that some aspects of this work are art, not science, and they label their advice as such. Each topic includes engaging examples both from life and from the law. Plus, the book includes handy summary charts making it easy to use the book to prepare for an argument. In short, this book gives great advice in an accessible format."

— Mariana Hogan, Professor of Law, Emerita and former
Director of Advocacy Programs, New York Law School

"As a 3L law student, I wish that I had read this book before my moot court competition. I love that *Point Well Made* has synthesized information in the form of easily referenced tables that contain suggestions as to what to say in a variety of commonly occurring situations. The book also provides concrete advice about structuring arguments and answering a judge's questions. Reading through *Point Well Made* is a no-brainer for law students who want a leg up in their oral advocacy competitions!"

— Jordan C. Lee, 3L Maurer School of Law, Indiana University, Bloomington, Indiana

"Without much (or any) analysis, I had always taken 'oral advocacy' as *argumentation* that merely happened to occur in court and that didn't differ (or didn't differ very much, anyhow) from advocacy that might occur in a meeting, a debate, or a boardroom. *Point Well Made* doesn't buy that; it zeroes in on argumentation *in court* and how to argue better *there*.

"The authors offer myriad suggestions as to what actually to say *in court* and how and when best to say it *there*: Organization, use of language (including body language), emphasis and re-emphasis, professionalism and courtesy (whose importance the book stresses heavily), 'reading the room,' furthering your arguments by making use of what opposing counsel or the court may be indicating, pivoting to accommodate in-court developments (both positive and negative), recovering from mistakes—all of it is covered. I was particularly impressed by the authors' insistence on the all-but-imperative use of clear, and clearly presented, *themes* in in-court oral arguments; especially as they go on to provide advice for developing them.

"What's not to like?"

— Rafael Madan, General Counsel of one of the U.S. Department of Justice bureaus, and Adjunct Professor at Christendom College

POINT WELL MADE

Persuasive Oral Advocacy

SECOND EDITION

Nancy Harris Vaidik

Indiana Court of Appeals

Rebecca Diaz-Bonilla

Lumen8 Advisors, LLC

NATIONAL INSTITUTE FOR TRIAL ADVOCACY

Address inquiries to:

Reprint Permission

National Institute for Trial Advocacy
325 W. South Boulder Rd., Ste. 1
Louisville, CO 80027-1130
Phone: (800) 225-6482
Fax: (720) 890-7069
Email: permissions@nita.org

ISBN 978-1-60156-942-4
FBA 1942
eISBN 978-1-60156-943-1
FBA 1943

Library of Congress Cataloging-in-Publication Data

Names: Vaidik, Nancy, author. | Diaz-Bonilla, Rebecca, author.
Title: Point well made : persuasive oral advocacy / Nancy Harris Vaidik,
    Rebecca Diaz-Bonilla.
Description: Second edition. | Boulder : National Institute for Trial
    Advocacy, 2021. | Includes index.
Identifiers: LCCN 2021008632 (print) | LCCN 2021008633 (ebook) | ISBN
    9781601569424 (trade paperback) | ISBN 9781601569431 (kindle edition) |
    ISBN 9781601569431 (mobi)
Subjects: LCSH: Oral pleading–United States. | Trial practice–United
    States. | Appellate procedure–United States. | LCGFT: Trial and
    arbitral proceedings.
Classification: LCC 7F891cbcb .V35 2021 (print) | LCC 7F891cbcb .V35 2021
    (ebook) | DDC 347.73/72–dc23
LC record available at https://lccn.loc.gov/2021008632
LC ebook record available at https://lccn.loc.gov/2021008633

Printed in the United States.

Official co-publisher of NITA.
WKLegaledu.com/NITA

SUSTAINABLE FORESTRY INITIATIVE

Certified Chain of Custody
Promoting Sustainable Forestry

www.sfiprogram.org

DEDICATION

To our families, particularly our husbands, Jim and Mariano, for their endless support and love. To Daniel Diaz-Bonilla for his research, edits, and fresh perspective. To Chris Lopez for the use of her DC home and her delicious meals. And to each other for the lifelong friendship we have developed through teaching together and writing this book.

CONTENTS

PREFACE

Our favorite review of the first edition of *Point Well Made* described it as "a cookbook for motion practice." For the two years that lawyers devoured the recipes for success in that original motion practice book, we were continually asked to write a similar cookbook for appellate oral argument. We debated whether enough differences exist between the skills necessary to deliver a motion and oral argument to necessitate two separate menus. There are so many similarities, in substance and style, that covering both motions and oral arguments together here in this second edition allows for the moot court law student, the seasoned trial lawyer, and the experienced appellate practitioner alike to sharpen skills and understand how they personally need to improve, all in one unified place. We decided to blend the two recipes with this new cookbook, and we hope you find the meals fortifying and delightful.

The frequency and complexity of your advocacy may vary. In certain aspects, the core components of how to think about and prepare for a motion hearing and an oral argument are the same. But there are also differences that require unpacking. This book is organized by the categories that unite motion practice before a trial bench and oral argument before an appellate bench. Within each chapter, we point out the differences and additional considerations you as an advocate need to succeed.

With regards to motion hearings, this book is not an instruction manual on when or how to file or respond to certain motions. This is not a book about how to draft pleadings and motions, nor a book about litigation strategy. This is not a book about how to prepare and call witnesses. *Point Well Made* is a book about how to spark a fruitful discussion with the court during a hearing. When a lawyer properly understands the art of masterfully persuading and applies it appropriately to a motion hearing, he is afforded the chance to discover what matters to the judge and, hopefully, cause the judge to find a way to rule in his favor.

Likewise, an oral argument before an appellate court is an opportunity to discover what matters to a panel of judges, to convince each one of your side, and to secure a ruling that will both help your client immediately and set precedent for future litigants. An oral argument is generally built from a static record, allowing for deep intellectual strategizing. The timeline leading up to the argument allows for excellent performance preparation, and the more formal nature of this history-making event means that advocates are expected to be in their most perfect state.

This book was written with the implicit recognition that each advocate brings their own education, experience, talents, fears, physicality, voice, and personality to an argument. These factors influence which recommendations are always followed, sometimes followed, and never followed for each individual. This book helps flesh out the rules of the road for advocates, and points out when the rule must be followed—*science*—and when the rule can be softened or broken—*art*. Throughout the book, we will alert you whether a principle is *science* or *art*.[1] To apply these principles, we refer to cases on record and our own mini-case files, including one based on the Humpty Dumpty nursery rhyme. We found through many years of teaching together that busy lawyers do not have time for a 200-page fake record.

The book is co-authored to bring you two perspectives. Judge Nancy Harris Vaidik was the Chief Judge of the Indiana Court of Appeals for six years and still serves today on the court. As a prosecutor and a private practitioner, she argued hundreds of motions. She served as a trial court judge for eight years before being appointed to the Indiana Court of Appeals, where she has served for over twenty years. Judge Vaidik has been an adjunct professor of law at Indiana University Maurer School of Law for the past twenty years, teaching trial advocacy and depositions. She developed the motion training and appellate advocacy program for the National Institute for Trial Advocacy (NITA) and teaches internationally.

Rebecca Diaz-Bonilla is an international communications consultant, strategic advisor, and an attorney. She has coached litigators for over a decade in motion and appellate practice. Mrs. Diaz-Bonilla systemized oral advocacy preparation for clients, bringing her experience in developing substance, voice, and body language for advocates of all levels. She was an adjunct professor at University of Virginia School of Law and now teaches as an adjunct at the Scalia Law School and serves as a communications faculty member for NITA. She authored the award-winning book, *Foolproof: The Art of Communication for Lawyers and Professionals*.

---

1. Certain chapters are almost entirely self-explanatorily science or art (i.e., The "It Factor") and will not have each point designated.

CHAPTER ONE

"10,000-FOOT VIEW"

Your heart races, brain fogs, hands shake, and stomach turns. You stammer: "Uh, I'm not certain Your Honor. I mean, I wish I had thought of that . . . ."

The judge interrupts: "This case was cited several times in your brief, counselor: Am I remembering that correctly?"

"Oh, um, no, I mean, yes, Your Honor. My associate researched that case, and I knew the facts, I mean, um, I thought . . . ."

"Is this a waste of our time? Why are you wasting my time today?" questions the judge.

Train wreck. Take two.

Your heart races, brain fogs, hands shake, and stomach turns.

"If Your Honor could give me a moment, I will review those facts." (Ten second pause as you consult your notes.)

"This case was cited several times in your brief, counselor. Am I remembering that correctly?" asks the judge.

You calmly reply, "Yes, Your Honor. You have that correct. The facts in *Smith v. Texas* are indeed close to the dispute before Your Honor today. Procedurally, the trial court in *Smith* disagreed with the government, but the Department of Labor won on appeal. Those facts are similar to ours. A Freedom of Information Act request must be narrow in scope. Here, the citizen wants records spanning fifty years."

The judge nods. You transition and sense success.

1.1 The Neglected Art of Oral Persuasion

Although one would hope that the lawyer in the first scenario exists only within the confines of a hypothetical example, this kind of lawyer is all too common. Despite the clear need for oral skills in the legal profession, most attorneys are inadequately trained in the area of oral advocacy; as a result, many lawyers end up as the lawyer from the first scene. The arena of oral advocacy exposes the common weaknesses found in attorneys who are untrained as oral advocates. Awkward. Unpolished.

Underprepared. This more common breed of lawyers is the unhappy product of an education system that emphasizes the written word rather than the spoken word. Lawyers often possess sharp writing abilities, but dull oral skills. When the weapons in legal battle shift from the pen to the mouth, many lawyers are left unready with little idea how to prepare and train, costly traits when a ruling in your favor could simply depend on your oral abilities. In these scenarios, the first lawyer would lose; the second would win. That is simply how it is. The degree to which you are a persuasive oral advocate could determine the success or failure of your case. This book reveals the tools of success, tried and true, that you need to become a persuasive oral advocate. Our goal is to transform you from the first lawyer to the second.

1.2   Two Types: Prepared and Spontaneous

Great oral advocacy in an argument rarely happens naturally. It takes logic and trustworthiness; confidence and charisma. To convince the court, the attorney must be a beautiful blend of substance and style. It is not enough to have a good case; you need a good presentation. In a trial, a well-argued motion can mean the difference between a document review that gravely increases costs for the client, crucial evidence in or out, or jury instructions that change the outcome. An appellate court does not have to grant an oral argument, so when they do, the judges want to hear what you have to say. The skill of the advocate often determines the outcome of the appeal. The oral advocacy matters.

Oral advocacy is the opportunity to not merely convince the court through logic and facts—those are contained in the written briefs—but to convince the court with emotion, through a sense of justice or fairness, and through the most ancient method of resolving disputes, oral persuasion. The human voice has an uncanny ability to persuade. It brings the case to life, humanizing names and dates on a page. The attorney must either possess a natural ability to excel in both *prepared* and *spontaneous* rhetoric styles or learn the skills necessary to excel. This book focuses on both genres, prepared and spontaneous, offering these skills to both the natural rhetorician and lawyer who has a simple desire to learn. Like anything else, these skill sets require development and practice. Master the rules and best practices of communication and persuasion—and know how and when to break those rules. Breaking the rules requires a keen self-awareness and an instant read on the moment at hand. A great litigant stays flexible. She relies on the prepared material but abandons the game plan when the circumstances demand. She shifts when needed to successfully persuade. Oral advocacy requires a firm grasp of the principles underlying preparation, but also the ability to quickly respond with spontaneity.

1.3   Rhetoric

At the heart of oral persuasion is one key concept: rhetoric. Many know it, but few master it. This book relies, in large part, on the ancient art of rhetoric as its guiding star. The art of rhetoric has its roots in the rich intellectual soil of the Ancient Greeks and Romans. Famous Greeks like Aristotle heralded the merits of rhetoric as *the* tool of persuasion in a society without printing presses and computers. Oral persuasion is still key in the digital age if an advocate wishes to prevail. Aristotle defined rhetoric as the discovery of the available means of persuasion and explained how to assess the success of a rhetorician through the metrics of ethos, pathos, and logos. Aristotle defined these as:

1. Ethos—manifesting good character,

2. Logos—appealing to the reason of the mind, and

3. Pathos—exciting emotion, with the right amount at the right time.

If that sounds like Greek to you, here's the translation:

1. Ethos—When people trust and rely on you, you may have a good level of ethos. We believe people we respect. Ethos is a means to cultivate that respect.

2. Logos—We have hearts, but we also have heads. We are reasonable creatures who want to have a *reason* to believe the speaker. Logic. Clarity. Cogent thinking. This is particularly important when speaking to a judge who prides himself on being logical and following the law. The level of Logos in an argument determines the level of reasonableness the argument contains.

3. Pathos—We have all experienced a moment where a speaker touches our hearts, when the speaker makes us feel like the only person in the room, like the message was custom-made, and is delivered with the right emotions dosed at the right times. Humans are emotional beings. We have hearts. Pathos is how we touch the human heart. As a newsflash to some, judges are people too. They respond to the right amount of pathos necessary to sway them your way.

In the digital age, with low attention spans and fast-moving media-inputs bombarding us, lawyers need to execute the age-old ethos, pathos, logos model by having laser-sharp substance and delivering with credibility, clarity, confidence, likability, and persuasiveness. Simply put, rhetoric is not about changing the content, it is about using it better. In this book, we have drawn on this ancient wisdom to strengthen our modern techniques.

1.4   Road Map

With these three principles of Aristotle serving as the pillars of our approach to oral advocacy, these are the "ten commandments" of great oral advocacy:

- Understand the audience (Judge or Judges) (Chapter Two)

- Carefully prepare for arguments (Chapters Three and Ten)

- Know the law, facts, and theme (Chapters Four through Six)

- Understand questions and know how to answer them (Chapters Seven through Nine)

- Integrate knowledge of the judge's motivations into your argument (Chapter Ten)

- Have a good structure that starts and ends your argument strongly (Chapter Eleven)

- Appreciate the opponent's arguments so as to refute them (Chapter Twelve)

- Master not only the substance, but the style (Chapters Thirteen and Fourteen)

- Practice your argument aloud (Chapter Fifteen)

- Become proficient in the "new normal"—remote arguments (Chapter Sixteen)

Throughout the book we will explore these ten bulwarks upon which the persuasive lawyer rests her arguments. The structure of the book is loosely based on this outline. With these foundations in mind, let's begin.

Chapter Two

Know Your Audience: The Judge(s)

Six thousand of Hollywood's star-studded elite gathered in the chic Beverly Hills Hotel to witness the live performance of the 2020 Golden Globe Awards. Ricky Gervais, a well-known and generally well-liked comedian, as emcee, delivered the opening monologue. He riffed about the ending of season one of a TV series called "After-Life" in which the protagonist allegedly commits suicide, jesting; "season two is on the way, so he obviously did not kill himself, just like Jeffrey Epstein." As the camera panned to the audience, there was little laughter and many shocked faces. Sensing the awkward reaction of his audience, Gervais followed up with, "Shut up, I know he's your friend, but I don't care." Cue round two of the shocked faces. Needless to say, the monologue was not well-received by the live audience.[1]

This is a crystal-clear example of an oral performance destroyed by twenty seconds where a speaker was unmindful of his audience. Think of the hours of preparation undone by a twenty-second mistake. All it takes to undermine an oral presentation is a mere moment where the audience is offended or made uncomfortable. While you may not find yourself speaking to an audience of stars, lawyers are just as susceptible to that ill-fated twenty seconds. It is critical to understand your audience. Socrates once said, "the unexamined life is not worth living." Applied to oral arguments let us say "an oral presentation with an unexamined audience is not worth giving."

If there is a self-destruct mechanism that destroys a lawyer's chance at delivering a polished, effective oral argument, it would be neglecting to understand his audience. And a lawyer's audience in oral advocacy is the court—with one or more judges.

Judges, like all people, have their strengths, idiosyncrasies, opinions, attitudes, and philosophies that impact how they see the world and how they will see your case. Except for the totally unprepared judge, most judges, consciously or unconsciously, arrive at an argument with a gut call as to how to resolve the issue soon to be heard. Malcolm Gladwell calls it the "blink reaction";[2] Daniel Kahneman refers to it as

---

1. *See* https://www.youtube.com/watch?v=LCNdTLHZAeo. We acknowledge that Ricky Gervais may have intentionally planned this moment, but he did offend the live audience and underestimated the reaction. Either way, it is never a good idea to intentionally offend a judge.
2. Malcolm Gladwell, Blink: The Power of Thinking Without Thinking (2005).

"thinking fast."[3] As an advocate, trite as it may be, you need to put yourself in the shoes of the judge(s) before whom you are arguing.

Persuasion requires the input of the judge. You provide information and arguments to her, and she processes them through her personal filters and comes to her own conclusions. To convince, you must understand the judge. Persuasion is not telling a judge how she must rule; you must show her. Let the judgment in your favor be her own revelation. Persuasion means understanding the judge's view of your case, meeting the judge where she is, and speaking directly to her so she wants to rule in your favor.

Think about the likely judicial reaction to your arguments. Make those arguments that your judge is more prone to accept and stay away from those that repel. The more you learn about a judge, the more likely you are to understand what will influence her. Personalize your advocacy. You may have the most logical, eloquent, or compelling argument, but if it does not speak to that judge, you lose. You become Ricky Gervais.

At a more basic level, persuasion also requires understanding the mannerisms and logistical preferences of each judge. Despite your perfectly tailored arguments, you may not be heard because you unwittingly annoy the judge. You may act informally in a formal court or tell a joke to a somber judge.

We begin this chapter by identifying common concerns of most judges. We then categorize characteristics peculiar to judges and give you suggestions on how to find and use this knowledge to customize your argument to both a trial and appellate bench. We recognize that in some appellate courts you may not know who your judges are until immediately before the argument. Courts who do not reveal the panelists keep specialized appellate lawyers busy because they have studied all the judges in the pool. We assume here that you know the panelists beforehand.

2.1   The Judge's Motivating Concerns

All judges are, to some extent, motivated by fairness, a fear of reversal, a desire for resolution, the real-world consequences of their decisions, and the need to be consistent. Speak to one or all of these concerns in your argument or ignore them at your peril. How much you do depends on how much each factor influences your judge. These motivating interests are so universal and important that we devote an entire chapter to molding your argument to each of these concerns.[4] We briefly mention them here.

---

3. Daniel Kahneman, THINKING, FAST AND SLOW (2011).
4. *See* Chapter Ten: Appeal to the Concerns of the Judge.

2.1.1   *Fairness and Justice*

Most judges desire to be fair and just in their decisions. Judges want to get it right. They want to leave the courthouse at the end of the day with a sense of satisfaction. They want to be respected for ruling justly. Well-intentioned attorneys and judges often disagree on what should be considered fair in a case. Respectfully convincing the judge of your position and assuming she desires fairness will achieve the best long-term results for you and your client. Do not underestimate how the possibility of achieving a just and fair result impacts the ruling of a judge. Because fairness is often subjective, your job is to convince the judge that a result in your client's favor is the right decision—a decision she can be proud of.

2.1.2   *Reversal*

Judges generally do not want to be reversed. Some judges disdain reversal, while others are merely annoyed by it. The level of sensitivity depends on a judge's personality or her ambitions. Nevertheless, most judges are sensitive, even if slightly so, to being reversed. The judge who may be indifferent to reversal may not be persuaded, but it is worth a try, as you are also appealing to the interest of the judge to follow the law.

2.1.3   *The Parade of Horribles*

All decisions have consequences. The "parade of horribles" is a method of argument whereby you warn the court of the negative consequences of a ruling for your opponent. To a trial court judge, the consequences may be a life of pain for the plaintiff or the demise of a business. To an appellate court, the consequences reach far beyond the case before them. Ruling for the opponent may disrupt a long-standing and workable procedure for handling all future patent claims. Or it may impact a large swath of criminal defendants. *Art:* This mode of argument can be potent—but be careful that the "parade of horribles" argument does not descend to mere hyperbole.

2.1.4   *Desire for Consistency in Rulings*

Judges want to be predictable—some more than others. Predictability is important to attorneys and their ability to advise clients. Attorneys advise businesses and individuals to chart a course of conduct or avoid another based upon the probability of an outcome. Judges know this. Predictability also makes a judge's life easier because parties settle their cases based upon their expectations of a judge's ruling.

Most judges also want to be internally consistent. Even justices at the International Court of Justice (ICJ) or the United States Supreme Court fight for stare decisis to preserve the integrity of the highest court's previous decisions. Where appropriate, appeal to a judge's desire to issue rulings consistent with her previous rulings. Argue that ruling for your client will follow the way she ruled in a similar case, and therefore gives predictability to the attorneys who appear before her in the future.

Finding judges' prior opinions demands groundwork. Luckily, now more than ever, access is easily obtained through internet searches.

2.1.5   Concern for Time, an Overloaded Docket, and Clarity

All judges in all cases want resolution. You may think that is an overstatement. It is not. Judges are busy; their job is to resolve conflicts in an efficient way. Judges understand this mission.

Trial court judges are exceptionally concerned with resolution because of pressing and congested dockets. Decisions on motions dispose cases and encourage settlement. Disposing cases is a happy event for judges. Judges are evaluated, in part, by their peers, themselves, and their superiors based on the annual number of cases closed or pending. Plus, resolving a case to a judge is like fixing a sink to a plumber—gratifying.

Appellate judges are also concerned with resolution. When there is a split decision below, appellate judges strive to give clear direction to future litigants, preferably with unanimous decisions. Unanimous decisions on close cases require compromise among the judges.

This is not to say that judges favor resolution, clarity, or efficiency over justice. But resolution is one factor lurking in the minds of judges.

2.2   A Judge's Knowledge: A Sliding Scale

What the judge knows when she walks into the courtroom to hear your argument will significantly affect your presentation. Talking to a prepared judge differs from talking to one who is ill-prepared. Likewise, discussions with an expert in the law are on a different plane than discussions with a novice. When delivering an oral argument, great advocates learn to be accordions at expanding and contracting detail and generalities based on the individual expertise of each judge.

2.2.1   Reads Nothing, Little, or Everything

What has your judge read before the hearing? Has she pored over every paper you filed and researched the cases cited? Has she cursorily reviewed your papers? Or has she read nothing? Although you never will really know beforehand, most judges follow a pattern. Find out the judge's habits.

Make an educated guess about the amount of preparation the judge has done instead of asking the judge directly. This is *science* in oral advocacy: do not ask the judge if she has read the papers. That question reveals what you think of the judge—she is unprepared. The judge will not appreciate it. If you wait a few minutes into the argument, you may be able to tell how prepared the judge is without asking. Look for a quizzical face, avoidance of eye contact, or silence; these may be clues indicating lack of preparation.

The typically ill-prepared judge will probably not disappoint expectations in your case. Prepare a thirty-second fact wrap-up to bring her up to speed, and dive in without fanfare. Even the prepared but busy and distracted judge appreciates a recap:

"Here's how we got here, Your Honor . . ."

"To sum up the course of events so far . . ."

"As Your Honor knows . . ."

"To recap . . ."

Prepare to dig deeper into the cases and facts with a prepared judge, and usually she will dive directly into the issue she needs to discuss with you. She does not want you to merely repeat the content of the pleadings. She wants to probe the nuances of the arguments. Even so, do not forego the crucial facts of your case with the well-informed judge. And know the two or three key cases cold. Be able to discuss the similarities and dissimilarities of those cases with the facts in your case.

Neither the ill-prepared nor the well-prepared judge wants to look stupid. It is easy to slip into talking down to an ill-prepared judge. Never oversimplify your argument as if the judge cannot understand your point. Do not mock or belittle a question from the bench. Do not say, "That is not the issue here, the better question is . . .," or "This is an interesting question, but not relevant here." After a dumb question, do not give the judge a shocked look. Keep your poker face and answer the question as best you can.

Science: Make the judge appear smart by using her words in your response. When answering a question, weave the judge's words into your answer. Take this exchange, for example:

Judge: Counsel, isn't personal jurisdiction met here?

Counsel: Yes, Your Honor, personal jurisdiction is met here.

 Use the judge's words in other parts of your argument as well:

Counsel: As the judge said when discussing this with my colleague, "the issue boils down to the amount of contacts in the jurisdiction. The contacts here show . . ."

The techniques to answer these questions and others are explored further in Chapters Seven and Eight.

2.2.2 Expertise in Area of Law

Your judge may know nothing about the law in your case, may know a moderate amount, or may be an expert in the field. Discover where on the spectrum of knowledge your judge lies.

If the judge is a novice in the area of law, spend some time explaining the law. Explain the policy reasons behind the law. Begin your discussion at a 10,000-foot level with general concepts. Build on those concepts with more specifics but break down the explanation using plain words. Simplify without appearing to condescend. Do not preface your sentences with, "Let me explain to you." Do not slow your cadence down to a crawl thinking that the judge needs slowness to capture your point. *Science:* Do not robotically repeat the same point using the same words. Instead, mimic the most engaging teacher you have seen.

On common issues likely to often come before the court, do not waste your time on the basics. Instead, zero in on the flashpoint. For example, on a motion for a preliminary injunction, do not waste time outlining the elements that must be proven by the petitioner. If your strongest argument is that the petitioner is unlikely to succeed on the merits, go directly there.

If a judge is an expert in the area of law, there is no need to begin with the basics. Plunge headfirst into the conflict at hand. Plan to have a profound discussion about the nuances. Plan for more than a superficial conversation about the law and focus on your facts.

With a panel of judges, advocates should investigate ahead of time whether any judge has an expertise or ignorance about the type of case. You need to know before the argument that one judge was an antitrust lawyer with the Department of Justice, one judge was a criminal defense lawyer, and one judge was a contracts law professor before being appointed to the appellate bench. In Chapter Six: The Law, we delve into how to have a discussion with panelists of various levels of knowledge while keeping everyone interested.

2.3   A Judge and Opinions, Attitudes, and Beliefs

Life experiences result in opinions, attitudes, and beliefs. Two people can see the same group of protesters walking down a city street in an entirely different way. One is convinced the group is unpatriotic—about to destroy property and cause havoc. The other is convinced the protesters are passionate about the direction of the country and peacefully exercising their First Amendment rights. All of us, including judges, view the world through the prism of our experiences. Knowing the framework through which the judge interprets the world helps you to craft more persuasive arguments.

2.3.1   *Judicial Philosophy*

Judges form strong opinions about legal issues. Those opinions may have been formed through personal experiences with the law or lawyers, in law school, or may have been formed through practicing law. But judges, like most people, have attitudes and beliefs that shape their judgments. Judges may have witnessed a nasty divorce proceeding in their childhood, seen a family member or friend struggle through the legal system, been public defenders or prosecutors, or both. They may have practiced either plaintiff's personal injury work or insurance defense. Whatever their prior personal and legal experience, they develop judicial philosophies.

Judges also have views on procedural matters. Some judges are liberal in discovery; others are not. Some judges are more likely to grant or uphold summary judgments, dismissals, or default judgments. Some are generous on attorney fee awards, while others are stingy.

If the judge is prone to agreeing with your position, use it to your advantage without flaunting it. If you are not so lucky, find a common ground and build from there. Start with the judge's preference on the issue, and then differentiate your case. For example, if the judge generally grants discovery requests, begin by explaining that most discovery should be granted. With this start, you align yourself with the judge, making it more likely that she will listen to your argument. However, if you want to limit the discovery requests, then explain why this is not the typical discovery case.

Consider this sample language:

Counsel: "Your Honor, I understand that discovery should be liberal in most instances. Open discovery normally promotes settlement. While discovery should generally be liberal, here disclosure would interfere with the attorney-client privilege and work product. In this shareholder-derivative action, the shareholders are demanding the complete written report of the special-litigation committee. The report was prepared to determine whether to pursue the shareholder's claims. We have provided the report to the shareholders but redacted those portions of the report prepared by the corporation's counsel advising the committee of the likelihood of the suit's success. The material deleted from the report is attorney-client privileged information and work product in preparation of litigation. We've given them what we could."

2.3.2 *Conservative versus Liberal Views*

Political views impact judges' decisions. Reams have been written by political scientists about the effect of conservative and liberal beliefs on the decisions of appellate courts and the United States Supreme Court. Less has been printed on the influence on trial court judges.[5] Nevertheless, trial court judges have considerable discretion in determining the facts and applying the law, allowing political views to influence their decision making.

Where a judge lies on the continuum of political views may impact the judgment. In criminal sentencing, admissibility of evidence, and dismissals, the conservative judge is more likely to impose and affirm stricter sentences, less likely to suppress

---

5. For a scholarly work summarizing this issue *see* WHAT'S LAW GOT TO DO WITH IT? WHAT JUDGES DO, WHY THEY DO IT, AND WHAT'S AT STAKE, CHARLES GARDNER GEYH (Stanford Univ. Press 2011).

the government's evidence, and less likely to dismiss or uphold the dismissal of an indictment. Political views impact business cases, with liberal judges more likely to hold against a corporation and tending to be more favorable to plaintiffs in personal injury and medical malpractice cases.[6]

Judges may cross party lines issue by issue. Some may be conservative in criminal cases, yet liberal on cases involving corporations and personal injuries. Determine where your judges stand on the political spectrum regarding the issue at hand. If before a single judge, understand the judge's view, then either convince the judge that a favorable ruling aligns with her philosophy or gradually pull the judge toward your position by helping her see it a different way.

2.3.3   A Word About Handling Differing Opinions, Attitudes, and Beliefs in an Appellate Court

With a panel of judges, carefully thread the needle by finding the common ground among the panelists. For all judges, appeal to their other concerns such as resolution, reversal, and fairness, hoping that those factors will override their conservative, moderate, or liberal viewpoint. *Art:* Develop an argument that will attract all judges.

The fabled friendship between the late Justices Antonin Scalia and Ruth Bader Ginsburg is well documented and provides a fantastic example of how individuals on the extremes of the political spectrum can still put aside differences to be friends. But even more interesting than their unlikely friendship are the Supreme Court decisions where these two legal giants—who each are considered champions of their respective jurisprudential philosophies—ended up on the same side of contentious questions. When decisions were decided 5–4, Ginsburg and Scalia were on the same side a scarce 7 percent of the time. For that reason, bringing these two unlikely bedfellows together was quite the achievement. To secure this end, the lawyer had to construct an argument that brings together a Catholic-Conservative male with a Jewish-Liberal female. In short, he must *know his audience* and prepare an argument specifically for that audience. By understanding the judges and their individual biases, experiences, personal characteristics, and political leanings, the prepared oral advocate can effectively argue the case and win it. Consider such an argument, one that brought Ginsburg and Scalia together in a close 5–4 opinion (the rare 7 percent) in *Maryland vs. King*—a case in which the court ruled that conducting a DNA test as part of the arrest procedure did not violate the Fourth Amendment. Arguing on behalf of King, counsel framed his argument thus:

> I would say two things about the privacy interests at stake here. First
> of all, there is an intrusion into the body, and that is what triggers the

6. Many works do not define liberalism and conservatism in the context of trial judges. Even though USLAW Network does not define these concepts, its website at https://web.uslaw.org/classifies every county in each state by liberal, moderate, or conservative benches.

applicability of the Fourth Amendment here, to be sure, but it is also a relevant intrusion for Fourth Amendment purposes. But, second, and perhaps more importantly, there is a legitimate expectation of privacy in the contents of an individual's DNA.

His argument consists of a "right to privacy" argument—clearly aimed at the more left-leaning Ginsburg—and an argument about how the actual physical intrusion without a warrant constitutes a Fourth Amendment violation—obviously directed at Scalia. Both justices were able to connect to something in the argument. Ginsburg was attracted to the privacy argument and Scalia was attracted to the physical intrusion argument. As a result, they ended up on the same side, dissenting.

Try to find common ground that the panel can agree to and start from there. Be careful though that in finding common ground with one judge, you may lose the others. Now, this is not to say that you must frame an argument that makes everyone happy. Most of the time, you cannot. The point is that you need to thread an argument which sews together the views of a majority of the judges on the panel.

2.4 A Judge's Relationships with Others

The friendship between Justice Ginsburg and Justice Scalia exhibits how important it is to understand a judge's relationships with others and her preconceptions about various types of attorneys. Further, at an appellate court level, understanding the dynamics between judges is crucial to managing the courtroom discussion in a productive way. Arguing in front of three judges instead of just one presents new obstacles that must be overcome in order to effectively argue your case.

2.4.1 *The Judge and the Public*

When standing for election, a judge may be swayed by public opinion on issues before her that are of public concern. Depending on the judge, the time in the election cycle, or the issue, the election may or may not impact the judge's decision. An appointed judge can also be influenced in her decision making by the importance of the decision to the party or parties responsible for her appointment.

Know these potential influences. Argue the other interests of the judge aggressively to counterbalance the effect of politics. Justice and the rightness of the ruling tug strongly on a judge concerned with political affairs because her future could be at stake.

2.4.2 *Alignment of the Judge with Opposing Counsel or You*

Sometimes a judge will have a relationship with the attorney on the other side of the case; that relationship may cause the judge to like or dislike the attorney. Relationships vary—maybe they attended school together, maybe they belong to the same Inn of Court, maybe they practiced law together at one time, maybe they serve on the same board of a charitable organization. Relationships can be worrisome for several reasons. First, the attorney knows what is likely to persuade the judge and how to push those buttons. Second, the court likely finds the attorney credible and so the attorney's arguments carry extra weight with the judge. Third, the relationship may engender favoritism—but remember, it may also create animosity. Short of recusal, there is not much you can do but be aware of the relationship. If you show the judge you are not ruffled by the relationship and assume she will be fair despite the connection, you will earn the judge's respect.

If you are the attorney with a relationship with the judge, or one of the judges, avoid presumptive behavior intimating a familiar tone. You do not want opposing counsel to pine away for recusal, nor do you want to act aloof with a judge who knows you outside the courtroom. *Art:* To strike the right balance, behave respectfully and confidently and respond in a friendly manner when and if the judge refers to your history together.

Likewise, judges have preconceptions about categorical types of attorneys. Some judges favor attorneys from large law firms, while others favor solo practitioners. Maybe your judge is inclined toward more experienced attorneys over less experienced ones or local counsel over out-of-town counsel. Many judges appreciate the young lawyer who argues a case accompanied by a seasoned lawyer. These judges will assist the young lawyer as much as they can, to the point of giving slightly more favorable rulings. Be aware of a judge who champions giving younger lawyers an opportunity to speak in court. Many trial teams make the mistake of not allowing younger lawyers opportunities. If you are not able to add the type of attorney favored by your judge to your team, then buck the stereotype about the type of attorney disfavored by the judge. *Science:* As the out-of-town attorney, faithfully follow all local rules with alacrity, including any dress code preferences.

2.4.3 Fellow Judges

If an NFL football player had an issue with an assistant coach—a small disagreement about the game plan—would the player as a solution go to the head coach and begin bashing the assistant coach? Absolutely not. A player understands that you do not win favor with one coach by demeaning another. The head coach and the assistant coach both know how hard designing an effective game plan is, they both know how difficult their respective jobs are, how easy it is to get a game plan wrong. Further, the head coach has, at some point, been an assistant coach. For those reasons, a head coach will not want to hear a player's belittling criticisms of an assistant coach. In the same way, judges want to stick together and will not stand for an attorney disparaging another judge. Consider a real-world example:

One argument in the Indiana Court of Appeals started with the appellant's attorney saying that while the trial court judge was a wonderful person, he was in a small rural community and probably had never had a complex case such as the one before the court. Judge Ezra Friedlander stopped him saying, "If you lose before us, what will you be saying about us to the Supreme Court?" Judge Melissa May joined in and said, "I know and respect Judge Smith. He and I serve on a judicial committee together." There was no way out of the hole counsel had dug for himself.

When you argue in front of an appellate court, it is critical to avoid berating the judge of the lower court who, in your mind, "got it wrong." *Science:* Do not speak ill of any judge.

Always be respectful and focus on developing a strong argument for why you should win, rather than simply complaining about the judge who got it wrong. Avoid the criticism. It will not do you any favors.

2.4.4 *Multiple Judges*

When you argue in front of multiple judges, understand the rules of the game have now shifted. You are no longer dealing with one person's individual inclinations, belief systems, political leanings, personality, etc. Now, you deal with several and their combination. The variables have increased exponentially. For that reason, it is important to consider a few things:

First, be polite to all judges. *Science:* If one judge's questions express hostility, do not react.

Keep your calm and professional demeanor. If you snap back, the other judges will side with their fellow judge, despite the disrespect you endured.

Second, give all judges your attention. Do not just focus on one. *Science:* Aim for paying attention to all judges equally, whether by simple eye contact or body position. No one wants to be ignored or left out. There is a tendency of certain advocates to habitually pander to only the more seasoned judges or the male judges or the female judges or the judges they perceive to be on their side. Giving in to that inclination is not only impolite but does a disservice to your client and his chances of prevailing. Judges on a panel serving together recognize when their colleagues are being slighted and could punish you for it.

Third, recognize that judges who may not agree with each other may use their questions to you as an opportunity to hash out their personal disagreements. The argument may be the first time the judges talk about the case; they know the case will probably be decided at the panel conference immediately afterwards. They want their view to be the majority view. So, they try to convince each other during the hearing. Simply put, you may turn into the go-between. Tread lightly in these situations. When possible, avoid taking a side with one judge or another. *Art:* Look for a possible reconciliatory solution you can offer. Do not alienate yourself from one judge in order to gain favor with another.

Fourth, know that judges want consensus. Appellate judges know that the law is better served when it is agreed upon—predictable. Tailor your presentation by stitching your argument together to accommodate all the judges' views. Or at least, if not the view of all judges, something all can live with.

Lastly, an appellate court may get heated. *Art:* The prepared attorney understands that part of the job description is knowing how to cool the temperature of the room, to smooth over the emotional wrinkles in the courtroom. A clever comment or a smartly inserted smile help to lower the volatility. If you gain emotional consensus and build likability with all the justices, you will at least make it harder for a panel of judges to rule against you.

The table below summarizes how to create a snapshot of the judge(s) and determine how to integrate your substance and style to react to the judge before you.

THE JUDGE AND THE CASE	
Reads everything or reads nothing	Prepare to dig deep into the issue with the prepared judge. Have a thirty-second fact wrap-up for the ill prepared. Do not make the judge look stupid.
Expert or novice	If an expert, no need for the basics. Delve into the issue. If a novice, spend time explaining the law and its reasons. No lecturing.
Judicial philosophy in area	Identify it. Start with the judge's opinion, and then differentiate your case from the norm.
Conservative or liberal	Identify it. Convince the judge that ruling aligns with her view. Argue other factors that may influence the ruling.
Elected versus appointed	Recognize the influence of public opinion. Argue justice, fairness, and the correctness of the ruling in your favor.
Stereotypes about attorneys	Buck the stereotype the judge has about the type of attorney you are by acting respectful and professional in all ways.
Alignment with opposing counsel or you	If the relationship is intimate, consider a change of judge or recusal. Do not show any concern. If not, show no sensitivity to the judge's familiarity with opposing counsel.
Multiple Judges	Be respectful of all judges. Avoid taking sides in a judicial argument.
Fellow Judges	Don't bash the lower court judge, who you think got it wrong.

2.5   The Judge and the Court

Each judge has their own logistical preferences about how to run their courtroom, from punctuality to courtroom attire. Learn the judge's courtroom practice and procedures. A successful advocate stays flexible and adapts his presentation to the judge's preferences.

2.5.1   The Extent of the Judge's Questioning

Your judge(s) may or may not be an active questioner. If the judge is known to be an active questioner, odds are that you will be extensively questioned. Prepare for that reality. Anticipate questions and prepare responses. On the other hand, if you know the judge to be a silent observer, prepare to monologue.

2.5.2   Argument Day

Motions-call day means the judge's brain is on overload. The courtroom is full of litigants and their attorneys, patiently (or impatiently) waiting their turn. Numerous hearings are held—one after another, without a break. During the hearing, the judge is listening to your argument while at the same time signing agreements that have been reached by other litigants scheduled that day. In a word: chaos. *Science:* Get to the point quickly.

Go immediately to the heart of the matter on argument day in an appellate court. Often courts schedule back-to-back arguments in one day because the judges are coming from their hometowns to the court. Utilize brief and memorable arguments that are easy to grasp. We cover the complexities of remote arguments in Chapter Sixteen.

2.5.3   Energy and Humor

Most judges want to enjoy the arguments of counsel. *Art:* An attorney is not a stand-up comedian, but it is important to be energetic and entertaining. The next time a judge falls asleep during your argument, consider that the problem might be you. Create interesting phrases. Be innovative in problem-solving. Make exhibits colorful. Speak with energy, stressing what is important so the judge will follow your lead. Distinguish yourself from the mass of attorneys moving through the courtroom that day. You want the judge to say to herself, "That was well done. This is why I do this for a living."

Always laugh at a judge's joke. Laugh with the same intensity the judge does—not more or less. Do not be funnier than the judge. A little self-deprecation can be effective but avoid false humility. For example, do not pretend to be less intelligent than you are: "Your Honor, I can hardly understand this regulation." Instead: "We all understand the regulation, but the engineer on the ground can't consult with us every time a government change order is needed to complete the electrical project."

Certain types of humor should always be avoided. *Science:* Do not use humor at the expense of the parties or other counsel. Avoid sarcasm in general, and never engage in racial, gender-based, or cultural jokes.

Beyond that, it depends on the judge. *Art:* If you are before a judge who appreciates the clever exchange between quick-thinking trial attorneys, employ a reasonable balance between taciturn exchanges and humor. But the humor should not be prearranged; it should come naturally from the circumstances of the hearing. If used properly, humor energizes a bored judge, makes your arguments memorable, and reveals you to be the intelligent and clever person you are.

2.5.4   Dealing with Opposing Counsel

Do not disparage opposing counsel during the argument. Phrases like "opposing counsel is disingenuous" may sound civilized, but they are not; they are fighting words. When the name calling begins, it is a bad day for the court. All the judges see are two toddlers in a bathtub fighting over a rubber duck.[7] Rather tell the court the details of what opposing counsel did. Example: "Opposing counsel misconstrues the holding in *Smith v. Jones*. The holding is . . . ."

Also, always speak to the judge during the hearing. Do not turn to the opposing counsel and speak your problems with his argument to him. Do not say, "Mr. Green, you know this is objectionable because . . ." Instead, when it is your turn explain that opposing counsel's argument has no merit and why.

2.5.5   Law Clerk

Many judges have a law clerk who listens to the arguments and helps write the judge's order. Some judges heavily rely on their clerk; others do not.

If a writing clerk is present during the hearing and the judge relies on the clerk for research and/or the clerk's opinion, you may be speaking to two audiences. During your argument, your eye contact should remain with the judge. You do not want the judge to think that you believe her clerk is more important than she is. But you may briefly look at the clerk to see his reaction when you release your eye contact from the judge or when the judge is reading. If the judge runs a more casual courtroom and likes to include the clerk, then occasionally make eye contact with the clerk.

When your opponent argues, survey both the judge's and clerk's reactions to your opponent's arguments. You may catch some of the nonverbal communication between them. The nonverbal information you gain may allow you to modify the direction of your argument and develop your rebuttal.

---

7. We borrowed this analogy, with permission, from Andrew Lillie, a very skilled and seasoned trial attorney from Hogan Lovells.

2.5.6 *Formal versus Informal*

Appellate courts are very formal. *Science:* Never deviate from the formality of the setting. Dress appropriately. Do not lean on the podium. Do not walk around to the side of the podium. Do not call the judges "you guys." That reference drives female judges crazy. Address each judge by name if you can. Use the title chief judge or justice where appropriate.

If the judge conducts formal hearings, follow the protocol. Some judges are taskmasters for decorum in a courtroom. Learn the rules. If your judge is a stickler for obedience in the courtroom, disobedience can be costly. The judge may believe you are being disrespectful to her and to the institution. Your credibility will be diminished.

Do not confuse formality with coldness. A more formal judge may be more concerned with efficiency and knows that formality keeps things moving on an argument day. Judges appreciate your adherence to the rules as a sign of respect.

Certain trial judges tolerate a little deviation from the rules, which allows you more flexibility in your argument. The trial judge who prefers a more casual atmosphere will encourage more small talk, include her clerks in conversation during a proceeding, and readily switch the schedule at a hearing depending on the circumstances. Some judges permit you to speak even when not called upon. Others allow you to speak beyond your time. In the more laidback court, if the judge is particularly interested in a topic, surrebuttal and sur-surrebuttal arguments are routine. Often the judge will invite surrebuttal, even with only a slight glance in your direction; sometimes not. But if the judge is interested, the conversation may continue well beyond your preordained turn.

 Even if the judge is more casual in the courtroom, show respect. For example, the practice may be that the attorneys sit at counsel table while presenting their arguments. Even so, do not address the judge while sitting. Out of respect for the judge and the position, rise to your feet. Standing indicates how serious you are taking the matter. If she asks you to remain seated, comply.

Some judges hold motion hearings in chambers. If the hearing is held in chambers, the good news is you will be more relaxed and able to better connect to the judge and her concerns. The bad news is often these in-chamber discussions are not recorded. For any number of reasons, including the possibility that your client may want to appeal, you need to preserve an accurate record.

If you find yourself in an informal trial court chamber and need to capture the discussion, politely ask for the court reporter to join you or ask that the hearing be held on the record in the courtroom. If you absolutely know you will win or have no intention of appealing, then go with the flow and let the other side take the heat for being record-hungry.

You will rarely offend a judge by erring on the side of respectful decorum in delivery and dress. Even if the judge prefers a more casual atmosphere, treat every party with good manners and present yourself in a polished, professional way.[8] A courtroom is a judge's office. Consider yourself a guest in her space and act accordingly.

THE JUDGE AND THE COURTROOM	
Formal versus informal	Stick to formality even if in an informal setting. Get your record.
Decorum in the court	Stick to the rules with the judge who demands obedience. Energize the courtroom with your enthusiasm. Laugh at the judge's jokes. Sparingly use self-deprecation.
Argument Day	The shorter the time and the more chaos, the simpler and more succinct. .
Law clerk	Depending on if the judge relies on a clerk, you may be speaking to a second audience.
Active questioner versus no questions	If active, spend time predicting questions and answers. If no questions, have a bullet point prepared script and watch the judge.
Humor	Never be funnier than the judge.

2.6 The Judge's Personality

Every judge is a human being. They each have their unique personalities. They want to laugh; they dislike boring experiences; and they possess their own unique levels of common characteristics such as caution, ambition, thoughtfulness, etc. Tailoring the presentation to the judge as a human being is crucial. The last thing you want to do is to lose a hearing because you failed to understand the judge's human side. This is why part of knowing the judge is adapting your presentation to her personality.

2.6.1 Personal Attributes

Let's look at some common characteristics and discuss how to modify your argument based on the personality of the judge:

Cautious:

- Give the judge courage to rule in your favor. Highlight the fact that ruling in your favor is in keeping with settled law. Emphasize how the decision will be solid and right.

Easy-to-change positions:

- Keep the conversation going. Try for the last word. Ask for surrebuttal.

Thinks out loud:

- Listen. Adapt your argument to what you hear.

---

8. Be careful to dress proportionately to your client or the opposing party. If your client is being sued by a nonprofit, best to avoid wearing the Armani suit and cufflinks to court.

Processes silently:

- Do not be scared by silence. Nonverbal cues are key here. Watch for them.

Big picture:

- Paint the landscape. Do not drill down to the details. Give the big view.

Detail-oriented:

- Know the details cold. Make sure you correctly state the facts and law. No errors.

Industrious:

- Help the judge write the order. At the end, explain what you want and how to get there.

Creative:

- Think outside of the box. Propose creative solutions.

Lazy:

- Prepare impressive briefs and, to a trial court, findings of facts and conclusions of law. Track your argument to the proposed order.

Curt:

- Do not let it shake you. This judge is curt to everyone.

Ambitious:

- Show the judge that a ruling for you will not be reversed on appeal—and a ruling for you is within the mainstream.

Shoots from the hip:

- Try to slow down the argument. Slow your pace. Appeal to broad principles of fairness and justice.

Wants to make a big statement:

- Show how this case is significant and will have a lasting effect on the law.

2.7 How Do You Research the Judge?

If you have been in front of the judge numerous times before, you will not have to do much research. Better yet, if you have served as a law clerk for her or for a colleague of hers, then you have even more insight. However, if you do not know the judge, use the resources at your disposal to gather information. Learn your judge's preferences on the issues of your case through research. Read the judge's decisions and any law review articles or other law publications she has written. The internet provides formal and informal insights into a judge's positions and preferences. Look at the court's website and her biography to learn what the judge wants you to know. Search generally for her name online. You will be surprised what you may learn from a simple internet search. This may provide newspaper articles about her speeches she has made, or her favorite community organizations. You may discover she has ambitions for a higher court or that she is in limbo, awaiting appointment, at the time of your hearing. Find the local bar's rating of her. Go to websites where attorneys rate and comment on judges like www.robingroom.com. Use the various litigation services available that profile judges. Be cautious about using social media sources to research a judge. Social media creates a fingerprint every time you view and follow and being connected to a derogatory comment about a judge by an attorney whom you "follow" can come back to bite you. Talk to attorneys in your firm or your attorney friends. Email advising them you will be appearing before the judge, asking them if they have any insight into her. Write the email in a way that if it is forwarded to the judge you will not be embarrassed. You would be surprised how often emails are forwarded and wind up in the hands of a judge. Ask for a phone call in return, as opposed to an email response.

Talk to former clerks. Make blind calls to attorneys whose names appear on the court's decisions. Attorneys love to talk about their cases. If they do not call you back, you have lost nothing.

Go to the courtroom. Sit through a proceeding or two. File a pleading in-person with the court staff. Engage in small talk with the staff about the judge's favored practices. In an informal conference with you, opposing counsel, and the judge (no ex parte discussions please), ask the judge about her preferences. Judges are delighted to speak about what they consider to be their own unique and efficient procedures. A happy by-product of your court visit is that you will develop a relationship with the judge and her staff. *Science:* Never underestimate how important her staff is to a judge. Be nice to staff, never rude. Your discourteous comments will be repeated to the judge.

Go to the judicial qualifications board in your state and get a copy of her statement of economic interest. Each year, a judge must file a report indicating income and gifts she receives from any source. If the judge is elected, go to the local election board and get a copy of her campaign financing report. It will tell you who has contributed to the judge's election campaign. One bit of caution: judges often know personnel in the offices that keep these materials. Send someone who cannot be connected to you to retrieve the information.

If your client has the resources available, hire local counsel, someone who has repeatedly been in the court. Brainstorm with local counsel about the judge(s).

Once you find reliable sources to learn about your judge(s), begin creating a snapshot of them. This snapshot should shape your substance and style.

Below is a spectrum graph to compile the research you have done.

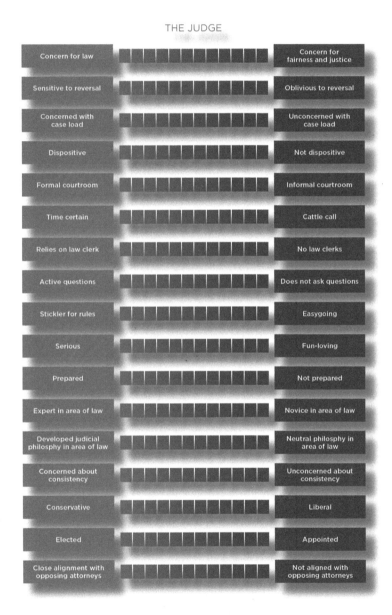

Having researched the judge(s), we now turn to other essential preparation for the winning argument.

Chapter Three

Preparing for Arguments

Film study all night. Avocado ice cream as the one dietary treat. Making receivers stare into the sun by catching balls from the direction where the sun will shine during the game. These are just a few examples of the extent to which Tom Brady, the greatest quarterback of all time, goes in order to be perfectly prepared for every game. Brady thrives on an obsession with practice. Playing at the age of forty-three in the most athletic league on the planet, Brady is as sharp as ever—in part because he gets all the little details right. There are countless stories of his legendary commitment to be better prepared than every single one of his opponents. As one story goes, after winning the AFC championship game that sent the Patriots to the Super Bowl, Tom Brady went home and studied hours of tape on his next opponent, the Atlanta Falcons. To be the best football player he could be, Brady prepared and planned for everything he could. While this book does not expect a diet comprised of avocado ice cream, the same principle of dedicated preparedness applies.

To keep improving your skills or to learn them afresh all together, dedicate the same time and attention as Tom Brady would. Successful planning involves preparing for spontaneity. It may well be you deliver an uninterrupted monologue that you have carefully prepared in advance of the event. A more likely scenario, and the one that is ultimately better for your client, is that you engage in a conversation with the court—one that you may or may not have *precisely* anticipated, but one you anticipated nonetheless. A successful presentation is a prepared yet spontaneous delivery from a credible attorney who quickly gets to the point, converses persuasively with the court, and has anticipated and prepared for possible disasters.

Planning for your next argument depends on your experience, the opponent, the complexity of your issues, the time allotted by the court, and the stakes involved. Nevertheless, all good advocates, whether seasoned at arguments or not, must spend some time planning and practicing. If you are a prosecutor handling several motions every day before a familiar judge, your preparation will be quite different than for the intellectual property litigator preparing for a *Markman* hearing in Washington, D.C., or from a criminal defense attorney arguing before an appellate court. Sometimes you will prepare with little time, but other times you will have months to get ready.

We begin with the basic elements you need to prepare. You must substantively know the legal theory, factual theory, and a theme that explains why you win and why the court should care. Deliver this content through two or three strong arguments, pinpoint your Achilles' heel, anticipate questions and potential concessions, recognize the long-term and short-term consequences of the outcome, and contemplate a fallback position.

3.1 Know the Legal Theory and Its Support

Before the argument, review the legal theory supporting your position. The legal theory addresses what must be legally proven or disproven, including the legal elements, cases, rules, and statutes upholding your stance. Undoubtedly, you already decided on a theory before you filed the motion and its accompanying papers or replied as respondent.

Review the legal theory and the law cited in your briefs, making yourself comfortable with those crucial three or four cases your argument turns on, including the few strongest cases relied upon by the other side. Be able to show why the facts of these cases are similar to or different than yours.

The judge does not want you to read the entire case to him. He wants a concise and relevant understanding of the case law, statutes, or regulations that govern the legal theories presented. Be ready to discuss the law, not just report it. Prepare a case "crib sheet" with each critical case, which should include a sixty-second fact and procedural history summary, a thirty-second description of the holding and legal theory, and talking points to show reliance on or distinctions of each case. We discuss this preparation technique further in detail in Chapter Eleven.

The day before the argument, check the cases upon which you rely to ensure that none of them have been refined or overruled. When you walk into the courtroom, you need to have a legal theory, actual theory, plus a theme, all of which yield the substance of the argument.

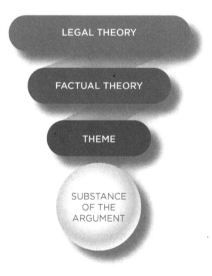

3.1.1   Magic Words

A dialogue with the judge about the law is easier to understand if you concentrate on the "magic words" of the case. Key phrases like "excusable neglect," "likelihood of success on the merits," "abuse of discretion," and "reason to believe that criminal activity is afoot" can be the foundation of a successful argument. Prepare the law of the argument by learning the key words and phrases of the supporting law. These are not full sentences. Repeatedly practice them aloud. You must be able to say them without hesitation.

Magic words allow you to find the universal language of the issues and reduce complex legal theory into memorable and clear phrases. Rarely is the case the first one of its type heard by the court. If you appropriately use this familiar language, judges do not need to work hard to understand your legal arguments and can categorize your case into the appropriate legal box. In the absence of these well-known phrases, however, you run the risk of complicating the law, making it more difficult for the judge to understand your points and rule in your favor. These magic phrases are especially helpful for bringing the ill-prepared judge quickly up to speed.

Sometimes, the issue is unusual, and the law is unknown to the court. In this case, there are no common magic words. Nevertheless, find the critical language of the cases on which you are relying. To make the legal issues understandable for the court, pluck simple phrases from the case and use them to your advantage. Not only will this preparation make your arguments clear and understandable, but upon reading the cases cited, the judge or clerk should hear your words reverberate in his mind, enhancing your credibility.

3.1.2   Understanding the Rationale Behind the Law

Investigate and identify the rationale or public policy behind the law. Research the law's legislative history and the regulatory application since its inception. Ask yourself why the law is written as it is. Knowing the reasons behind the purpose of the law allows you to develop commonsense arguments supporting your position. Oftentimes the practical outcome of the law fails to advance the purpose of the law or overreaches beyond the law's target.

Suppose in a motion in limine hearing your opponent asks that certain business records be excluded from evidence as hearsay. Of course, you will argue for their admission under Federal Rule of Evidence 803(6), but it is even more compelling and persuasive if you also argue that the purpose of the rule is driven by a company relying on the records to conduct its business, which makes the records inherently trustworthy.

In an appellate oral argument, the judges are waiting for a robust discussion about the rationale or public policy behind the law precisely because their decision may change precedent for future cases, since the law's application will be modified by the decision.

3.1.3   *Knowing the Law = Credibility*

Credibility depends in large part on your knowledge of the issue before the court. When the judge looks for an answer, you want to be the go-to person on whom the court relies. You may serve that role only if you are prepared with a full and complete understanding of your case and the law underpinning it. A judge will detect your level of understanding based on your grasp of the legal theory. You cannot hide. A judge knows when you are pretending, and a panel of judges can smell an unprepared lawyer from a mile away. As you prepare, it is essential to learn and fully understand the law. There is no replacement for good old-fashioned elbow grease. Do the work necessary to be ready. Do your homework. There is no room for "winging it." The goal is to preserve the trust between you and the judge(s) at all times, so never pretend to know the legal theory of your case. *Science:* Think long-term relationships over one-time transactions.

3.2   Review and Refine Your Factual Theory

Thoroughly understanding the facts also establishes and maintains your credibility. Prepare to be credible by knowing the facts underlying your argument. Some advocates think that judges are not interested in facts. Not so. Judges are experts in the law, but you are the expert of the facts. It is the advocate's job to shape the legal argument and weave the critical facts into the argument throughout. Have the key facts, both good and bad, at your fingertips during the hearing. Keep relevant quotes from documents in your portfolio so there is no fumbling during your discussion with the court.

Before the argument, review and refine your factual theory. The factual theory is why the composite of your facts results in you *winning*. Know the good facts that support your theory, the neutral facts that neither support nor harm you, and the bad facts that hurt your position.

The facts may be relatively few, as in a motion to dismiss for failure to state a claim upon which relief can be granted. Because a motion to dismiss tests only the legal sufficiency of the pleading and not the facts supporting it, the facts are limited to the complaint and its attachments. On the other hand, a summary judgment motion or a motion for injunctive relief may involve many facts from many sources, including those from depositions and affidavits. And appeals may have even more facts recorded in a lengthy transcript.

For fact-intensive cases, many attorneys engage in brainstorming sessions before both writing and arguing their case. With a whiteboard, an hour's time, and possibly a colleague:

- Write the legal elements.

- List the facts, in a nonjudgmental way, as being good, bad, or neutral to the case. Place good facts in one column, bad facts in another, and neutral facts in both columns. Be sure to list only facts and not conclusions. To stay away from conclusions, put on your journalist hat and answer "who, what, where, why, how, when, to what extent."

- Identify the three best facts and three worst facts.

Eventually, a factual theory develops which must explain your good and bad facts and be believable and simple while addressing your legal elements.

Consider this example in which this technique is applied to a motion. You represent Sam Smith in a bad-faith claim against Acme Insurance Company, Inc. Sam sustained injuries in a car accident. The tortfeasor's insurance company paid its policy limits to Sam, but this amount did not fully compensate Sam for his damages. Sam was insured by Acme Insurance Company. His policy provided underinsured motorist coverage with limits of $50,000. After investigating the claim, Acme refused to pay any money to Sam. You filed an action alleging breach of contract and breach of Acme's implied covenant of good faith and fair dealing.

Two months later, you served a request for production of documents demanding a copy of all complaints filed in any court against Acme by its insureds for bad faith claims arising out of underinsured motorist coverage. You also asked for a copy of all claim forms submitted, depositions taken, or affidavits of adjustors, supervisors, or company officers given in those suits. Your request covered all litigation filed five years before Sam's accident and one year after.

Thirty days passed and you received no response from Acme's counsel. You mailed a letter to counsel reminding him of the request. As there was no response, you sent a second demand letter. Finally, three-and-a-half months after serving the request for production, you asked the court to compel discovery. The hearing was scheduled and only one week before the date the insurance company moved for a protective order, claiming the request was not relevant and unduly burdensome. Two days before the hearing, the insurance company finally contacted you to try to resolve the dispute. No agreement could be reached.

Attached to Acme's protective-order motion is an affidavit from an employee of the company stating that to comply with your request, the company must perform a manual search of its records costing upwards of $100,000. Ten verdicts in the time period in question have found bad faith on the part of Acme. Acme has a computerized filing system for most claims, but not for most of the documents you want.

Your brainstorming board may look like this with good facts in one column, bad facts in another, and neutral facts in both columns:

THE LAW
The request must be relevant to our claim and proportional to the needs of the case.[1] The court may issue an order to protect a party from oppression, undue burden, or expense.

GOOD FACTS	BAD FACTS
Served the request	Will cost $100,000 to produce
There was no answer to first request	Request is for complaints (public records) filed against Acme for bad faith
You wrote the first reminder letter thirty days later	Documents requested include claim forms that may implicate privacy concerns
There was no response to the letter	The request is for a six-year period
Wrote second reminder letter	Want records after Sam's accident
Opposing counsel contacted me two days before the hearing to resolve the discovery dispute	Ten verdicts in the six-year time frame have found that Acme engaged in bad faith
Filed motion to compel three-and-a-half months after request	
Did not hear of the $100,000 cost until the protective order request was filed two weeks before hearing on motion to compel	
Most files are computerized	
A manual search is required	A manual search is required

Your factual theory must explain what happened and why you win under your legal theory.

Perhaps your factual theory is:

- The insurance company's pattern of denying valid claims makes it more likely that your client's claim was unjustly denied.

- You did all you could in good faith to resolve this dispute without bothering the court. You waited three-and-a-half months to ask for the court's help, during which time you wrote to opposing counsel multiple times.

- After your repeated informal requests, the insurance company first advised you of its objection through a court pleading. The insurance company's lack of cooperation is the reason you stand before the court—the insurance company should not be rewarded for its conduct.

---

1. For this example, we assume that the case is in federal court. Many states' rules will include the magic words "reasonably calculated to result in discoverable materials."

- It is the insurance company's policy that causes the retrieval of the documents to be so costly. It could easily have stored this information electronically but chose to keep the files in hard copy only.

3.3 Create Your Theme

A theme is the heart of your case. It explains why you should win and why the court should care. It is the moral imperative that explains why your prayer for relief is just. Your theme is the essence of your argument, stated in one or two sentences. The theme is what you would tell your mother to convince her that you should win your case. The theme puts aside the facts and the law for a brief second and appeals to the moral fabric of the judge. From a first-year law student arguing in a moot court competition to a seasoned Supreme Court advocate, the theme is crucial. Furthermore, when you lay out a strong theme, the justices may embody that same theme when they write their own opinion on the case. The test of a winning theme is whether or not your theme ends up in the ruling.

Developing a strong theme is discussed in detail and numerous examples are provided in Chapter Four.

3.4 Know Your Timing

Time is important in three respects: how much time you have to prepare, how much time you have to speak, and what time of day the hearing is. A hallmark of great advocacy is preparation, and it is your responsibility to set aside the requisite time needed to substantively develop your argument and practice the delivery. Good planning demands you find out the amount of time allocated for your hearing. Preparing for a two-hour argument is very different than planning for a ten-minute one. Your goal is to make two or three points maximum explaining why you should succeed. Longer arguments allow you more time to expand on the details that support your main points. A rule of thumb is no more than one argument for each ten minutes of a hearing.

From a judge's perspective, it is frustrating to sit through a hearing where the attorney decides to tackle all issues in her pleadings. Here, the attorney speaks at the judge at supersonic speed. Judges tend to shut down, not ask any questions, and hope for the presentation to end. To avoid this reaction from the court, make the most of the time you speak to the judge. Plan your points carefully. Do not merely repeat the points you made in your papers—the judge or his clerk can read them. Pick the points that require further discussion or explanation that you will need to win.

Find out what time of day you will be heard. Be in the court ready to go fifteen minutes before the hearing is scheduled. Do not get upset if the court is running late. Resist the urge to whine to the judge's staff. Judges do not view time in the same manner as attorneys do and will not appreciate your complaints.

If your case is scheduled during a "motions call" morning—or as judges affectionately call it, during "cattle call"—you will have the limited attention of the court. Even if the judge has read your papers before the hearing, chances are he may not remember the nuances of your argument or, less charitably, may not remember anything about your motion in the sea of motions he will hear that day. If you are crammed into a motions call, immediately get to the point, be brief, and distinguish yourself in some way. You must stand out from the pack. Make your theme catchy or begin with a clever, yet appropriate, metaphor. But remember, be concise and to the point.

The time of day may also affect the decision of the court. Studies have found that when a judge is hungry or tired, he is more likely to resort to his default position when deciding your case. In his groundbreaking book, *Thinking, Fast and Slow*,[2] Daniel Kahneman opines that we have two systems of thinking: a fast brain and a slow brain. The fast brain makes decisions with an initial, intuitive, "gut call," while the slow brain conducts a careful, thoughtful analysis. Kahneman reports a study of the decisions of eight Israeli parole officers. All day the officers heard parole cases, and the default decision was to deny parole. The study showed that the officers were more likely to grant a parole request after a morning, lunch, or afternoon break. Nothing explained the increase in releases except that the officers were less hungry and more alert.

This study has implications for an attorney scheduled on a "cattle call" day. If you want a ruling against the judge's default position, it is best to get the hearing scheduled first thing in the morning or immediately after lunch, when the judge is fresh. If that is impossible, grab the court's attention with a memorable theme and then slow down the judge's thinking process. Take time to explain why your case is different than the norm. You can shift the judge from his intuitive gut call and into a deliberate and more thoughtful analysis.

In an oral argument, timing is even more critical. Your assigned time is not yours. You must share that time with all the judges on your panel, including their speeches disguised as questions, their cross-judge debate and commentary, and the transition time wasted with multiple interruptions from many speakers. This time squeeze means an advocate facing an oral argument must be even more efficient, concise, and organized. Only then can you manage the court and make your oral argument sound like a conversation.

The formality of an oral argument means that time will be less flexible in an appeal. Appellate panels properly presume that advocates will be prepared, practiced, and polished. The strict adherence to time ensures a fairer playing field. It means that hard work will pay off for the lawyer who can take the big thoughts and pages of briefs and weave them into simple, compelling discussion.

---

2. Daniel Kahneman, Thinking, Fast and Slow (2011).

As the French mathematician and philosopher Blaise Pascal closed one of his letters in 1657, "*Je n'ai fait celle-ci plus longue que parce que je n'ai pas eu le loisir de la faire plus courte*," which translates famously, "I have made this longer than usual because I have not had time to make it shorter." Likewise, a panel of judges expects an attorney to use the time wisely. *Science:* Prepare to be concise.

3.5   Pick Your Strongest Two or Three Arguments

Your strongest two or three arguments should be independent arguments that support each other. The optimal arguments are like guy wires—strands of intertwined steel. Each strand is strong, but when knitted together, their tensile strength increases exponentially.

Consider this example. A company purchased a piece of property to develop a residential neighborhood knowing that a utility company had a 300-foot easement running through the property. On the easement were electric transmission towers with uninsulated wires that provided electricity from one major U.S. city to another. The developer placed the only road access to the subdivision entirely within the easement without consulting the utility. The utility moved for summary judgment in the trial court, which was denied. On appeal the utility argued that 1) the developer unnecessarily burdened its easement as a matter of law and 2) the developer did not present any evidence demonstrating that there was a genuine issue of material fact for trial.

Each of the arguments complement one another—one requires a review of the utility's evidence and the other, the developer's evidence. Each argument looks at the evidence from different perspectives but either way the utility prevails.[3] This example highlights the need to craft your arguments so that even if one fails, the others will survive. Independent, supportive arguments are successful, but domino arguments are not, because when one falls, they all fall. To avoid this outcome, always plan for a consistent backup position.

3.5.1   *How to Order Your Arguments*

Emphasis in oral delivery may be different than in the written pleadings and briefs. Even though the order of delivery may shift from written to oral, start with your strongest argument. This is your offense. You may not have another chance to showcase it to the court. Collect your weaker arguments and decide which ones will be chosen for the argument. Pick either the weaker arguments that you need to win or the ones the judge(s) will predictably struggle with. This is your defensive strategy. Allow the papers to cover the rest but be prepared to address those issues if

---

3. Duke Energy Indiana, LLC v. J&J Development Company, LLC, 142 N.E.3d 916 (Ind. Ct. App. 2020).

the court so chooses. Spend time strategizing the offensive and defensive approaches and how they fit together.

The time spent on your points may be determined by the likelihood of success on that issue. If you know one of your issues is settled law in your jurisdiction, do not waste much time and energy focused on that winning issue. Start with the winner to solidify the agreement between you and the judge(s), then quickly turn your focus to issues that require more persuasion.

To keep the court interested, find something of value to argue that was not included in the papers. Maybe it will be a different way of saying the same argument or a different way to frame the issue but find that twist. The twist is precisely what causes the judge(s) to leave the hearing or oral argument thinking the time was well spent.

3.5.2 *Prepare to Get to the Point*

From a court's perspective, this may be the most important point of advocacy. Get to your point quickly. Trial judges abhor wasting time, and on busy days they simply do not have the luxury of spending time being led down a seemingly endless path. Appellate judges who grant you an oral argument expect you to take advantage of the opportunity by not wasting their time and yours.

Getting to the point takes preparation. Repeatedly cut down your argument until you reach its essence. The essence is the core struggle between the parties and why your client should win. Do not wallow in the detail. Instead, focus on the big picture.

Consider the motion to compel discovery example, *Smith v. Acme.* Suppose you start out by saying, "Mr. Smith is entitled to receive documents that are relevant and proportional to the needs of the case. Rule 26 says so. The leading case of *Jones v. XYZ* confirms this." The judge is already asleep before you have begun, and you have not told him anything that he does not know.

Get to the point to show the court that you honor its time. You will also capture the judge's attention, thereby generating some interest in what you are saying. Try saying, "The insurer is hiding behind a problem it created. The insurance company has painted itself into a corner by not storing its data electronically." A brief yet focused argument is no easy task and takes time and preparation. Once you have chosen your arguments, begin by simplifying them for oral delivery. Simple messaging has fewer syllables, memorable phrasing, and eliminates the foundation established in the papers. Your goal is to make the court's job easy—summarize the final take-away point of the argument. You will likely be reducing three pages of persuasive writing into three lines of oral delivery.

Exercise

Practice reducing a written argument into an oral argument. Pick a written motion or response you have authored. Choose the strongest argument for oral delivery. Boil down the argument into a simple, understandable form. Practice delivering this argument in ninety seconds. (*Hint*: A regularly paced delivery should be 160 words per minute.) Can you give the reasons why you win in sixty seconds? In thirty seconds? Take the same argument and change the wording or angle so it does not sound the same. This accordion exercise will force you to choose only the pivotal facts needed, and then allow you to add context and essential details, all in keeping with a tight time frame.

3.5.3 *Inconsistent Arguments*

Watch out for inconsistent arguments. Judges have the capacity to accept some inconsistency in arguments, but too much inconsistency dilutes the strength of your strongest points. Imagine representing someone charged with murder. At trial, the attorney argues to the jury: "John did not kill Ann. But if you think he did, it was in self-defense. If you do not believe it was in self-defense, then it was an accident." There comes a time when you dilute the strength of your strongest argument by adding conditions and "if/then" reasoning. It looks like you are hoping that something—anything—sticks.

The logic and the credibility of the advocate are lost with too many inconsistent arguments. There are times when you need inconsistent arguments, but if you have too many contingencies, then the holes in the original proposition become too large.

Exercise

Practice identifying inconsistent arguments. Take the following example and note at which step you think the original and strongest argument loses strength.

STEP 1: There was no meeting of the minds for the contract.

STEP 2: If you find there was a meeting of the minds, then there was no consideration.

STEP 3: If you find there was consideration, then the contract is ambiguous.

STEP 4: If you find the contract is not ambiguous, then it is void because of impossibility of performance.

Most listeners would accept Steps 1 and 2, but not Steps 3 or 4. That being said, a Plan B can save you if you sense the judge is disagreeing with you. Pivot to a pre-determined fallback position. A fallback position may be a different argument, or it may be a concession that you and your client have agreed upon before the hearing. Usually, presenting a fallback argument is not problematic so long as you do not present a plethora of inconsistent arguments that undermine each other. *Art:* Knowing when that one additional argument undermines your stronger ones.

3.6   Know the Other Side's Case

Before making her move, a good chess player maps out her opponent's potential moves in her head to determine the most effective move possible. The same principle applies here. Once you choose your strongest arguments, step into the shoes of your opponent. Outline her arguments. Anticipate what she will present to the court. If you have colleagues working with you on the matter, ask one to draft the other side's argument so you can freshly react and rework yours. Further, as an exercise, ask yourself how you would argue the case if you were the opponent. After this, sharpen your arguments to overcome the opponent's anticipated arguments. You can never effectively argue your case without knowing the other side. As the famous Chinese military strategist Sun Tzu said: "If you know the enemy and know yourself, you need not fear the result of a hundred battles."

For example, as the petitioner in a preliminary injunction motion, you must predict what the respondent will argue to the court. After you have argued that your client is likely to succeed on the merits and that the balance of harms favors him, the respondent might alert the court of the difficulty associated with enforcing such an injunction. As the petitioner, you need to be ready with talking points that preclude the respondent's argument. "Your Honor, enforcing this injunction is no more difficult than enforcing any TRO or injunction. But here, we meet the requirements necessary to grant a preliminary injunction."

Likewise, if you know the appellant has a solid precedential case in his favor, but the facts are clearly distinguishable, you must predict how the appellant will argue around the differences in facts. You must build a defense by predicting their best argument and then build an offense by reworking your argument to attack this precedent in the best way possible.

Exercise

Before your next argument, argue aloud the other side's case. Say the arguments with conviction. Now, plan how you will respond to these arguments. Are they all worthy of a response? If not, which are? Build your counterarguments.

National Institute for Trial Advocacy

3.7   Consider Calling Witnesses—In a Motion Hearing

After picking your strongest arguments and understanding the likely arguments of the other side for an upcoming motion hearing, you may discover that you must call one or more witnesses. With most motions, it is unlikely that calling a witness will be necessary. Many motions are decided on the affidavits, depositions, or other papers submitted to the court before the hearing. Some, however, routinely require testimony; for example, motions to suppress evidence in a criminal setting, or *Daubert* hearings.[4] Examining witnesses is beyond the scope of this book, but the same techniques used in court to examine and cross-examine witnesses at trial should be used with witnesses in motion hearings. Make certain you are well versed on these skills.[5]

3.8   Consider Exhibits and Demonstratives

Visual aids and demonstratives are often wrongly forgotten by advocates. When your message can be more efficiently and powerfully shown and remembered by the court through a visual aid, use one. Many wise advocates prepare such demonstratives to use during the hearing, even if the advocate knows they are unlikely to become part of the record. The judge(s) will look at it anyway.

Decide beforehand whether an exhibit will make it easier for the court to follow your argument. The exhibit must highlight an important point that the judge must understand for your client to win. The exhibit may be as simple as a copy of the complaint, a map of the area in dispute, a copy of a critical case, a list of documents needed to be produced, a genealogical chart of descendants, excerpts from a deposition, timelines, a decision flowchart, or pictures that focus the court's attention.

Simple and clean is always better than complicated. For example, consider a wife's motion to set aside an agreed property settlement because her husband did not disclose the true value of the parties' assets. Wife's counsel may create two foam boards to be displayed side by side to the judge. One foam board itemizes the property disclosed to the wife through discovery, which adds up to a net worth of $1.1 million. The second foam board shows the same property with the values the husband provided to his bank for purposes of obtaining a loan showing the total value at $1.8 million. Only the figures of $1.1 million and $1.8 million are circled on the boards.

At the appellate level, demonstratives focus the court's attention quicker than paragraphs of words. Often the attorneys place the exhibits inside the briefs, but sometimes the exhibits are brought to the argument. If you plan to bring an exhibit to an appellate court, contact the court staff and your opponent ahead of time.

---

4. Daubert v. Merrell Dow Pharmaceuticals, Inc., 509 U.S. 579 (1993).
5. *See* Steve Lubet & J. C. Lore, Modern Trial Advocacy (6th Ed., 2020) for a good discussion on direct and cross-examination techniques.

Following are three photographs used in the above-mentioned utility case which effectively showed that the developer unnecessarily burdened the utility's easement:[6]

The transmission towers transmit 345,000 volts on one line and 138,000 volts on the other.

The utility needs room to access the towers because the equipment necessary to maintain the wires is enormous:

---

6. Duke Energy Indiana, LLC v. J&J Development Company, LLC, 142 N.E.3d 916 (Ind. Ct. App. 2020). Counsel, who capably argued for Duke, was Maggie L. Smith, Frost Brown Todd LLC.

The subdivision plat shows the yellow boundaries of the easement and the sole road access to the subdivision:

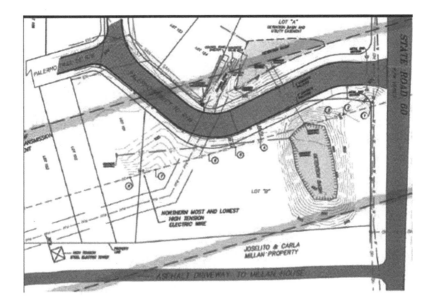

The images above showcase the efficient and illustrative use of demonstratives, and how much time would be wasted if the practitioner attempted to verbally describe the pictures to the court. The practicality and logistics associated with having demonstratives created and reproduced mean you need to think of them early to avoid a fire drill. Prepare well in advance so you have time to practice with the exhibits before the argument.

3.9 Anticipate Questions

We have talked about how preparing for an argument is preparing for spontaneity. The spontaneity generally does not come from the other side, as you have a pretty good idea from the papers what your opponent will argue. Rather, the spontaneity and its accompanying fear arise from the prospect of the judge(s) asking questions you have not anticipated.

Questions allow a window into the judge's mind to discover the struggles of the court. When you are asked a question, the court is inviting you to assist in the problem solving. Most judges appreciate attorneys who act as their partners in resolving disputes. Judges ask questions to clear up misunderstandings, clarify thinking, and learn about the facts and the law. Appellate judges also ask questions to tease out and understand how the court's decision will affect future litigants.

There may be questions that you are unable to answer, but with some thoughtful planning, you should be able to anticipate many of the questions that you may be asked. If you can predict the questions, you can and should prepare the responses to those questions.

Anticipating questions requires you to place yourself in the court's shoes. Think back to the first time that you heard the facts of the case. What questions did you have? What worried you? What struggles did you have? Were the facts the problem? Or was the law the problem? Or, heaven forbid, both? What is your likelihood of success? The court is likely to grapple with the same issues. As we delve deeper into a case, our natural tendency is to become more convinced we are right. Take a step back to your initial impressions. From this vantage point, you can anticipate many of the court's questions.

This is one of many instances where developing and maintaining great collegial relationships bears fruit. Get fresh perspective from a trusted colleague who can put on the hat of a judge and brainstorm areas of concern and provide a blueprint of what a judge is likely to ask you at a hearing or oral argument.

Creating a list of potential questions is only the first step; you must also prepare the answers. Chapters Seven, Eight, and Nine are devoted to the types of questions you may be asked and how to effectively answer them. If you spend time anticipating likely questions and practicing picture-perfect responses, your comfort level and confidence will increase.

3.10   Be Ready to Negotiate

Judges want to resolve disputes. That is their job. A motion hearing provides an opportunity for the judge to collect all the lawyers together in one place, and most judges cannot help urging the parties to settle. When all opposing attorneys are in one room, there is a chance for resolution. A motion hearing is one of those opportune moments. Judges cannot resist the temptation to negotiate.

The judge may subtly, or not so subtly, direct the parties to negotiate. Who has not heard at the beginning of a hearing, "Counsel, why haven't you settled this case?" Alternatively, in the middle of a hearing, the court may directly negotiate with you: "Counsel, do you really think that the noncompete should be enforced in a fifty-mile radius? Isn't twenty miles sufficient?" In either situation, decide ahead of time if you and your client have a fallback position or ready concession. Prepare a spectrum of possibilities to discuss with your client ahead of the hearing if you expect to have a judge who will urge a meeting of the minds. Are you willing to accept less than you are asking? This decision must be made beforehand, with your client's approval.

Before the hearing, explain to your client the result of the motion, win or lose. Describe how the judge may push for settlement or a plea deal or ask for compromises or stipulations. Find out the client's boundaries. Determine how much leeway you have to negotiate on the spot. Explain that this is just a battle in the longer war, and together decide if it is time to die on the sword.

Let us return to the request for all documents pertaining to claims against the insurance company for bad faith in *Smith v. Acme.* Suppose the court seems concerned with the volume and confidentiality of some of the documents you have requested. Consider agreeing with the court that the order should compel redacted documents excising any confidential information. Or, on the other side of the continuum, you may agree that the order should compel only the names, addresses, and telephone numbers of those people making bad-faith claims against the insurer, along with the title of any action filed, the court it was filed in, and the cause number. The final compromise may end somewhere in the middle, and you should obtain your client's consent for any agreement. Your client will be comfortable with a certain range of solutions, and you need to know those boundaries before negotiations start in a hearing.

Although rare, appellate courts have been known to press for settlement, especially in cases where the outcome will make neither side happy. More often in appeals, the judges will let an advocate know that they are not swallowing the advocate's hardline position but might be willing to accept a middle ground. On the spot, the advocate must decide whether to accept the judges' compromise. Some appellate courts give the advocate a chance to backpedal her ask if the result from the bench will be ultimately displeasing to the client. "Are you sure you want to ask for attorney's fees for the prevailing party? This is not being asked by the other side." This question should warn the advocate that she may indeed be the loser and then be on the hook for both invoices. Of course, compromise must be only with the client's consent, which the attorney must receive before the oral argument. This requires preparation and ample time set aside to discuss the hearing with your client. *Art: Know when to fold.*

3.11   Short-Term and Long-Term Consequences

Before you filed your motion, you considered the long-term and short-term consequences of the request. Is it being filed at the client's insistence? Are you filing it to educate the judge(s) for future motions, and it does not matter if you win or lose? Will it only result in a cranky judge for the entirety of the case? Was your intention to delay? Is it dispositive? Is the motion one you are likely to lose at the trial court, but have a reasonable shot at the appellate level?

Your answers to these questions will affect your delivery in the courtroom. Decide before the hearing what tone you will use. If the motion is dispositive, you may be more passionate in your delivery. If you have little likelihood of success at the trial level and are convinced you are destined to appeal, your tone may be the professional tone of one merely making a record.

In an appellate court, you may file your appeal knowing that the request is futile at the intermediate level but wish to pursue the issues to the highest court. Try a professional tone. Or is there an issue that continues to arise in your area of the law that needs the court's direction? In that case, more zeal may be appropriate. Adjust your tone depending on your long- and short-term wishes.

3.12   Planning Worksheet

Completing this Oral Argument/Motion Planning Worksheet before your hearing should help you to clarify your thinking, develop a logical presentation, and anticipate and plan for the unexpected. Ultimately, you need to develop a personalized preparation worksheet that fits your practice and delivery style. The same worksheet can be used for a motion hearing or an appellate argument.

The completed worksheet below is an example of one used in the motion hearing to compel the insurance company to give documents of previous bad-faith claims in *Smith v. Acme.*

MOTION PLANNING WORKSHEET	
Legal Elements	**Statute, Cases, Law**
1. Relevant to the claim	Rule 26 (Tab 1) .
2. Proportional to need	Rule 37 (Tab 1)
3. Not unduly burdensome	
Critical Good Facts	**Bad Facts**
1. Request for production (Tab 2)	1. Complaints are public
2. 1st demand (Tab 3)	2. Claims form confidential info
3. 2nd demand (Tab 4)	3. Six years requested (Tab 2)
4. Motion to compel (Tab 5)	4. Manual search (Tab 7)
5. Protective order first learned of problem (Tab 7)	
6. $100,000 cost—speculative (Tab 6)	
7. Most files computerized (Tab 7)	
8. Ten verdicts against Acme	
Theme and Sub-Themes	
Insurance company hiding history of bad faith	
Burden is of its own doing	

Time Allotted	**When**	**Where**
10 minutes	August 15 motions call	ND Indiana-Hammond

Witnesses	**Subpoenaed Date**	**Exhibits**
None	N/A	1st demand letter
		2nd demand letter

(Continued)

MOTION PLANNING WORKSHEET	
Questions	*Responses*
How is request proportional to needs?	The information is relevant to pattern.
How can $100,000 in costs be justified on claim that may be worth less than $100,000?	Claim is worth more than $100,000. Even if not, insurance company caused its own problems.

Strongest Argument
Pattern of denying bad-faith claims is highly relevant to this bad-faith claim.

Argument 2
Burden on the insurance company is of its own doing.

Argument 3
The plaintiff has tried in good faith to resolve this matter outside court; the insurance company has not.

Opponent's Argument 1 and Response
Unduly burdensome. Discovery costs more than the claim.
Insurance company caused burden by keeping claims in hard copy instead of computerizing. Deliberately done in an attempt to hide its bad conduct.

Opponent's Argument 2 and Response
Request not proportional to the needs of the case.
Proportional because of the highly relevant nature of the information.

Fallback Position	*Client's Approval*
Court pleadings from cases for two years	Yes

See Appendix A for a blank Oral Argument/Motion Planning Worksheet. You will find instructions to download the worksheet as a Word document that you can then customize for your own use in oral argument or motion practice.

3.13   Prepare a Long and a Short Script

Decide how much paper you need at court to feel comfortable with your oral presentation. You need as much supportive material as necessary at your fingertips to guide you through your planned scheme and rescue you should you get thrown off your game. Some people are content with thinking through their argument, outlining it in their head, and jotting a few notes on an envelope. Most are not.

An effective tool is to prepare a long script and a short script. A long script is the lengthy version of what you want to say in court, organized by theme, strongest arguments, issues likely to concern the court through questions, and conclusion. A short script is a condensed version.

Creating a long script clarifies and organizes your thought process. Ideally, you will never deliver your long script because the judge will ask you questions about what interests him. But if the judge is not engaged, you will have the long script as a backup.

Learn how to turn your long script into a short script. A general rule is to shorten each page of your long script to one or two sentences. This becomes your "elevator speech"—what you would say to someone during an elevator ride about why you should win your argument. Creating a long and short script will help when you find yourself with less time in an oral argument than you hoped because of very lengthy or multiple judicial interventions. We deal in depth with long and short scripts in Chapter Eleven.

3.14   Know the Architecture of an Argument

In preparing for your argument, know the structure of the final product. Below is our recommended architecture for a successful argument. We discuss all the component parts of the argument and how to put them together in detail throughout the rest of the book.

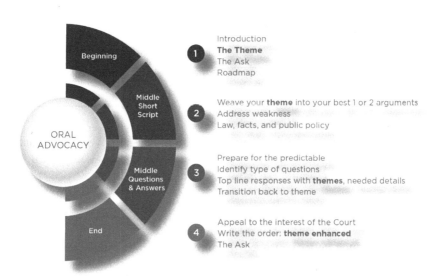

3.15   Prepare the Materials You Need for Court

Put together a three-ring binder to take to the lectern when addressing the court. Make sure you can easily open your binder and remove the pages. If your materials are bound like a brief, you will not be able to quickly find the information you need during the hearing and, once found, will not be able to keep it open on its own at the page you need. Detailed instructions with a photo example about how to create a proper argument portfolio are included in Chapter Eleven.

Alternatively, write your main outline notes in a large-tip marker on the sides of a file folder. For example, if you organize your main outline by issue, devote each side of the folder to an issue. Then create additional file folders for each section that you would tab if you were using a three-ring binder. The goal is to be able to easily retrieve your information.

Note: When we refer to notes throughout this book, we mean paper or electronic. As most courtrooms are becoming digitized, tablets are more widely used by advocates. We still recommend a back-up paper version in case of a technical failure.

CHAPTER FOUR

THEMES: THE WHAT, THE WHY, AND THE HOW

On March 3, 2009, Theodore B. Olson stood at the podium before the members of the United States Supreme Court for his fifty-first argument in the Court. The case, *Caperton v. A. T. Massey Coal Co.*,[1] was the second of four cases before the Court he would argue in just twelve weeks. He represented Hugh Caperton, the petitioner.

Caperton had sued Massey Coal and received a jury verdict against the company for $50 million. While an appeal filed by Massey Coal pended before the West Virginia Supreme Court, the chief executive officer of the company contributed $3 million to the campaign effort of Brant Benjamin. The $3 million was more money than Benjamin and his supporters had raised from all his other donors combined. Benjamin won the seat, ousting the then-sitting West Virginia Supreme Court Justice. Caperton moved to recuse Justice Benjamin from the case; Benjamin refused, and became part of the 3–2 majority vote for Massey Coal.

Before the U.S. Supreme Court, Ted Olson calmly—some would say matter-of-factly—spoke: "In the Magna Carta, the king promised: 'To no one will we sell justice.'"

He nailed it. Few words. Huge impact.

Themes have long been used effectively in trial work. The most well-known theme in modern legal history is largely remembered by all attorneys, young and old, more than twenty years later: "If it doesn't fit, you must acquit." This theme worked and became the mantra of the O. J. Simpson case worldwide because it simplified a complex issue, evoked a picture, and was memorable.

Likewise, themes are essential in arguments before a trial judge or appellate panel. This chapter explores what themes are, why they are important, what constitutes a good theme, how to create them, and what to do with them.

4.1 The *What*

A theme is the main point—the take-away of the case. If you had to boil down your case to one or two sentences, what would you say? A theme is the essence of

---

1. Caperton v. A. T. Massey Coal Co., 556 U.S. 868 (2009).

your argument—why you should win. It is a powerful, pithy statement that explains not only the logic of your argument, but also the heart of your argument—why the judges should care about ruling for you. The theme summarizes the entire argument in a few memorable phrases. A good theme is catchy and clever. It should remain in the judges' heads and become the water-cooler line repeated between judges and clerks as they deliberate. Themes predict the issue the court will struggle with. And a great theme will inspire the judge(s) to action.

Consider these examples of themes:

- On a motion for preliminary injunction: "A trade secret lost is lost forever."[2]

- In a case regarding the applicability of the First Amendment to false speech: "The remedy for speech that is false is speech that is true . . . . The response to the straightout lie is the simple truth."[3]

- In a case about the limits on a government's eminent domain power: "Every home, church or corner store would produce more tax revenue and jobs if it were a Costco, a shopping mall, or a private office building. But if that's the justification for the use of eminent domain, then any city can take property anywhere within its borders for any private use . . . ."[4]

- In a child abuse case: "This case is about a mother's love. Her love of cocaine and herself."

- On a summary judgment motion in a patent infringement case: "They may as well have handed our product to the [competitor] and said, 'Here, make one for us.'"[5]

 There is no reason to umbrella your entire case under one theme. *Science:* Subthemes are permissible and often advisable. Multiple themes work particularly well in a complicated matter such as a *Markman* hearing, multidistrict litigation (MDL), class action, or appellate case, but also in the simpler cases with more than one facet.

As an example, in a motion to set aside a default judgment, the overarching theme may be, "Every person deserves his day in court." However, we know that Federal Rule of Civil Procedure 60(b) requires more than the platitude that every person deserves his day in court. It requires that there be excusable neglect on the part of the defendant in not answering the complaint. So, a subtheme may be, "An attorney's neglect should not be visited on his unwary client." You do not need a theme

---

2. FMC Corp. v. Taiwan Tainan Giant Indus. Co., 730 F.2d 61, 63 (2d Cir. 1984).

3. United States v. Alvarez, 567 U.S. 709, 727 (2012).

4. *See generally* Kelo v. City of New London, 545 U.S. 469 (2005).

5. *See generally* Stryker Corp. v. Zimmer, Inc., 782 F.3d 649 (Fed. Cir. 2014).

that perfectly wraps up all issues in your case. Start with the theme of your strongest argument and integrate the subthemes when those additional issues arise.

Themes can also be created for fallback positions. *Art:* If you see that a judge will not agree with you on your main theme, have alternative themes prepared and ready. For example, you start with a theme in a whistleblower case: "Mr. Doe is being punished for cooperating." As the hearing develops, you see that the judge is completely unsympathetic toward Mr. Doe, and you decide to shift focus to the company. "The company should take responsibility for its biased research."

4.2   The *Why*

Why use a theme in an argument? First, the act of disciplined simplification focuses your thinking. It helps you to find your most concise, perfect argument. Not only does it focus you, but it focuses the judge's attention on what you see as important, gives her a framework to look at the case, and simplifies difficult concepts.

Second, getting immediately to the point will be well received by the court. Judges feel overburdened by their caseload and have little patience with attorneys who do not get to the core of the argument immediately. The detailed, foundation-building argument should have taken place through the papering of the motion. The hearing is a chance to boil it down and give the court the crux of why you win. Themes help you quickly reach the heart of your argument.

Third, a theme straightaway captures a judge's attention, and with a captive audience you have a greater chance to keep the audience interested—at least for a while. Imagine sitting on the bench after reading all the papers and hearing a lawyer begin with, "We are here on the issue of whether Congress can require health insurance." You have lost the judge by repeating the obvious before you have even begun. A judge's life is boring, at least on the bench. *Art:* Add a little fun to it with a theme. Be clever; add some spice.

Fourth, in communications, the rule of primacy and recency teaches that a listener remembers what is said first and last in a presentation. If your first words are the essence of the case, then the judge will remember what you think is the foundation of your case. Start and finish with the theme, developing it as needed based on the judge's reaction. Many advocates follow the sage advice that sums up the importance of primacy and your theme: "Don't bury the lede." A clever theme reverberates in a judge's head well after the argument, and if *your* theme is resonating, you are more likely to prevail. Resonating themes are also discussed among court staff. A properly crafted theme is memorable. It can be replayed without struggle—"Sanctions should be a last resort option," for example. This theme insinuates that the moving party is premature and dramatic. It calls for reason and fairness, without whining for them.

Lastly, a good theme invokes a moral imperative. It compels the court to act. Usually, the theme speaks to a judge's inner sense of fairness and justice. For example, "Equity does not reward those with unclean hands" and the petitioner has "unclean hands because . . ." clarifies that a ruling for the petitioner would be unfair. Yet, at the same time, it addresses the very issue the judge must resolve. Likewise, in a discovery dispute, using a theme such as "They are asking for too much, with too little value, at too high a cost," tells the court where justice lies.

A strong, memorable theme serves as a foundation for an argument, one that grounds you throughout and resonates with the judge.

4.3 The *How*

Begin by thinking about the underlying principles behind your argument. Begin with your broad theme before you decide on your memorable theme.

Here is what Ted Olson's creative process developing the *Caperton* theme may have looked like:

Unlike appellate cases, many motions are rule driven, so the broad theme derives from a rule, making theme creation effortless. Broad themes for common motions include the following:

MOTION	MOVANT'S THEMES	RESPONDENT'S THEMES
Motion to Dismiss	• Taking the allegations together still does not add up to a claim.	• We have pled enough. Sufficient notice has been given.
Motion for Summary Judgment	• The facts are so clear we can only get to one result.	• There only needs to be one factual dispute. Let me count the ways.
Motion to Compel Discovery	• Discovery rules are broad. This information is important to our case and may help us to settle.	• What is being asked for is overly broad. Discovery is bound by the notion of proportionality. The request is burdensome.
Motions in Limine (exclude)	• Educate the judge on what will happen at trial if this comes in.	• Let's see what happens at trial. Indicate to the judge you need a context that only a trial can give.
Motions for Sanctions	• The process is important, and the court needs to gain control of it.	• Sanctions are unduly harsh, considering the circumstances.

MOTION	MOVANT'S THEMES	RESPONDENT'S THEMES
Motion for Interlocutory Appeal	• (Worry the judge.) • If this is not fixed now, then there is a bigger problem later. • If we are right, then we will have wasted an incredible amount of time and resources for naught. • We do not want to hold up the proceedings, but neither do we wish to duplicate efforts.	• (Argue the merits.) • The court was right. • Granting the request will result in piecemeal litigation. • If every ruling is taken up midstream, then chaos will result. • Balance is important.
Motion to Stay	• Judicial economy and fairness compel a stay. We are willing to compromise on the conditions for the stay. Suggest reasonable conditions.	• This is only a delay tactic. More time will accomplish nothing.
Post-trial motions	• You did not mean to make a mistake, but you did.	• The decision was correct in the first place.

You can see that in creating our broad themes for each of the above motions, we subconsciously slipped into a memorable theme. It is sometimes easier than it looks to take a broad theme and to turn it into something memorable. Consider a motion for post-trial error. A theme for the movant may look similar to this:

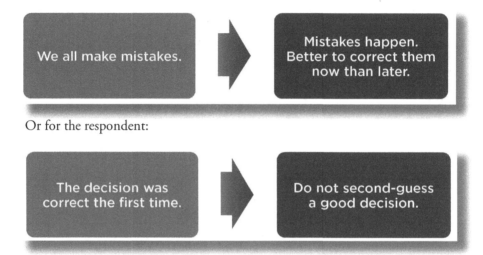

We all make mistakes. → Mistakes happen. Better to correct them now than later.

Or for the respondent:

The decision was correct the first time. → Do not second-guess a good decision.

4.3.1   *The Memorable Theme*

Once you decide on a fitting generic theory, create a memorable theme that personalizes your argument. Be creative. Inspiration can come from many sources. Here are a few examples of techniques for creating a memorable theme.

The Headline:
- Create a newspaper headline about your case. What would the headline or bumper sticker read?

- Examples:

    o "Put up or shut up." (Summary judgment)

    o "Congress doesn't have the power to create a market just to regulate it."[6]

Legal sayings:
- Call upon one of the hundreds of legal maxims that have survived the test of time.

- Examples:

    o "Justice delayed is justice denied."

---

6. National Federation of Independent Business v. Sebelius, 567 U.S. 519 (2012).

o "For every wrong, there is a remedy."

o "One who seeks equity must do equity."

Quotes from cases:

- Pick critical language that cannot be ignored and use it as your theme. This is especially helpful to use with a judge who wants to be affirmed on appeal.

- Example: "Reasonable suspicion to stop is missing here."[7] (Motion to suppress)

Other side's words:

- Turn the other side's words from their papers into your theme.

- Example: "We value judicial efficiency just as much as the defendants." (Defending motion for interlocutory appeal or prosecution of a preliminary injunction)

Quotations or Idioms:

- Quotes from books or the Internet.

- Example: "They are trying to make much ado about nothing." (Summary judgment)

Advertisements:

- Ads are so well-known to a wide audience they provide common material for themes.

- Example: "It's the real thing."[8] (Patent infringement)

Songs or poems:

- Find songs of the judge's generation to make your point. Do not quote Beyoncé, Jay Z, or Billie Eilish to an older judge. Stick with The Beatles, Lionel Richie, Bob Dylan, or even Roy Orbison for the mature judge.[9]

- Example: "You don't need a weatherman to know which way the wind blows."[10] (Expert testimony is not helpful to the trier of fact.)

---

7. Terry v. Ohio, 392 U.S. 1 (1967).
8. Coca-Cola advertisement, 1969.
9. *See* Alex Long, *The Freewheelin' Judiciary: A Bob Dylan Anthology,* 38 Fordham Urb. L.J. 1363 (2012), for an interesting discussion of opinions where judges cite song lyrics.
10. Bob Dylan, Subterranean Homesick Blues (Columbia Records 1965).

Rhetorical questions:

- Ask a question but be sure to know the answer and answer it. Do not let the question linger unanswered.

- Examples: "Is there a material issue of fact? Yes, there are four of them." (Summary judgment), "Who is the arbiter of what the Constitution says—the judiciary or the president?"[11] The Court of course.

Metaphors and Analogies:

- Comparing one thing to another simplifies complicated concepts.

- Example: "This government technology is like allowing the FBI to park in my bedroom."[12] (Motion to suppress)

The Rule of Threes:

- There is something magical about the rule of threes: "Father, Son and Holy Spirit." "Beginning, Middle, and End." "See no evil, speak no evil, hear no evil." "Never have so few given so much to so many." They are memorable and provide a natural structure to your argument, couple it with alliteration for extra impact.

- Example: "This case is about precedent, policy, and predictability."

Clichés (+):

- While clichés can be annoying, they often provide a quick way to brainstorm the right theme. Start with a tired cliché and then dress it up or change it to be fresh and unexpected.

- Example: "The plaintiff has cast his net too wide."

These are all examples of themes that strike the balance between being memorable without being cheesy or boring. For more examples, see Appendix A.

4.3.2 Bad Themes

In the same way a good theme elevates the argument, a bad theme eats away at the effectiveness of an argument. Judges remember good themes; they remember bad themes even more. Here are some common types of bad themes:

---

11. Leon Jaworski representing the petitioner in United States v. Nixon, 418 U.S. 683 (1974).
12. *See* George Lakoff and Mark Johnson, Metaphors We Live By (Univ. of Chicago Press, 2003), for an innovative look at how people think in metaphors.

Issue Restatements:

- The lawyer restates the obvious. You are wasting your time and the court's time. Say something the court does not know.

- Bad example: "We are here today to review the trial court's granting of summary judgment to the appellee." Yawn!

Name Calling:

- Counsel starts the argument disparaging the opponent, his counsel, or the trial court judge. With the name calling, the judge knows she is ready to watch a mudslinging contest. Everyone gets dirty in the process.

- Bad examples:

  o "Your Honor, Counsel is being disingenuous. There he goes again with more misleading statements."

  o "Counsel's arguments are frivolous."

Hyperbole:

- Exaggeration damages your credibility. Once lost, credibility is difficult to regain. If the case is so obvious or clear, why are you still in court?

- Bad examples:

  o "This is obvious."

  o "The answer is clear."

  o "This is a simple case."

Too cute by half:

- If the theme is too cheeky, it comes across as childish.

- Bad example: "The defense is runnin' against the wind"[13] (motion to suppress on a fleeing charge).

Overused Clichés:

- Triteness does not inspire any judge and causes lost attention. Can you guess how many times the typical trial court judge hears in a year, "This is a fishing expedition?" Let us leave it as once is too many.

- Bad example: "Justice is blind."

---

13. Bob Seger, *Against the Wind*, on Nine Tonight (Capitol Records 1981).

Easy to turn:

- Avoid using a theme the other side can flip and use against you.

- Bad example: In a medical malpractice case, the defendant's counsel uses a theme such as "Risk is part of life." There are a wide slew of comebacks available to the plaintiff's counsel: "Yes, life is risky, Your Honor, but I doubt my client would have taken the risk of ingesting poison had she known."

More than three sentences in length:

- The theme is a hook, not a dissertation. Think short and clever rather than long and intellectual.

- Bad example: "We have tried to negotiate with the other side, but they continue to throw roadblocks in our way. The defense will not budge on the dollar amount, and they won't consider a more creative settlement offer, blah, blah, blah."

4.4   What Do You Do with It?

Arguably, the four notes at the beginning of Beethoven's Fifth Symphony are the most recognizable notes of any classical piece of music. Even non-lovers of classical music know them. Beethoven used these notes as a theme to capture the attention of the listener and create a memorable introduction. Likewise, use your theme to capture the attention of the court immediately. State your theme during the first seconds of your argument. After your succinct, memorable theme, explain the broader theme, and only then tackle the intricacies of the law and facts.

At the point where you are mired in the details, come back to the theme to give the judge relief from the concentration needed to understand the complexities of your argument. Then plunge back into the subtleties of your argument. The judge(s) will be thankful for a short mental break. And just as Beethoven peppered his four-note theme through his symphony to bring the listener back to the familiar, so too will your theme bring the judge back to comfortable ground.

Rely on your theme to bring you and the court back to the strengths of your case after answering a question. Avoid the hesitation and look of panic when your answer is complete, and instead utilize effective transitions back into your theme and strongest arguments.

Let your theme serve as a rescue device for when you stumble. Instead of fumbling through your notes, hoping to find your next point, get back on track by reiterating your theme.

Conclude your argument with your theme, knowing that what is said last by you will be remembered by the court. Integrate your theme with your request for relief.

Repetition is a successful persuasion technique, so thread your theme throughout the argument. Themes are like a refrain in a song: they bring the listener back to the main chorus.

4.5   Avoid Theme Rot

Beethoven's Fifth Symphony repeats his four-note theme throughout. But, the theme mutates, and while still recognizable, transforms itself frequently to sound ever so slightly different. The theme remains visible and familiar, but not annoyingly repetitive.

Sometimes, if used too frequently, a repetitive theme can become irritating. Follow Beethoven's technique: avoid theme rot by pivoting before your theme has become its own cliché.

Revive your stale theme with elegant repetition. Find other ways of saying the same thing. Sometimes, this is accomplished by changing the words of the themes by using synonymous phrases.

Here is an example of synonymous themes for a discovery motion:

- "Hiding the ball prolongs litigation."

- "Not providing discovery wastes everyone's time."

- "At this rate, we will never resolve the real issues."

- "The more arguing over these minor matters, the more the court's time is chewed up."

- "This is not a game of hide 'n seek."

Or, as another example of tweaking your theme:

- "When you ain't got nothing, you got nothing to lose."[14]

- "Hypothetical injury is not enough for standing."

- "Plaintiff must have something to lose in order to sue."

- "Standing is fundamental."

- "No harm, no remedy."

---

14. Sprint Communications Co. v. APCC Services, 555 U.S. 269 (2008).

Many advocates are faithful to the principles of primacy and recency. They maximize the effectiveness of their theme by saving the best iteration to close the argument and use their second-best synonymous theme to open it.

Another effective strategy available to maximize synonymous theme usage is to give the theme in rapid succession. It was used in the aforementioned case, *Caperton*, where Ted Olson chose rapid succession delivery of synonymous themes to finish his argument with a bang. He first said: "To no one will we sell justice." He then ended his argument quoting Blackstone, "For injury done to every subject, he may take his remedy by the course of law and have justice freely without sale."

 Art: Another method to avoid the monotony of the same theme is to change the style of the delivery. For example, you can put heavy stress on certain words:

"There are *six* requirements, and the government has met *each* and *every one*."

You can also slow down certain groups of words:

"*There are six requirements*, and the government has met each and every one."

Finally, you can make the same wording sound fresh while showing emotion in your voice by raising your pitch or volume through a different section:

"There are six requirements, and the government *has met each and every one*."

4.6   Theme Affirmation

Strive for theme affirmation. Create a theme so good that it appears in the decision of the court. A good theme aids the judge in writing her own opinion. Your theme may even appear verbatim in the court's decision. When an attorney effectively establishes a theme, the judge will often reflect on that theme as she writes the decision. As an example of this, consider William Kunstler's arguments on behalf of Johnson in *Texas v. Johnson.*[15] Kunstler argued:

> I understand this flag has serious important meanings. The Chief Justice has mentioned many times that it is not just pieces of material, blue and white and red. It has real meaning to people out there . . . . (This case) goes to the heart of the First Amendment, to hear things or see things that we hate test the First Amendment more than hearing or seeing things that we like. It (First Amendment) wasn't designed for things we like. They never needed a first amendment.

Kunstler established a theme—that we cannot suppress things we merely do not like—and this theme was strong enough that it was embodied in the majority opinion written by Justice Brennan. Brennan echoes the theme:

---

15. *Texas v. Johnson*, 491 U.S. 397 (1989).

The way to preserve the flag's special role is not to punish those who feel differently about these matters. It is to persuade them that they are wrong . . . . We can imagine no more appropriate response to burning a flag than waving one's own, no better way to counter a flag burner's message than by saluting the flag that burns, no surer means of preserving the dignity even of the flag that burned than by—as one witness here did—according its remains a respectful burial. We do not consecrate the flag by punishing its desecration, for in doing so we dilute the freedom that this cherished emblem represents.[16]

Themes are persuasive tools in your toolbox of advocacy skills. So, too, are facts. Once you develop a memorable theme, it is time to focus on the facts. Weave them together with the law, and you have a high chance of a promising ruling.

---

16. *Id.* at 419, 420.

CHAPTER FIVE

FACTS

After Japan attacked Pearl Harbor, sixteen B-25 bombers and a ninety-man crew converged on the deck of the naval aircraft carrier the U.S.S. *Hornet*, readying for an aerial attack of Tokyo. Lieutenant Colonel Jimmy Doolittle, later General Doolittle, led the charge. The weight of the bombers and the short runway made the take-off risky. None of the pilots had ever launched from a carrier. But there was no choice; the B-25s had range restrictions and the U.S. had no allies close enough to Japan. The take-off was successful. The psyche of the two nations dramatically changed. Morale in the U.S. skyrocketed, and the Japanese realized their vulnerability to sneak attacks. The Doolittle Raid, seventy-five years later, became the inspiration for the development of the B-21 stealth bomber commissioned by the U.S. Air Force and scheduled for completion in 2025. While no bomber is completely invisible, the B-21 is said to avoid detection more than any other bomber made to date.

Facts are the stealth bomber of oral persuasion. Facts invisibly persuade. Telling a judge how to rule does not work; showing a judge does. Through facts you show the judge why your client should win. The decision becomes the judge's creation, not yours. And all of us, even judges, are more resolute in our convictions if they are our own.

Look at any well-written appellate decision. After reading the facts, you should know who wins. You may not know until you have read the decision in its entirety *why* the party wins, but you will know *who* wins. Let us look at Justice Elena Kagan's recitation of the facts in *Miller v. Alabama*.[1] Evan Miller received a mandatory sentence of life without parole. The issue was whether a mandatory sentence of life without parole for a juvenile offender violated the Eighth Amendment's prohibition against cruel and unusual punishment. Justice Kagan recites the facts:

> Evan Miller was fourteen years old at the time of his crime. Miller had by then been in and out of foster care because his mother suffered from alcoholism and drug addiction and his stepfather abused him. Miller, too, regularly used drugs and alcohol; and he had attempted suicide four times, the first when he was six years old.

---

1. Miller v. Alabama, 567 U.S. 460 (2012).

One night in 2003, Miller was at home with a friend, Colby Smith, when a neighbor, Cole Cannon, came to make a drug deal with Miller's mother. The two boys followed Cannon back to his trailer, where all three smoked marijuana and played drinking games. When Cannon passed out, Miller stole his wallet, splitting about $300 with Smith. Miller then tried to put the wallet back in Cannon's pocket, but Cannon awoke and grabbed Miller by the throat. Smith hit Cannon with a nearby baseball bat, and once released, Miller grabbed the bat and repeatedly struck Cannon with it. Miller placed a sheet over Cannon's head, told him "I am God, I've come to take your life," and delivered one more blow. The boys then retreated to Miller's trailer, but soon decided to return to Cannon's to cover up evidence of their crime. Once there, they lit two fires. Cannon eventually died from his injuries and smoke inhalation . . . .

Relying in significant part on testimony from Smith, who had pleaded to a lesser offense, a jury found Miller guilty. He was therefore sentenced to life without the possibility of parole.[2]

Did fourteen-year-old Miller win his appeal? Of course. Why did Justice Kagan introduce Miller as a fourteen-year-old in and out of foster homes because of his addicted mother and abusive stepfather? Before we learn of Miller's crime, why are we told that Miller attempted suicide four times, the first at age six? We know why: facts drive the justice of the case. Facts convince us why fairness lies with one party or another. We conclude from reading the Justice's delivery of the facts that imposition of a mandatory life sentence on Miller would be unjust. We want the court to hold for Miller.

5.1   The Power of Facts

To fully comprehend the power of facts, consider this hypothetical:

Person A draws a gun, aims it, and deliberately shoots and kills Person B. Person A is a murderer. But what this statement only illustrated was the action—shooting at person B—and the intention—to kill person B. If you only look at the action and the intention, Person A is guilty of first-degree murder. But what if you now introduce the circumstances, the facts. Person A is awakened in the middle of the night by a window breaking. Person A peers down the stairs and sees a masked Person B. After shouting, "Who are you?" Person B shoots at Person A. Person A avoids the bullet, rushes to the house safe, and grabs a gun. Person A returns, shoots, and kills Person B. Now, Person A is not a murderer; rather he simply defended himself. The difference between the two scenarios is the first scenario neglected to outline the facts.

---

2. *Id.* at 468–9.

Facts contextualize. Facts drive decisions.[3] Facts tell us who wins or who loses. But facts are also subject to interpretation. Sometimes they can be spun to fit multiple narratives. The goal is to persuade the judge to view the facts through your prism—to place your spin on what occurred and why.

Judges need to hear the facts from you. *You* are the expert of the facts, not the court. *You* have lived with your client's cause; the judge has not. *You* have interviewed your client, studied the documents and exhibits supporting your client's position; the judge has not. A persuasive presentation of the facts is vital to the success of any argument.

Not talking about the facts during the argument is like not talking about the facts to jurors during a closing. But at least with jurors, you know they have heard the facts during testimony and foreshadowed during the opening statement. With a judge, however, you never can be sure that he has read the papers in advance—and you certainly do not want to be so impertinent as to ask the judge if he has read them.

Good lawyers highlight facts in two different ways: in a dedicated fact section or a few sentences at a time interwoven with the legal issues. Both work. If you write a separate fact segment, do not start out by saying, "The facts of this case are . . . ." The judge will shut you down as soon as he hears this phrase as a sign you will repeat the facts written in the papers. If he has read them, you will waste his time; if not, he does not want you to know that he has not done his homework. Instead go directly to the essential facts. If you choose to lace the facts through your argument, condense the pertinent facts for each legal point into two or three sentences. Whatever organizational structure you select, this chapter offers techniques to persuasively present your facts to the court in the hope that the court will want to decide for your client.

Exercise

Read trial court or appellate court opinions. Begin with the facts. After reading the facts but before the analysis, try to decide who won. Consider what facts brought you to your conclusion, and then check to see if you guessed correctly.

5.2   Be a Storyteller

The guiding star of oral argument is a story. Humans understand the world in terms of stories. Whether it is a fairytale or a parable from Jesus, a simple story has immense power in conveying meaning to human minds. Because of this, consider

---

3. Louis Brandeis, later an Associate Justice on the United States Supreme Court, is known for writing the Brandeis Brief. It consisted of 100 pages—ninety-eight pages devoted to the facts and two pages to the law.

yourself a storyteller. *Art:* The characteristics of a good story are the characteristics of a good oral argument. The same do's and don'ts apply.

5.2.1 Create a Hero and a Villain

Your cases, like all legal disputes, are stories about people. Stories have characters—some good and honorable, others evil and flawed. These characters have reasons why they act as they do. Your audience, the judge, will assign a hero and a villain to the story at hand and make logical causal connections based on the facts you deliver. You need to control the narrative and present your argument so the judge reaches the conclusion that your side wears the white hat while the other side wears the black one. Tell the story showing the noble motives of your client and the nefarious ones of the opposing party. Frame your client as the protagonist and the opposing party as the villain. *Science:* Every good story clearly indicates who is who. The same principle applies to an oral argument.

One simple technique to portray the client as the likeable hero is how you talk about the client. Avoid calling your client "plaintiff," "defendant," "petitioner," "respondent," "appellant," or "appellee." First, it is confusing to the court. The judge, with each reference, must remember who is who. Second, it dehumanizes your client. Your goal is to make your client likeable. Start by using the client's actual name and avoid using "my client." The term "client" emphasizes that you are a hired gun. Your relationship to the client is not what is important. Who the client is, what the client did, and why the client acted a certain way is what really matters.

Instead, dehumanize the other side, but do not do so by constantly calling them "defendant" or "respondent." This confuses the judge and is too blatant an attempt to demonize. Instead, call the opposing side by his full name: John Wayne Gacy, for example, or simply his last name, Gacy. Call the opponent by their full corporation name: Campbell Soup Corporation, Inc. or Allstate Fire and Casualty Insurance Corporation, Inc. But after that first time, shorten the name to a commonly used word or phrase—Campbell's Inc. or Allstate Insurance—so you do not get tongue-tied.

This is not to say you may not judiciously call the opposing party *plaintiff, defendant, petitioner,* or *respondent.* At times, the reference clarifies matters or strengthens your argument: "This is the twentieth discovery motion brought by the petitioner. Each and every time, this court has denied the motion. Here we are again."

Your argument should continually build on this narrative that your client is the hero. As you deliver the argument, understand that every little detail has that purpose—to make your client the hero.

5.2.2 Contextualize

There is a reason every fairytale begins with "Once upon a time in a faraway land, there lived. . . ." Context. Every storyteller needs to acclimate the listener to the setting of the story. In the same way, in court, you must contextualize your facts.

Give context for the facts before you recite them. For example, "Mr. Blackburn drove home safely and followed every rule of the road. The police officer had no reasonable suspicion to stop him and no probable cause to search his car." Telling the court upfront allows the court to understand the facts in the context of the issue. Otherwise, the judge is asking himself, "Why is this important? Why are you telling me this?"

Further, context often gives the listener the opportunity to empathize. As an example, let us reexamine Justice Kagan's *Miller v. Alabama* opinion, discussed earlier in this chapter. We know that Miller struck Cannon repeatedly over the head with a baseball bat and then set fire to his trailer, causing his death. Yet, Justice Kagan humanized Miller by giving us the context for his conduct . . . he was a young kid trapped in a horrific environment. Before she mentioned Miller's crimes, she talked about the drug addiction, the suicide attempts, and the events leading up to Miller's crime. Context softens the blow.

5.2.3 Crucial Facts Only

Science: Do not waste time. Every detail has a purpose. In a story, too many plot threads over-complicate the narrative of the story. In an argument, too many unnecessary facts muddy the waters and confuse the court.

Distill the facts to the crucial facts relevant to the issues. Delete facts that are not important. Be picky; do not dump data on the court. Otherwise, the important facts of the case are lost in a morass of irrelevant facts. You have only limited time before the court, so use it wisely. Otherwise, the judge will become disinterested—or worse, aggravated.

Decide what facts are crucial by doing the good-fact/bad-fact analysis we discussed in Chapter Three. After you have brainstormed all the facts, good and bad, decide which facts are essential. With each fact on your table of facts, ask yourself, "Is this necessary for the court to know to resolve this case?" *Science:* Your presentation should include both the crucial good facts and bad facts relevant to the issues.

When choosing the facts, remember that uncontroverted facts, those agreed upon by both sides, are the most convincing. Stress the agreed facts. Stay away from facts not in the record or testimony. You will be seen as cheating.

You may be tempted to include unrelated facts that engender sympathy for your client. Proceed with caution. Blatantly appealing to a judge's sympathy seldom works. Obvious, overt, and open appeals to emotions may backfire. Judges are human beings who are influenced by the emotions of a situation. A light sprinkle of emotional facts may be appropriate.

For example, suppose you represent the plaintiff in a negligence case and are arguing against a motion for summary judgment. The issue is duty, but your client was seriously injured in the accident. A brief mention that your client "is paralyzed and will never walk again" will suffice. A judge does not need to be told repeatedly that your client was seriously injured; he understands. Talking about your client's injuries any more risks aggravating the judge and potentially hurting your cause. Judges pride themselves on making logical decisions. Of course, sympathy and fairness factor into a judge's decisions, but clear attempts to appeal to a judge's emotions usually tell him your legal argument is weak.

 Art: Generally, the more dramatic the facts are, the fewer of them you need and the less emotion you need to inject during delivery. An advocate needs to carefully choose facts when describing a gruesome murder and deliver those selective facts without much emotion. The more intense and dramatic the facts are, the less dramatic you should be. That said, you may need to dress up your facts and dial up the emotion discussing a corporation's S Corp tax status or the employee benefit dispute within a complicated corporate takeover, or the judge will suffer.

Another common mistake is to delineate every date of every event. Do not start your sentences with the default that "on such and such date, this occurred." Be sure you want the judge to focus on the exact date if you mention it. For example, if a statute of limitation tolls on June 1, that date is a crucial fact that must be mentioned. Most of the time, exact dates are not important. Do not clutter the judge's mind with them. Doing so sends the judge down a path of irrelevancy. He begins to think that the dates are the important facts to remember. Instead, focus on the sequential relationships: what events came first, second, and third. And do the math for the judge to drive home your points. Instead of saying that on June 24 a default judgment was entered, and the following year on February 23 a motion to set aside the default was filed, tell the court it was almost eight months after the default judgment before the motion to set aside was filed.

5.2.4 The Goldilocks Principle

Too many facts are problematic, but so are too few facts. The danger of knowing too much is that you assume the judge shares that knowledge; as a result, you tend to start the story in the middle. If the judge is not confident, he is unlikely to ask you to backpedal. If the judge does not stop you for clarification, then you have lost him. To avoid this, tell your story to someone who has never heard it to ensure that you have not omitted necessary facts. Follow the Goldilocks principle: not too many, not too few, just right.

Consider a motion for summary judgment. Imagine you represent a local restaurant, Chicago Burger. John Smith sues the restaurant for negligence for breaching its duty of care to its customers. One customer was killed and five were injured, including Smith, when a truck owned by Kenneth Levy crashed through the window of the restaurant. Levy also died in the accident. You filed a motion for summary judgment on Chicago Burger's behalf alleging that it owed no duty to the plaintiffs because Levy's actions were not reasonably foreseeable.

This story of the motion gives, quite simply, too many facts:

Counsel: Chicago Burger is a wholly owned subsidiary of Partial Foods Inc. Chicago Burger was incorporated in 2012. Partial Foods purchased the restaurant premises on July 20, 2012, and rented it to Chicago Burger soon thereafter on July 31, 2013. The organic meat restaurant is on the corner of Western and Chicago Avenues in Chicago in the up-and-coming and trendy Ukrainian Village. The restaurant is positioned twenty feet from the west side of Western Avenue and twenty feet from the north side of Chicago Avenue. Between the curb and the windows of the restaurant is a five-foot-wide sidewalk, and a one-foot-wide grassy area. On both Western and Chicago Avenues, the restaurant's façade is entirely covered with picture windows. Inside the restaurant, tables abut the windows so that the patrons may view the city landscape while eating. There is an outdoor seating area with ten tables.

On July 25, 2020, at 9:00 p.m., six patrons were sitting in an outdoor table right next to the sidewalk facing Chicago Avenue.

Meanwhile, Kenneth Levy had a fight with his wife at his home at Rockwell Street and Chicago Avenue, which was three blocks away, and left in his 2017 Dodge Charger traveling east down Chicago Avenue. Before he got into his car, Levy consumed a six-pack of beer in the preceding three hours. Their fight was about his frequent drinking.

As Levy drove down Chicago Avenue at forty-five miles per hour—twenty miles per hour over the speed limit—he crossed the centerline of Chicago Avenue immediately before Western Avenue and, at exactly 9:05 p.m., crashed into the seating area facing Chicago Avenue. Jenny West died, as did Levy, before the emergency crew arrived. The other five patrons suffered multiple injuries: Clive Gentry, a broken leg; Paul Bayou, a fractured pelvis; and Kathy Kite, Mandy Lopez, and Henry Aster, minor cuts and bruising.

Levy's autopsy revealed a blood alcohol content of .18. Levy had no insurance, so all the patrons sued Chicago Burger for negligence, alleging that Chicago Burger breached its duty of care to them.

Yawn . . . . if you read through this excerpt in its entirety, mazel tov. This version of the story wastes time on facts that are unimportant to the question of whether Chicago Burger could have reasonably foreseen the accident. It sends the judge on a wild goose chase through irrelevant matters, such as the relationship between Chicago Burger and Partial Foods, Inc.; the dates of incorporation; the dates of purchase of the restaurant; and the injuries sustained by nonplaintiffs. These diversions take the court's focus off the main issue, weakening the argument.

Now let's look at sample language with the opposite problem: it divulges too *few* facts.

> Counsel: Chicago Burger had no duty to the customers of its restaurant. Levy was drunk when he crashed into the restaurant's seating area, causing the plaintiffs injuries. He was speeding. There is no way that Chicago Burger could have foreseen Levy's actions.

Huh? This rendition of the facts leaves the listener wondering if he came into a story already in progress. Perhaps the judge read the papers before the hearing, but perhaps not. Even so, with a busy docket that day, the judge may not remember the facts of this case. Counsel assumes the court knows as much about the case as she does. In addition, the skeletal facts fail to paint a picture for the judge that he can remember.

Just as Goldilocks discovered at the house of the three bears, there is a happy medium for you. Not too many facts, not too few . . . just right:

> Counsel: Chicago Burger could not have reasonably foreseen that the drunken Kenneth Levy would crash into its outdoor seating area, killing one of its customers and injuring others. Chicago Burger is at the corner of Western and Chicago Avenues. Here is a diagram of how the restaurant is situated at that corner [*showing a map of the location*]. You can see the outdoor seating area complies with city ordinance.
>
> July 25 was like any other night at Chicago Burger. Customers were enjoying the food and outdoor area when Levy, after fighting with his wife and drinking six cans of beer, got behind the wheel of his car, drove eastbound on Chicago Avenue, crossed the center line, went across the westbound lane, jumped the curb, sped across the sidewalk, and crashed into the plaintiffs' table. Levy was driving 20 miles per hour over the speed limit, with a blood alcohol content of .18, which is over twice the legal limit. Chicago Burger could not have foreseen the actions of Levy and thus had no duty to the plaintiffs.

Note that although the "just right" version of the facts has fewer facts than the "too much" version, the "just right" version contains additional facts crucial to the issue of foreseeability. For example, included in the facts are that the restaurant was in compliance with city ordinance and that Levy went across the westbound lane, jumped the curb, and sped across the sidewalk, before crashing into the restaurant.

If the court has no patience to hear the long rendition of the facts, then the crucial facts must be interwoven into the law. Counsel might separate the facts as follows:

Counsel: For Chicago Burger to be liable for the injuries to the appellees, the appellees must show that the restaurant had a duty to them. Duty is a question for the court and there is no duty to anticipate unforeseen events. Chicago Burger could not have foreseen that Levy, after drinking six beers, would speed down Chicago Avenue, cross the centerline, jump the curb, barrel over the sidewalk, and injure its customers.

               Duty is a question of law that this court determines. Levy drank six beers and had a blood alcohol content of .18—two times the legal limit. He was driving twenty miles per hour over the speed limit seething after having had an argument with his wife. *Chicago Burger could not have foreseen Levy's actions and therefore, it had no duty to its patrons.*

               While complying with all laws does not necessarily mean that Chicago Burger had no duty. Chicago Burger did comply with all ordinances of the City of Chicago regarding outdoor seating. All the uncontroverted facts in this case point to no duty here.

Exercise

For every case, practice both zeroing in on the facts and staying broad. Do this once a month. To zero in on the facts, set a three-minute timer for yourself and describe the facts in detail. To stay broad, retell the same set of facts in thirty seconds and force yourself to select the key facts. Audio-record yourself and listen for ways you can eliminate extraneous facts and summarize others.

5.3   Playing Chess

When a good chess player thinks about her strategy, she often uses the counterfactuals and small inferences to construct a winning game-plan: "If I moved here, he will take my Bishop" or "If I move my Knight forward, he will infer I'm going after the Queen." *Science:* In the courtroom, an oral advocate must build into her argument counterfactuals and inferences to strengthen her argument.

5.3.1 Reasonable Inferences

Sticking with the facts in a hearing does not mean you cannot make reasonable inferences from the facts. You can, and must, connect the dots for the judge. Your job is to help the judge infer favorable conclusions from the facts you present. Once again, let us look at the Justice Kagan example.

The structure of Kagan's delivery forces the audience to infer an understandable cause for Miller's crime. Justice Kagan artfully presents the facts so that the reader unconsciously makes a causal connection between Miller's neglected childhood and his act of murder. Making a causal connection between two events is a natural tendency. It could very well be that young Miller mutilated animals when he was four or committed any number of horrendous acts. But, because we hear only limited facts, we naturally connect those facts as cause and effect. *Art:* Provide the trail of breadcrumbs for the court to make the connection by explicitly announcing the reasonable inference or implicitly inferring it.

5.3.2 Coulda, Shoulda, Woulda

Use the counterfactual to your advantage. Sometimes highlighting what did not happen is an even stronger way of showing what did happen. Facts include what did occur as well as what did not occur. Think about what could have or should have been done but did not happen. Once you think through the possible choices that were not made, point them out.

Take this simple discovery dispute as an example:

> Your Honor, the court ordered discovery to be completed on June 1. I sent a set of interrogatories and a request for production of documents to opposing counsel in January of this year. Opposing counsel had six weeks to respond. When nothing was sent, I talked to opposing counsel on the phone two weeks after the deadline. He told me *I would have* the responses the following week. The following week came and went without a response. *He could have* called me to tell me he could not make the deadline. *He did not*, so I wrote a letter asking again for his responses. *He could have* answered my letter by phone explaining his problem with complying. *He could have* told me his administrative assistant was sick, and *I would have* understood. *He did not. He could have* told me his dog ate the documents and *I would have* extended his deadline. *He did not.*[4] At this point, Your Honor, opposing counsel is months past the discovery deadline, and I had to file this motion to get a response from him.

---

4. Okay, kidding. But sometimes adding a slight, sarcastic bit of humor is a better way to register your complaint about opposing counsel than to adopt a whiny tone.

National Institute for Trial Advocacy

This tactic requires the creative genius of the attorney and can be used in many types of arguments. When arguing that a complaint should be dismissed for failure to state a claim upon which relief can be granted, list all the facts that were not alleged in the complaint. When arguing *Daubert*,[5] specify all that an expert could have done, but did not. Did the expert conduct his own investigation, or rely on the raw data of another? What test did the expert use, and not use? If the issue is the suppression of evidence in a criminal case, what could, or should, the police have done but did not? Did the police talk to this witness? Did the police take fingerprints, record a confession, or send the samples for analysis? If arguing that the court has no personal jurisdiction, specify the contacts the company did not have with the state.

Search for the omissions. What is missing is many times as important as what is there. Include those crucial omissions in your factual analysis.

5.4   Employ the Senses

Art: A good storyteller paints a picture with phrases that touch on our five senses, memory, or imagination. You hear the suspenseful pauses and the deliberate speed; you see the waving of the arms and the dramatic facial expressions. The senses are powerful agents. Use them to your advantage.

5.4.1   Exhibits

Study after study confirms the old adage that a picture is worth a thousand words. 65 percent of the population learns visually, yet most communication in a courtroom is auditory. Visual aids increase understanding. Consider an automobile accident lawsuit. Displaying a picture or diagram of where the accident occurred increases the judge's comprehension. Likewise, looking at a complaint to show its deficiencies assists the judge's understanding.

Visual aids also make facts more believable. It is one thing to say that a debt was paid in full and quite another to show the canceled check. Testifying about an agreement is less convincing than seeing and reading it. Visual aids stay with the judge.

Take advantage of these tools: create and refer to exhibits to make your important points. When possible and appropriate, increase the court's understanding by using a visual aid. Maps, diagrams, tables, pictures, models, slideshows, depositions, decisional trees, and affidavit excerpts are all effective.

Some demonstratives will come from the papers you have submitted or witnesses you will call. Others, like slideshows or timelines, will summarize the evidence or

---

5. Daubert v. Merrell Dow Pharmaceuticals, Inc., 509 U.S. 579 (1993).

law. As a matter of courtesy and efficiency, make sure you have extra copies for the court, opposing counsel, and witnesses.

Art: Use exhibits to enhance, and not distract from, your presentation. *Science:* Do not discuss an exhibit as the judge is rummaging to find it. Multitasking is difficult for all of us; judges are no different. Before continuing to speak, wait until the judge lets you know that he has found the exhibit and the portion you wish to discuss. Then orient him to the exhibit. Tell him what he is looking at before you highlight a specific portion of the exhibit. If the exhibit is a map, tell him what direction is north. If showing a picture of an accident scene, let him know that the picture was taken immediately after the accident, looking to the south, before you zero in on the skid marks. If it is a document, explain what it is before you turn to paragraph ten. In other words, let him get his bearings before you describe the particulars.

Exhibits should be clear and understandable. Here are examples of pictures of street scenes, listed in order from the clearest to the most unhelpful.

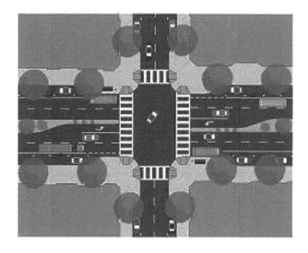

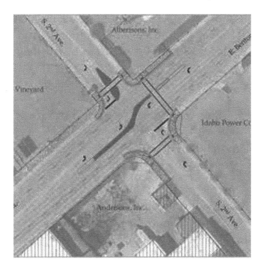

The more abstract the exhibit, the more the judge will need your assistance in understanding what he is looking at. Show the exhibit to a colleague and practice explaining it to avoid floundering in front of the judge.

5.4.2 Creating Visual Pictures

You want the judge to remember your version of the case facts. You want a good image to stick. To make the memory of the facts of your case stay in the judge's mind, create visual pictures with your words.

In *Moonwalking with Einstein*,[6] Joshua Foer tells the story of how he rose to the finals of the USA Memory Championship. The competition requires the contestants to memorize the order of cards in two decks in five minutes. To perform this Herculean task, Foer assigned a person, place, or action to each card. So, the king of hearts may be Einstein, the eight of diamonds moonwalking, and the three of clubs the Louvre. If the above cards came up, Foer would create in his mind a picture of Einstein moonwalking in the Louvre. Through a series of visual images, he memorized both decks.

Our brains are made to remember pictures. Judges' brains are too. Paint pictures in the judge's mind by using sensory language—language that helps the judge see, hear, feel, smell, touch, remember, and imagine. During an appeal of a denial of a motion to suppress the drugs found in your client's car, paint the picture of your client waiting on the berm of a busy expressway at rush hour in ninety-degree weather for half an hour until the drug dog arrives. Or, in the middle of discovery, paint the

---

6. Joshua Foer, Moonwalking With Einstein: The Art and Science of Remembering Everything (Penguin Books 2011).

mental picture of thousands of banker's boxes of documents being scanned, digitized, and electronically filed, but a few boxes—those containing bad-faith claims—being left on the side. These images will not be forgotten by the judge.

5.4.3 Word Choice

Use plain English—simple words that clearly and succinctly convey your meaning. Use "cars," not "vehicles;" "deals," not "transactions;" "before," not "prior to;" "agreements," not "memorandum of understanding;" "sign," not "execute;" "home," not "residence;" "ask," not "inquire;" "so," not "therefore;" and the list goes on.

Use words that create pictures in the mind of the judge. "Car" not only is a simpler word than "vehicle," but it conveys an image. A vehicle could be a tractor, semi-truck, motorcycle, or car. Tom Singer, a trial attorney, longtime professor of trial advocacy at Notre Dame Law School, and lover of poetry, uses a story about President Franklin D. Roosevelt to make the point that words should be simple. During World War II, FDR was given a placard to place in over a thousand federal offices. The placard said: "It is obligatory to extinguish all illumination before leaving the premises." FDR's response? "Why the hell can't we just say, 'Put out the lights when you leave'?"[7]

5.4.4 Speed-Crafting

Pay attention to the rate of your speed when delivering your facts. The rate of speed is the number of words per minute that you speak. Extremely slow talkers speak at 145 words per minute or less, while fast talkers speak at 180 words or more per minute. Many people speak too quickly and need to slow down; far fewer are slow talkers and need to speed up. More speed techniques are discussed in Chapter Thirteen. But for now, know that variety of your speech rate keeps a listener interested. If you are consistently slow paced, the listener falls asleep. If you are consistently fast paced, the listener cannot keep up with you and loses interest. Variety maintains interest.

When delivering your facts, when should you slow down and when should you speed up your rate of speech? *Slow down* when you make your most important points. *Speed up* on less important points or when you wish to build momentum or show enthusiasm, passion, or conviction.

Return for a moment to the Chicago Burger case. Here is an example of when counsel should slow down and speed up her delivery:

[Begin at a measured pace.]

---

7. Lawrence S. Bartell, True Stories of Strange Events and Odd People: A Memoir (iUniverse 2014).

Chicago Burger could not have reasonably foreseen that the drunken Kenneth Levy would crash into its outdoor seating area, killing one of its customers and injuring others.

[Pause.]

[Quicker pace.]

Chicago Burger is at the corner of Western and Chicago Avenues in Chicago. Here is a diagram of how the restaurant is situated at that corner.

[Pause, then a measured, regular pace.]

You can see the restaurant's outdoor seating complies with city ordinance. [*Showing map of location.*]

[Pick up the pace.]

July 25 was like any other night at Chicago Burger. Customers were enjoying the food and outdoor area when Levy

[measured build in speed to make it sound like there were other out-of-control actions that led to this accident]

after fighting with his wife and drinking six cans of beer, got behind the wheel of his car, drove eastbound on Chicago Avenue, crossed the center line, went across the westbound lane, jumped the curb, sped across the sidewalk, and crashed into the plaintiff's table.

[Pause and then *slow pace.*]

Levy was driving twenty miles per hour over the speed limit, with a blood alcohol content of .18, which is over twice the legal limit.

[Pause.]

Chicago Burger could not have foreseen the actions of Levy and thus had no duty to the plaintiffs.

Alternatively, to use the facts as a way for theme variation, the speaker may slow down for the important information. The theme is: *Chicago Burger could not have reasonably foreseen Levy's drunken rampage.* Slowly delivering the premise of the argument will resonate with the judge. When the speaker begins to tell the judge about Levy's actions, the rate of speed can substantially slow down with a pause after each clause: "When Levy [*pause*], after fighting with his wife and drinking six cans of beer [*pause*], got behind the wheel of his car [*pause*], drove eastbound on Chicago Avenue [*pause*], crossed the center line [*pause*], went across the westbound lane [*pause*], ..." This slow cadence with pauses allows the court to digest the information, see Levy's actions, and realize there was nothing Chicago Burger could have done to stop the accident.

> **Exercise**
>
> Practice telling the plot of a movie or TV show in thirty seconds, then in three minutes. Plan where you will slow down your rate of speed for emphasis, and where you will speed up to show enthusiasm and conviction. Time your deliveries. Once satisfied with your ability to manipulate speed effectively, switch topics to the facts of one of your cases.

5.5   Pitfalls

When conveying facts, there are plenty of pitfalls attorneys fall into. Avoid these common mistakes.

5.5.1   Facts, not Conclusions

Facts are convincing; conclusions are not. We can see facts but cannot see conclusions. Facts lead a judge to his own conclusion. No judge likes to be forced into a corner. To persuade the judge, lead him to agree with the facts you develop.

Imagine you are at a hearing asking the court to compel discovery in a case. You argue that the defense has been dilatory in its responses. What does that mean? As a conclusion, the meaning is subjective to the listener. What is dilatory to one person may not be dilatory to another. Instead, set out the facts as we did earlier in the chapter:

> Your Honor, we asked the other side for these documents six months ago. They were due five months ago. We did not receive them. So, I called opposing counsel. He said I would receive them in one week. I did not receive them in a week, so the next week I wrote a letter to him again asking for the documents. I heard nothing. I called again. Still nothing. One month later, I filed this motion to compel discovery. Still nothing. Five months after these documents were due, and after repeated attempts to receive these documents, still nothing.

These facts can be seen by the judge. You are not merely moaning in a conclusory manner that you have been stonewalled by opposing counsel. The details convince the judge.

5.5.2   Overstating Facts

Joe Friday said it best: "Just the facts, ma'am."[8] If you embellish the facts, your opponent will be sure to let the judge know you are overstating. As a result, the judge will question the strength of your case, because attorneys with strong cases do not

---

8. *Dragnet* (NBC television 1951–1959).

need to overstate. More importantly, you will lose the trust of the judge. *Science:* Do not exaggerate the facts of your case.

Often the overstatement comes from conclusions like, "this was the worst violation I have seen" or "this is a clear case of . . ." Let the facts speak for themselves. Use them as the secret weapons they are.

5.5.3 Don't Hide

Hiding the bad facts is not an avenue of escape; it actually provides opposing counsel with an opportunity to expose. You want the judge to hear the bad facts from you with your spin on them to lighten the blow. Include the bad facts in your presentation. If you own them, you can minimize them. If you do not, you look afraid of those facts and will lose your credibility. *Science:* Your case's credibility is also at risk if you do not explain bad facts from your vantage point.

If you do not deal with them, the judge will believe that you cannot. Do not dwell on them, however; include them in your factual presentation, but spend at least three times as much time talking about your good facts as your bad ones.

In general, place bad facts in the middle of your story, surrounded by your good facts. Exceptions do exist, especially for the respondent or appellee who must tackle the hard issues out of the gate. When the appellant spends her time pounding your bad facts, you should face them head-on.

By way of illustration, let's return to Evan Miller's case. Justice Kagan cleverly positioned her bad facts, the details of the murder, between Evan Miller's childhood and Miller's accomplice receiving a reduced sentence for his cooperation. Suppose she had organized her presentation as follows:

> One night in 2003, Miller was at home with a friend, Colby Smith, when a neighbor, Cole Cannon, came to make a drug deal with Miller's mother. The two boys followed Cannon back to his trailer, where all three smoked marijuana and played drinking games. When Cannon passed out, Miller stole his wallet, splitting about $300 with Smith. Miller then tried to put the wallet back in Cannon's pocket, but Cannon awoke and grabbed Miller by the throat. Smith hit Cannon with a nearby baseball bat and, once released, Miller grabbed the bat and repeatedly struck Cannon with it. Miller placed a sheet over Cannon's head, told him "I am God, I've come to take your life," and delivered one more blow. The boys then retreated to Miller's trailer, but soon decided to return to Cannon's to cover up evidence of their crime. Once there, they lit two fires. Cannon eventually died from his injuries and smoke inhalation.

* * *

Evan Miller was fourteen years old at the time of his crime. Miller had by then been in and out of foster care because his mother suffered from alcoholism and drug addiction and his stepfather abused him. Miller, too, regularly used drugs and alcohol; and he had attempted suicide four times, the first when he was six years old.

* * *

Relying in significant part on testimony from Smith, who had pleaded to a lesser offense, a jury found Miller guilty. He was therefore sentenced to life without the possibility of parole.[9]

What a difference mere organization makes. By starting with the crime, the framework of the story highlights the vicious crime instead of the trapped boy who snapped. The lesson is to surround your bad facts with your good facts.

Now that we have dissected two major components of an oral presentation—theme and facts—we turn to another key component: the law.

---

9. Miller v. Alabama, 567 U.S. 460, 468–70 (2012).

CHAPTER SIX

THE LAW

Justice Antonin Scalia famously said, "A judge must be, above all else, a servant of the law—and not an enforcer of his personal predilections—about the issues that come before him."[1] Put differently, the judge is the servant and the law is her master. Well, sorta. The law is indeed the master. Judges must undoubtedly follow it. However, the law is not always black and white. It is full of ambiguities that allow a judge some wiggle room to come to the "right" decision—the fair one for all parties. The advocate has two jobs: first, to convince the court to want to apply the law in a way that results in a ruling for his client. We learned in the last chapter that facts motivate a judge to come to the fair decision. Later we will learn that appeals to the concerns of the judge do as well. It does not end there.

An attorney has a second job, to show the court the legal pathway. Theme. Facts. Delivery. None of it matters without convincing the court that the law is on the client's side. The law is the fulcrum upon which everything else rests. The lawyer's responsibility is to show the judge what his master dictates—namely, what the law ultimately will accept. To achieve these ends, it is not enough to simply know the law. This chapter explores the necessary techniques to deploy in order to effectively present the master to the servant.

6.1   Keep It Simple

True brilliance occurs when complicated legal matters are boiled down into simple sound bites. Keep your discussion of the law simple. Simple delivery should be clear and logical. A judge rarely accepts contradictory or circular legal positions. Complicated arguments require too much work for the listener. Once a judge has to fight to listen and pay attention, she shuts down.

A good judge may rightly use the power of her position to interrupt a convoluted argument with questions. Sometimes, questions are a way for the judge to help unpack the attorney's argument into digestible chunks. This can be done consciously or unconsciously. The judge may realize that the advocate is weaving

---

1. Antonin Scalia, Scalia Speaks: Reflections on Law, Faith, and Life Well Lived, 170 (Christopher J. Scalia et al. eds., Crown Forum 2017).

a complicated legal argument and stop him in his tracks to give him a chance to revise the delivery or to point out the advocate's error. Other times during an argument, the judge shows non-verbal signs of confusion, and eventually asks a series of questions, struggling to find logic in the advocate's legal theory. Either way, it is tough to resurrect an overly complicated legal theory. The back-and-forth question and answer that ensues takes time away from the only important issues at hand: a ruling for your client.

Some attorneys fight the advice to simplify a legal argument because they contend that the legal argument is unavoidably complicated. They keep fighting—and they keep losing because they are taking a top-down approach. Begin by simplifying foundational principles until you and the judge see eye-to-eye on each level before launching into the complicated argument. A judge knows speaking simply takes time, creativity, and intelligence. As Albert Einstein said, "If you can't explain it simply, you don't know it well enough."[2]

6.2   Cookie Cutters

Finding the right way to discuss the law simply and powerfully is a challenge. It requires creativity. But if the spark of creativity is lacking, there are ways to deliver the legal theory in frameworks that act as catalysts for creativity. Following are some cookie cutters—that is to say, pre-made frameworks—to help simplify legal theory in a creative manner.

Enumeration:

- Divide the substance into numbered sections. Give a simple name for each section such as my first argument is sufficiency; my second is a due process violation. By naming your arguments, you can quickly direct the court to each without an extended dialogue. Also, after the hearing, the named arguments will be more likely to be remembered by the court. Keep the list to no more than five divisions, and preferably two or three. If you cannot count the divisions on one hand, you need to boil it down further. Once a numbering system is established, stay faithful to that regime. Do not over-enumerate (i.e., no sub-numbering systems in oral delivery, "There are three reasons why the law supports our side. The first has seven parts . . . ").

- Example: "There are three reasons why the law supports our side. The first is . . . "

---

2. Attributed to Albert Einstein, https://www.brainyquote.com/quotes/albert_einstein_383803 (last visited 12/10/2020).

Step approach:
- Similar to enumeration, but here the numbered items build upon one another and create dependence on previous foundations.
- Example: "Now that we've satisfied the second prong of the regulation, we move to the third."

Compare and Contrast:
- Compare and contrast the pros and cons, the risks and benefits, the plaintiff's and the defendant's perspectives on the issue. Use this model to show the similarities or differences between two things, including between your case and the leading case in the area. Click off a list of similarities or distinctions.
- Example: "The Ninth Circuit takes [X] position, while the Sixth Circuit takes the opposite view."

Lay Foundations:
- Start with foundations that are well-known and build upon them.
- Example: "Your Honor, it is a longstanding Supreme Court precedent that defendants must be Mirandized. Let's talk about the nuance of whether an undocumented-immigrant defendant must be Mirandized."

Principle and Application:
- Set up a legal principle and apply it to the facts in the present case or the facts of a cited case.
- Example: "The First Amendment provides for freedom of speech. In the case of *Arizona v. Emperor,* the young boy's shouts during the parade were considered protected speech."

Repetition:
- Use a word-for-word recitation of a line or message similar to a refrain of a song. Alternatively, repetition can be the recitation of synonymous phrases. This is one way to avoid the danger of the court losing interest, because of drumbeat repetition.
- Example: Early in the argument: "A likelihood of success on the merits must be shown by the plaintiff." Later in the argument: "It does not look like the plaintiff could ultimately satisfy his burden, Your Honor."

Headline and recap:
- Tell the judge what you are going to say, explain it, and then summarize what you said. The headline signals to the judge that you are starting a new

topic. The headline could also be your theme. An explanation would follow. The recap restates the meaning of the headline.

- Example of a headline: "The attorney-client privilege should be protected."

- Example of a recap: "The default position should be to guard the privilege, not destroy it."

Visuals:

- Prepare a foamboard, PowerPoint, chart, table, or picture with any information better understood visually.

- Example: "Your Honor sees here the words of Justice Anthony Kennedy that control this case."

Sensory:

- Give examples that help the judge see the natural consequence of a principle or proposition. When giving examples, paint a picture for the judge that she will remember later. Use the senses when possible and/or a scenario dialogue.

- Example: "Imagine someone going to an attorney for a first visit. They sit across from one another at a small table, and the attorney says, 'Everything you say to me is confidential. Oh, except that the judge may review what you tell me today and what I advise you may not fall within the privilege.' What will that do to attorney-client communication?"

Exercise

Take one legal theory from an argument and spontaneously deliver it out loud, trying the different organizational options above. Keep the deliveries crisp. Decide what style best fits the particular legal theory.

6.3   Do Not Oversimplify

Imagine a spectrum of simple to complicated. It starts on the left, with an oversimplified argument, which offends the intellect of the judge. While it is true that the goal is simplicity, it is a balancing act and it should not be made *too* simple. If it is, then it sounds as if the advocate is talking down to the judge. The judge should not be left to think that the advocate thinks she is stupid. This is not related to the tone or vocal inflection you use with the court, which when improperly done can cause offense. This lesson hinges on the words themselves not oversimplifying the legal theory. You run the risk of patronizing a judge with the wrong words and/or the wrong delivery (we cover delivery in Chapter Thirteen).

OVERSIMPLIFIED   SIMPLE   COMPLICATED

On the other side of the spectrum is the complicated argument, which causes confusion and/or lends itself to misinterpretation. You will lose your judge if you speak like an encyclopedia.

In the middle of the spectrum is the balanced, simple argument. If you find yourself on the oversimplified side, the legal theory needs to be more sophisticated. If you find yourself on the complicated side, the legal theory needs to be made more elegant, precise, and basic.

Where you must land on the spectrum from simple to complex depends on the expertise level of the judge. If you have done your research on the judge before your hearing, you will know whether she is a novice, expert, or somewhere in the middle on your issues. Use this information to gauge where on the spectrum of complexity you should speak. If the judge is an expert, plunge deeply into the complexities of law. If she is a novice, lay foundations and build on them one layer at a time.

If you do not know ahead of time the level of expertise of the judge, start in the middle of the spectrum. Then listen and watch the judge for cues. Through her body language and questioning, she will tell you the depths of her knowledge. Adjust your argument accordingly.

Let's take a look at some examples:

Example—Too Complicated

Counsel: Your Honor, the crime-fraud exception to attorney-client privileged communication allows disclosure of communications in the furtherance of future illegal conduct. The exception applies when the client strategizes a fraudulent scheme when consulting an attorney's advice to further the stratagem.

Huh? Even the judge, familiar with the crime-fraud exception, will find this explanation difficult to understand. Now let's turn to the overly simplistic argument that insults the judge's intelligence.

Example—Too Simple

Counsel: Your Honor, conversations between attorneys and their clients are confidential. This is called the attorney-client privilege. There is an exception to this rule. When a client seeks advice from an attorney to further the client's fraudulent plan or crime, then the conversations are not privileged. This is called the crime-fraud exception.

Duh, of course. The court knows that attorney-client communications are confidential. And the judge also knows that the conversation is generally privileged. This simplicity risks the judge shutting off from listening to anything else this advocate says. A balanced approach simplifies, but not overly so.

This example strikes a good balance:

Example—Simple, but Not Too Simple

Counsel: Your Honor, as we all know, an exception to attorney-client privilege is the crime-fraud exception. When a client seeks advice from an attorney for the purposes of committing a future fraud or crime, the communication is not privileged. Can you imagine if attorneys could help their clients embezzle?

Exercise

Take one legal theory from a brief and draft three different ways to present the theory:

1) Complicated

2) Over-simplified

2) Simplified

Art: Sometimes you may encounter a case where the law is complicated, and to win you want to show how complicated and confusing the law is. Perhaps you are arguing that the law is ambiguous or impossible to interpret. In that case, strategically choose to present a complicated presentation of the legal theory. But for this to work, simplify all the connecting transition phrases to a clear and casual level. Avoid using "therefore" when "so" would work just as well. Try transitions that are rhetorical questions, which you answer for the court: "What did the legislature mean here? There looks to be seven possibilities. The statute is that unclear."

6.4 Spot the Difference

Science: If you cite a statute, rule, or regulation in your papers, be ready to discuss what it is, what it means, and why you used it. Know the holding of each of the cases cited by you or your opponent and how the holding impacts the decision. Also, be acquainted with the facts of all cases cited in the papers. Know the facts well enough that you can distinguish the cases that hurt you and use the cases that help you. Plan how you will discuss the cases. Your discussion of a case changes depending on whether it is good or bad for you and whether the facts are the same or different than yours. Simply put, understand the difference between cases that strengthen or weaken your position. To do this, construct a simple table like the following:

GOOD CASES		BAD CASES	
Same facts, same holding	**Different facts, same holding**	**Different facts, different holding**	**Same facts, different holding**
Quote the cases, weave into the theme.	Use carefully; show comparisons and admit distinctions before your opponent does.	Distinguish facts, show how if the facts in that case were the same as the present facts, the holding would have been different.	Distinguish holding or how it was applied, argue public policy.

Before the argument, prepare brief talking points about the similarity of the facts to your case or the irrelevance of the dissimilarities. Take limited information about the cases to the podium with you. We talk more about what to bring to the podium in Chapter Eleven.

6.5   Use the Law Elegantly

Just because you are prepared to discuss all the cases cited does not mean you *should*. Focus your discussion of the law. Judges appreciate an attorney who sets out a legal principle and then applies the principle to the facts of the case. *Art:* Many times, the legal principle has become a powerful "magic phrase," used and repeated throughout the hearing. These magic phrases encapsulate the legal holding or summarize the statute or regulation. The phrases become like comfortable shoes, easy for the judge to wear. If the judge is not comfortable with the law controlling your case, then a succinct and memorable phrase should help in the education process. Use repetition, either through exact quoting or synonymous phrasing, to make a once unfamiliar legal phrase into a familiar one for the judge.

Be discerning when discussing the case law. Use one or possibly two cases for each point you wish to make. Citing laundry lists of cases does not impress a judge; instead, it makes her think that the law is not settled—or worse, that you do not know the difference between important and minor cases. Pick your best case and hit it hard. Unless you are asked, do not get into the weeds of the case. If you do, you will chew up the limited time you have. Set out the legal principles involved, then distinguish or apply them to the facts of your case.

Science: If you quote something from a case, do not misquote the law or take the case out of context. You immediately lose credibility, appear unintelligent, or open yourself up to an attack from opposing counsel. If you quote from a case where the holding cuts against your legal position, tell the court. Do not wait for opposing counsel to inform the judge. Be exact, even if you need to extrapolate your position from the exact words. You can use the exact words from the case or use similar or analogous language to return to your argument.

6.6   Argue the Purpose of or the Commonsense Reason Behind the Law

During your preparation, you identified the purpose or policy reasons behind the law. To create a convincing public-policy argument that persuades a judge to hold in your favor, ask yourself: What is the commonsense reason for the law? What policy implications does it advance? What reason behind the law is in concert with our position? Convince the judge that your preferred result will further the purpose of the law.

Commonsense, public-policy arguments are compelling. Illustrating the purpose behind the law helps orient the judge, giving the context of the law itself. If you know why/how a law came to be, it becomes easier to show where it ought to proceed.

For example, if you represent the petitioner in a preliminary injunction hearing to protect a trade secret from being used by the respondent, you are likely to succeed on the merits in the underlying action by arguing that the legal elements of a trade secret are met. To be even more convincing, argue that the very purpose of protecting a trade secret is to incentivize innovation, a purpose undermined by denying injunctive relief and allowing the respondent access to the trade secret.

Consider another example from the oral arguments in *District of Columbia v. Heller*,[3] the famous Supreme Court Case dealing with the question of whether handguns might lawfully be suppressed under the Second Amendment. To open their argument, the petitioners predicated their claim on a discussion about the purpose of the Second Amendment. They began with:

> The Second Amendment was a direct response to concern over Article I, Section 8 of the Constitution, which gave the new national Congress the surprising, perhaps even the shocking, power to organize, arm, and presumably disarm the state militias. What is at issue this morning is the scope and nature of the individual right protected by the resulting amendment and the first text to consider is the phrase protecting a right to keep and bear arms.

Understanding the origin of a law is key to seeing its reasonable destination. For that reason, the first thing the petitioners discussed was why the law came to be—to prevent disarming the state militias. Once the petitioners established this, they were able to argue that, since the law was designed to prevent military disarmament, the District of Columbia is perfectly within its limits to disarm regular citizens because they are not the military.

---

3. District of Columbia v. Heller, 554 U.S. 570 (2008).

A good oral advocate identifies the purpose or policy reasons behind the law to provide a source for convincing, persuasive, commonsense arguments—with the added bonus that these commonsense arguments are simple and easily comprehended and remembered by a judge.

Closely aligned with knowing the rationale behind the law is understanding the development of the law. A law's evolution informs its current status and future trends. Read the key cases chronologically to identify trends. Predict the natural future progression of the law based upon its history. For cases in which the law is not yet on your side but the equities are, this pioneering approach may provide your best argument. But do not wait for the judge or opposing counsel to surprise you with a question revealing that your interpretation of the law is not the current state of the law. Instead, address it head on and urge the court to act consistent with public policy.

Example

Counsel: Your Honor, a progressive interpretation of the law is needed to prevent an injustice here. The case law here is old and does not account for the constant and rapidly changing landscape of modern cybersecurity. The law's purpose is to protect information and encourage companies to do the same. It is not intended to punish a company that gets hacked despite its best efforts to prevent an intrusion.

6.7 The Real World

Many judges have been on the bench for a long time. Even the expert judge may have lost contact with the practicalities of how the law works in the real world. Be prepared to talk about the way the law operates in reality. As an example, suppose the law requires a medical malpractice claim to go through a review panel of doctors before a complaint can be filed with the trial court. The panel of doctors reviews the plaintiff's medical records, her allegations of malpractice, and renders an opinion. The complaint subsequently filed in court includes allegations of malpractice different than those submitted to the panel but based on the same medical records. The court will likely want to know if plaintiffs are trying to game the system by holding back allegations before the panel and ambushing the defendant with new theories at trial.[4]

---

4. McKeen v. Turner, 61 N.E.3d 1251 (Ind. Ct. App. 2016). Upon questioning, the defense attorney in the case, Michael O'Neill, told the court that the plaintiffs' counsel would have no incentive to game the system by holding back allegations from the review panel. Mr. O'Neill's credibility is forever golden with the judges on the panel.

Expert in the area of law or not, many judges need help with the practicalities of the case. It may have been a long time since the judge practiced in the area, or she may have never practiced in the field. Tell her how it actually works and the consequences of her ruling.[5] She relies on you for that expertise. Give her your know-how. When done properly, this becomes a way to collaborate with the judge so she joins your cause.

6.8   Practice Aloud

Figuring out whether you strike the right legal argument requires practicing aloud. *Science:* Do not speak your legal theory aloud for the first time in front of the judge. A reader can digest more complicated material than a listener. The written word gives a reading audience time to digest—and reread, if necessary. The judge is a prisoner to the speed and complexity chosen by the attorney. In preparation, talk about the legal theory out loud to hear whether it makes sense off the page; the argument will become clearer and more concise because you will hear the confusing sections and complicated words. Today's technology affords attorneys the opportunity to practice out loud and hear an instant recording. If you do not have a phone with an audio-recording function, invest in a portable recording device. Set a timer and record the planned argument. Play it back and listen first for clarity and simplicity. Put yourself in the shoes of a judge who did not have time to read the papers. Rehearsing out loud also gives you a sense for whether you are wasting precious time in front of the judge regurgitating the same information that was written and submitted to the court.

6.9   Practice Discussing the Law Conversationally

The law should be discussed conversationally. When discussing the law with the judge, pick the style that you would use to have a spirited debate with a friend at a restaurant. With that scenario in mind, you will be conversational and natural.

One of the unhappy results of our legal education system is the tendency to manipulate the language to make us "sound" like attorneys. Practice eliminating the legal jargon. Avoid pretentious language that would sound awkward in a dinner conversation. Certain language is appropriate for written briefs, but not fitting to be spoken to a judge. Think awkward transitional words such as "aforementioned," "hence," "moreover," and "notwithstanding." Words such as these have a place on the page, not on your tongue. Pretentious language is not a sign of intelligence; taking legal principles and transforming them into conversational speech is.

---

5. One of the authors had a conversation with Justice Souter about oralist Ted Olson. Apparently, Attorney Olson honestly conceded a question during an argument before SCOTUS that ensured his side would lose. Years after the argument, Justice Souter commented on the admirable credibility that Olson had built with all members of the Supreme Court because of incidents like this.

For those of you still reluctant to remove the legalese from your vernacular, consider the research of Daniel Oppenheimer, professor of psychology at Carnegie Mellon. He concludes that audiences perceive overly complex language as a sign of low intelligence.[6] A listener who must work hard to understand what an advocate is saying blames the advocate. If you feel like the judge failed to grasp the argument, the disconnect may be your own complicated language choices. Explain a legal theory in an organized, simple, and memorable way so that the message replays in the judge's mind. This can only happen with a conversational tone.

Exercise

Choose a legal theory within your motion or reply brief. Read the legal argument out loud as you record the delivery. Re-record the argument a second time, describing the legal theory in a dramatically different and conversational tone—as if you were describing the theory to your best non-attorney friend. Limit this conversational delivery to two minutes. After you listen to yourself, ask, "How will the judge talk to a friend or spouse about the case? Her staff? Which version could she easily remember and replay in her head?"

If possible, call one colleague unfamiliar with your case. (A phone call will prevent non-verbal influences from changing your colleague's interpretation of the message.) Tell her you want her to listen to a legal argument and resist taking notes during your delivery. Read aloud the section of your papers that describes the legal theory you have chosen. Call a second colleague unfamiliar with the case. Ask him, too, to listen to a legal argument and resist taking notes during your delivery. Read your simple, conversational delivery—of no more than two minutes—to your second colleague. Wait a few hours and call both colleagues independently. Ask them how much they remember from the description delivered earlier in the day and write down their responses. Compare the difference in the remembered content.

6.10   Do Not Flip a Stylistic Switch

Some advocates have a dividing line in their minds between the facts and law. Often, an attorney confidently and conversationally discusses the facts of the case, but the moment a legal argument begins, his voice or body language changes. The advocate's mental prejudice makes him change the delivery style when he talks about the law. Perhaps he thinks he should categorically morph into a crotchety law professor and

---

6. Daniel M. Oppenheimer, *Consequences of Erudite Vernacular Utilized Irrespective of Necessity: Problems with Using Long Words Needlessly*, Appl. Cognit. Psychol. 20: 139–156 (2006). Available at http://www2.psych.utoronto.ca/users/psy3001/files/simple%20writing.pdf (last visited October 20, 2020).

pontificate about the legal theories at issue. Perhaps he is less confident about the legal theories or is insecure about debating the law with a judge. Perhaps he thinks that anyone can deliver the facts, but only a bright attorney can discuss the law. The judge sees the change, and it raises a red flag. Is the attorney hiding something? Is there a problem with the legal theory? Is there something I do not understand? Why is the attorney acting so differently?

Common pitfalls of oral advocates who change their delivery style include the following:

Raising or lowering vocal pitch a note or two:

- Effect: The speaker shifts the register of the voice entirely. Going up signals excitement, anxiety, questioning, or stress. Going down signals patronization, defeat, seriousness, or nonchalance.

Inserting upward inflection when introducing a new term to the court:

- Effect: This vocal pattern is a cousin of the upward inflection that causes a lift in the pitch of the voice at the ends of sentences. With upward inflection, a speaker lifts the pitch of the voice, irregularly running the risk of sounding less intelligent or offending the judge by sounding patronizing. Either way, the advocate loses credibility and likeability.

Accent changing:

- Effect: At times, attorneys with regional accents reduce the intensity of their natural accent when they switch to a more intellectual subject matter. The accent becomes neutralized. Assuming that the attorney's natural accent is inoffensive and comprehensible, there should be no shift in accent when he discusses law, facts, or public policy.

Noticeably crisper pronunciation:

- Effect: Like accent reduction, attorneys often over-pronounce consonants when discussing the law as a way to force the listener to understand the theories.

Awkward vocal mistakes:

- Effect: Sometimes an attorney launches into a legal argument and clearly mispronounces names within the case. This breaks the rhythm of the speaker and makes the attorney look nervous or less prepared on the law. It would be better to take time on the difficult words that are universally hard to pronounce and regain the previous pace of delivery.

Vacant facial expression:

- Effect: Sometimes an attorney forgets to match his facial expression with the themes and words of the law. The facial expression flattens, and all expression is lost. There is not a better recipe for a boring delivery. Often, a judge loses interest in the legal argument section because the attorney removes all human connection or pathos with the information being delivered.

Marked change in posture:
- Effect: Some attorneys become so formal and rigid when discussing the law, they appear frozen and statuesque instead of confident and natural.

Marked change in size, rate, or scope of gestures:
- Effect: All attorneys have natural gesticulation patterns. A telltale sign of nerves or discomfort with a position is a dramatic change from natural to over-controlled or exaggerated gestures.

Art: Avoid the pitfall of changing the tone of your voice and/or your body language when talking about the law. Instead, stay consistent. Discussing law should be just as natural, comfortable, and seamless as discussing facts, greetings, and public policy. We examine more stylistic delivery techniques in Chapters Thirteen and Fourteen.

Exercise

Audio-record yourself discussing the facts of a case, then discuss a legal theory of the case. If you detect a noticeable difference in your vocal delivery, identify the change and practice saying the facts and law until both are discussed with the same vocal style.

Now video-record yourself discussing the facts of the case, then discuss a legal theory of the case. If you detect a noticeable difference in your body language, then identify the change and practice delivering the facts and the law until the same body language is used for both.

6.11 Do Not Read to the Judge

Judges, like most audiences, can read the brief and law more efficiently than having it read to them. When attorneys discuss the law, they often fall into the trap of reading large sections of case law to the court. The goal is to have an oral discussion, not a reading.

Science: Here is the proper way to read a holding or a portion of case law to the court:

1. Pick a powerful, on-point quote.

2. Limit the reading to no more than two lines, but ideally one.

3. Indicate to the court, with verbal and stylistic (body language and vocal) signaling, that you are quoting a statute, court, regulation, etc.

VERBAL SIGNALING
"As the court in *Hernandez* said . . ."
"As Judge Daniels determined . . ."
"As Chief Justice Roberts reasoned . . ."
"Congress clearly states . . ."
"The FTC gives us the standard of review . . ."

BODY LANGUAGE OPTIONS
Gesture to the front of your page as you begin to quote.
Show air quotes with your hands.
Change eye contact focus from the judge to the page.
Lift your eyes and re-connect with the judge immediately after or during the last moments of reading the quote.

VOCAL CHANGE OPTIONS
Raise or lower your pitch.
Slow down your delivery speed.
Pause.
Repeat a small portion (two to seven words) of the quote to launch into your next point with the court.

6.12 Dolphining: Speaking to a Panel of Judges

When speaking to a panel of judges, an attorney must be agile enough to hold their attention while educating them about the law of the case. One judge may be an expert in the area of law, another a novice. One judge may have read the briefs and the entire record, while another may have read nothing or possibly a bench brief prepared by her clerks.

Here is where you need to act like a dolphin. Dolphins repeat a cycle where they rise up to breathe air and then dive back down into the water. As they swim they follow a pattern: moving up and down, up and down. In the same way, be a dolphin during oral argument: rise up to the simple broad legal argument and then dive down into complexities of the law. *Art:* Moving seamlessly through the simple and complex keeps all the panelists engaged. Even the expert judge is relieved to have a break from the intensity of a complicated argument.

To illustrate this concept of "dolphining," let us return to *District of Columbia v. Heller.*[7] Arguing on behalf of the respondent, Mr. Gura exhibits "dolphining." Consider a piece of dialogue from the middle of his argument:

Mr. Gura: Your Honor, the extent recognized in *Miller* where the Miller Court asked whether or not a particular type of arm that's at issue is one that people may individually possess. It looked to the militia clause and, therefore, adopted a militia purpose as one of the two prongs of *Miller* [*engages in a deep dive discussion of the law*].

A few seconds later:

Mr. Gura: Your Honor, because the Second Amendment is the right of the people. And it would certainly be an odd right that we would have against the congress, if congress could then redefine people out of that right. Congress could tomorrow declare that nobody is in a militia, and then nobody would have the right against the government [*returns to his overarching broad argument—namely, "you cannot redefine a people out of their rights"*].

_____

7. District of Columbia v. Heller, 554 U.S. 570 (2008).

Again, a few seconds later:

> Mr. Gura: Oh, yes. Yes, Justice Kennedy. The right of the people to keep and bear arms was derived from Blackstone. It was derived from the common-law English right which the Founders wanted to expand [*dives back down into the details of the law itself*].

This is an example of good dolphining. Coming up from the complex to the simple and then back down into the complex. Now we turn to another important aspect of oral advocacy: questions.

CHAPTER SEVEN

THE QUESTIONING FORMULA

Forty-four U.S. senators grilled 33-year-old Mark Zuckerberg, the CEO of Facebook, for five hours. Many senators were former prosecutors and others adept at asking tough questions to witnesses. The topic that day was data security for some 87 million American Facebook users. Data mined from the website had been used in the 2016 presidential campaign. Zuckerberg began with his opening comments acknowledging there were enormous issues of privacy and security at stake, but before the "hard questions" were asked, he first wanted to talk about how Facebook "got here." He described Facebook as an "idealistic and optimistic company" that had organized the "Me Too" movement, raised $20 million in relief for Hurricane Harvey victims, and helped 70 million small businesses to create jobs and growth. Zuckerberg admitted that the company did not realize the responsibility it had, apologized, and concluded his opening remarks listing measures the company would take to ensure no further breaches. Then the third degree began.

Senator Thune questioned first, "After more than a decade of promises to do better, how is today's apology different?" After thanking the chairman, Zuckerberg incorporated his American Dream theme into his answer, "So, we have made a lot of mistakes in running the company, I believe to start a company in a dorm room and then grow it to the scale that we're at without making some mistakes (would be impossible). And because our service is about helping people connect and information, those mistakes have been different . . . ." When Senator Cruz aggressively pressed Zuckerberg to agree that a "great amount of Americans" believe Facebook has a "pervasive pattern of political bias," Zuckerberg began his even-toned answer with, "I understand where that concern is coming from." He ended with, "I am very committed to making sure that Facebook is a platform for all ideas. That is a—a very important founding principle of—of what we do." When Senator Graham asked if Zuckerberg thought that Facebook had a monopoly, he paused, and answered, "It doesn't feel that way to me," provoking a crowd-giggle.[1]

---

1. *Transcript of Mark Zuckerberg's Senate hearing*, WASH. POST, (April 10, 2018). Available at https://www.washingtonpost.com/news/the-switch/wp/2018/04/10/transcript-of-mark-zuckerbergs-senate-hearing/ (last visited February 2, 2021).

Despite the aggressive questioning, Zuckerman remained deferential to the senators—calling each their name prefaced with the title "Senator," maintaining eye contact, and keeping even-tempered. He often reverted to his themes of "a small guy makes good," "a company helping people connect," and "the company will do better in the future." The *New York Times* reported that Zuckerberg "appeared confident and answered questions directly." By the end of his testimony, Facebook's stock climbed 4.5 percent.[2,3]

Zuckerberg used the questions as his launch pad to answer the concerns of the senators and emphasize his own talking points.[4] While it may not seem so while you are in the proverbial hot seat, questions are your friends. Embrace them. Through questioning, you can glimpse the judge's mind, his thinking process, and his struggles. With this knowledge, you can respond in a way that addresses his individual and particular concerns. Nothing is more persuasive than meeting the judge precisely where he is—responding to the very sticking points he will have to decide the case in your favor. Welcome questions from the judge—even cheer them on. Be grateful. Every time the judge asks a question, say silently to yourself, "thank you, judge." This will put you in the right frame of mind to answer the questions and it will show in your responses.

But with questions come understandable anxiety. In the nerve-wracking tension of a hearing, many attorneys fear that not only will they not be able to answer a question, but they will also make fools out of themselves. To be sure, there is an improvisational element to every hearing, but there are ways to plan for the unexpected. Of course, one of the best ways is to spend some time either alone or with others anticipating the questions you might be asked and your best responses to those inquiries.

No doubt, many queries can and will be anticipated before the argument. However, in nearly every argument, there will be times when the unexpected question is asked. This chapter gives you tools to deal with spontaneity by giving you a formula for answering questions. In the next chapter, we talk about specific types of questions you are likely to be asked, and how you can effectively answer them.

---

2. *Mark Zuckerberg Testimony: Senators Question Facebook's Commitment to Privacy*, N.Y. TIMES, April 10, 2018. Available at https://www.nytimes.com/2018/04/10/us/politics/mark-zuckerberg-testimony.html (last visited February 2, 2021).

3. In the moment and for the short term, Zuckerberg's performance was charming and convincing. However, he is alleged to have committed the cardinal sin of communications, not being truthful. In the long term, if true, this decision was a devastating choice as his credibility with the lawmakers may never recover.

4. It was reported that Zuckerberg hired a team of experts and spent a couple weeks with them preparing for his testimony. *Zuckerberg Gets a Crash Course in Charm. Will Congress Care?* N.Y. TIMES April 8, 2018. Available at https://www.nytimes.com/2018/04/08/technology/zuckerberg-gets-a-crash-course-in-charm-will-congress-care.html (last visited February 2, 2021).

7.1 Formula for Answering Questions

Let's start with a six-step approach to answering questions. This formula should be used with every question asked.

SCIENCE: STEPS TO ANSWERING A QUESTION
Step 1: Listen to the end of the question.
Step 2: Pause before you answer.
Step 3: Ask clarifying questions, if necessary.
Step 4: Directly answer the question first.
Step 5: Explain your answer.
Step 6: Transition back to your argument and your strengths.

7.1.1 Step One: Listen to the End of the Question

An attorney's tendency is to formulate the answer to a question before the question is complete. As the judge is asking questions, your mind may naturally drift to how you will concisely, intelligently, and persuasively answer the question. You may think that if you can create a proper response before the question is over, you will avoid the pregnant pause while you formulate your answer. Because multitasking is difficult for us all, you may stop listening to the question midstream to create the perfect comeback. Do not succumb to this tendency. Listen to the question until the end. Breathe. Take in the question.

To do otherwise means that mid-question, while you are contemplating your response, the question may take a twist—and by the time you are answering the question, it is not the question you have been asked. The evolving and sometimes changing question occurs because the hearing is spontaneous for the judge as well. As he is thinking about the case, questions arise on the spot as thoughts occur to him. If he is creating his questions in the moment, then he will probably not be as succinct as he would be with planned questions. Questions twist and turn. To avoid answering the wrong question, listen until the judge is finished speaking. If you do not and the answer is a non-sequitur, you will lose your credibility—even if only slightly—with the judge, affecting your ability to persuade.

Further, even if you are firmly convinced that you know the question, do not answer the question before it is complete. Nothing is ruder and more annoying to a judge than for an advocate to be so sure she knows where the question is going that to save time, she cuts off the judge before the judge has finished speaking. Impoliteness rarely makes you persuasive. *Science: Never, never, never* talk over a judge.

7.1.2 Step Two: Pause Before You Answer

Pausing may be the most difficult part of this technique. Silence can be deafening and often seems longer than it is. Attorneys fill the space with chatter. Filler words like *"um," "so," "and," "well Judge"* are common. Also, attorneys say things like, "That was a good question, Judge" or variations to that response such as, "That is an interesting question," "I am glad you asked this question," "I appreciate the question," or "Thank you for the question." This inevitably leads the judge to say or think to himself, "Of course that was a good, interesting, fill-in-the-blank question, I asked it. Now answer it and stop wasting my time with false flattery."

Better to remain silent and take a deep breath to allow yourself a moment for your prefrontal cortex and its executive function to overtake the amygdala, the part of your brain associated with fear. Pause for two seconds. During the pause, categorize the question. Even if the question is an easy one to answer, take a two second pause before answering it. This two-second pause will become your "baseline pause," which allows you to appear with calm confidence before the judge whether you know the answer immediately or need a moment longer to think. You behave the same regardless of your level of confidence. You are cool and collected with a baseline pause no matter what. During this baseline pause, ask yourself questions such as: What issue is implicated by the question? What type of question is it? What does the judge need? Determine the judge's problem and where to go for its solution.

The judge is sincerely flattered that you are giving his question the thought that it is due. With his questions, the judge knows he is asking you to put together information in a way that helps him decide the case. He will appreciate the respect you show him with a careful and thoughtful response.

Exercise

In everyday conversations, practice a pause pattern before answering questions. During the two-second silent pause, ask and answer to yourself two key questions: *What are they asking? Where do I go after I directly answer?*

Friend: "Did you like the BBC version of Pride and Prejudice?"

[You, internally: Pause, and ask yourself, *What is he asking?* I know him well. He is interested in the quality of the acting. *Where do I go after I directly answer?* I'll discuss Colin Firth's performance.]

You, aloud: "Yes. It's my favorite version of Pride and Prejudice. Colin Firth is the perfect Darcy."

7.1.3 Step Three: Ask Clarifying Questions, If Necessary

If you truly do not understand the question, ask for clarification. You may indicate to the judge that you do not know what he is asking you. Or you can begin to answer by indicating to the judge that you are taking his question to mean thus and so. This technique is particularly helpful for the complicated hypothetical question. The judge will then tell you whether you are right or wrong in your interpretation of the question.

There are important rules for clarifying a question:

- **Use this technique sparingly.** If you overuse clarifying questions, the judge may perceive you as avoiding the question, unintelligent, or possibly argumentative.

- **Be interested and curious in your clarifying question, but do not apologize.** Many advocates apologize, which weakens their position. They sound like this, "Judge, I am sorry, but I really do not understand the question you are asking." Chances are that it is not your fault that you do not understand the judge's question, so avoid saying you are sorry. During your argument, there will be times you may need to apologize because you have misstated the facts, misconstrued a holding in a case, or otherwise misspoken. Save your apologies for the times you are truly wrong.

- **Do not use a clarifying question as a stalling technique.** If you understand the question, do not fill the silence of the pause while you think aloud with a clarifying question. Judges know when you are stalling. If you ask a clarifying question too often during the hearing, the judge will know you are delaying. Best to take a deep breath and relish in the silence while you construct your answer to a question you understand.

7.1.4 Step Four: Directly Answer the Question First

Often you will be asked a direct question that requires a *yes* or *no* answer. Do not say you will get to the answer later. The question is your first priority because it is the judge's priority. Answer "Yes," "No," or "It depends." If you do not, the judge will assume you are hedging. The judge's first impression will be that your position is weak; otherwise, you would confidently and straightforwardly answer the question. Evasion is also a catalyst for cross-examination. Remember, many judges are former trial attorneys. A judge who smells weakness will reflexively try out his rusty cross-examination skills—skills he was, or at least thinks he was, on top of at some point in his career.

Consider this scenario:

Judge: Does *Smith v. Smith* control the outcome?

Counsel: In *Smith v. Smith*, the husband had not paid child support for many years—

Judge: Counsel, is that a *yes*?

> Counsel: Well, it's not that simple. On the one hand, *Smith v. Smith* is very similar to this case and on the other hand—
>
> Judge: Then the short answer is *yes*?
>
> Counsel: I can't say that.

By the end of the colloquy, both the judge and counsel are frustrated. And the judge believes that counsel is vulnerable on the questioned point. Consider this conversation instead:

> Judge: Does *Smith v. Smith* control the outcome?
>
> Counsel: Yes, it does, Your Honor, and it supports our position because . . .

Or:

> Counsel: No, it does not, Your Honor, and the reason it does not is . . .

A good negotiator learns to utilize "and" instead of "but," whether in business, marriage, or in court. If you disagree with the judge, try to find a path forward that includes agreement on some level. Notice that even when the counsel above needs to say "no," we suggest it be followed with "and." Train yourself to find the "and" instead of the "but" in your phrases as you respond to the judge's questions. If you can, it is better to answer the question with a "Yes, and . . . " to build on your and the judge's point of agreement. "Yes, and" accepts the judge's premise and then adds more upon which you can agree. "Yes, and" is more powerful and strategically useful than a "no," "it depends," or a "yes, but" answer. Judges know that "yes, but" really means "no," and a "no" puts you at odds with the judge. The point of getting in front of the court is to get the judge(s) to agree with you, so wordsmith your answers like a good negotiator. Better to agree with him and work collaboratively to find a solution. You will gain the judge's trust and acceptance and appear reasonable.

Give the short answer to a question that can be answered with a *yes, no,* or *it depends* before explaining your answer. Be careful to match your answer to your argument. The stronger your argument, the more definitive your answer can be. If you are weak in your answer—replying, for example, "It seems so"—yet your argument is strong, you have undermined your position. If, on the other hand, your answer is definitive, such as, "It could not be clearer," and your argument is weak, you have diminished your credibility.

Here are some variations of the "yes," "no," and "it depends" answer:

Yes	No	"IT DEPENDS"
"It seems so."	"No, that is not the case here."	"It's possible."
"Of course."	"Those aren't the facts."	"It's probable."
"You are correct."	"That's not possible."	"It's likely."
"I agree."	"Certainly not."	"Maybe."
"It couldn't be clearer."	"Definitely not."	"Somewhat."
"Absolutely."	"Not at all."	"To some extent."
"Yes, and . . ."	"No, and . . ."	"It depends."

7.1.5   Step Five: Explain Your Answer

After you have answered the direct question, explain your answer. Rhetorically, decide how deeply you wish to cover the problem. Start where the judge is in his thinking process. Recognize the judge's inherent concern with the question. You will be more persuasive if, as you begin your argument, you show the court that you are on its side, even if briefly so. Consider the difference between these scenarios:

Judge: Explain why *Smith v. Jones* is not problematic for your client.

Counsel: *Smith v. Jones* is totally distinguishable from this case.

Or:

Counsel: I understand your concerns with *Smith v. Jones*. In *Smith v. Jones*, the facts were X, Y, and Z, where here we have X, Y, and B. B makes the difference here because . . . .

In the second scenario, counsel is more likely to persuade the court. In the first response, counsel is saying between the lines, "What's wrong with you, Judge? It is blatantly obvious that *Smith v. Jones* does not control at all—it's totally distinguishable." Much more persuasive was the second answer, when counsel acknowledged the judge's concern, validated it, and then gradually explained why the concern was unfounded. Begin your response by aligning yourself with the court, starting where the judge is. It allows the court to hear and be convinced by your argument. You can gradually return to your argument, weaving in the reassuring magic words of the law to show how the legal principles behind those magic words apply to your case.

Another rhetorical device to persuade the court of the legitimacy of your position is using the judge's or opposing counsel's words in your response. Incorporating the judge's words into your answer shows the judge you heard him, builds consensus, and shortens the distance you need to travel to persuade him.

Suppose counsel in the above scenario sits down, and opposing counsel is also questioned about *Smith v. Jones*. Opposing counsel may answer, "As the court pointed out before, *Smith v. Jones* is problematic for the other side because . . . ." By reusing the judge's previous characterization, opposing counsel aligns herself with the court to highlight the correctness of the court's initial position.

You can use the judge's words as an effective tool of persuasion. Be careful though not to be too obsequious. Do not say, "The court was absolutely correct that [XYZ case] compels a win for us." or "The court astutely understands the implication of [XYZ case]." Overt brown-nosing usually backfires. You may also use opposing counsel's words. Great advocates turn the other side's words into their arguments, showing the vulnerability of the opposing argument.

7.1.5.1   Pick a pathway

Just as there are cookie-cutter frameworks to simplify the law, there are cookie-cutter pathways to answer questions. Many of the pathways we described to simplify the law work equally well when answering questions. After the question is completed and during your pause, pick a pathway to explain your answer. Your answer will be easier to follow and more comprehensible. Effective options are enumeration, chronology, compare and contrast, problem-solution-next steps, or sensory. All these pathways will lead to a clear and organized answer. Start your answer with a headline telling the court where you are going, follow the chosen pathway, and then wrap up with a conclusion.

Enumeration: Tell the court how many points you wish to make and then make them. "Judge, I have three points I would like to make in answering your question. First, ... Second, ... Third, ..." Return to the three-point system during the argument. After being quizzed on point one, say, "our second point is . . . ," And deliver what you promise; if you say three points, make sure you deliver three, not four or five. The judge may stop listening at three. This phenomenon also occurs when an advocate states, "To wrap up," or "In closing," or "Finally," and then keeps adding more points. *Art:* In most situations, it is wise not to go beyond three—you may lose the judge.[5]

Chronology: This is a well-known and efficient method to learn new information. Darting back and forth in nonsequential order is confusing. When answering factual questions, present the necessary facts in chronological order. When asking the court to expand the law, show the court, step by step, the timetable of where the law has been and why the next step is logical, small, and inevitable.

Compare and Contrast: Compare and contrast is a listener-friendly method to learn information. It is human to compare and contrast—we compare our old cars with our new, the liberal with the conservative, and the plaintiff with the defendant. Use this technique when distinguishing or finding commonalities between cases. Quickly rattling off the differences or the similarities between your case and case law is persuasive.

Problem→Solution→Next Steps: Another effective pathway is problem→solution→next steps. Acknowledge the problem the judge is having with the point you are making. Then propose the solution and a path forward with specific next steps.

For example:

Judge: Counsel, setting aside the judgment will result in delay—a very unfortunate circumstance for Mr. Johnson given his medical condition.

Counsel: I understand your concern about delay [*problem*], and Your Honor, we will agree to place this case on the fast docket to reduce the delay [*solution*]. We are prepared to have an expedited discovery period finishing in October, with a trial if need be by November [*next steps*].

Sensory: Finally, the sensory path explains to the judge in vivid detail what the natural consequences of the implication of the question are.

Judge: Setting aside this judgment is not judicially economical. No further judicial resources should be spent on this case.

Counsel: If this judgment is not set aside, the court must set a damage hearing. At a minimum, the paramedics, plaintiff, his family, the emergency room doctor, his personal physician,

---

5. We recognize that certain motions and oral arguments require the litigant to respond to questions by referencing prongs of a legal test or regulatory requirements which may demand more than three points (ex: emergency injunction).

> and his neurologist must be examined and cross-examined. My client is likely to file a legal malpractice suit against his previous counsel for failing to respond, causing a cascade of motions and a lengthy jury trial. Setting aside this judgment is the most economical use of the court's time.

Choose the best explanation pathway with each question to deliver a logical, coherent, and polished answer.

7.1.5.2 Decide the Depth and Breadth of Your Answer

With each answer, decide how deeply and completely you want to delve into the problem. Through her questioning, a judge can hijack your argument. During your baseline pause, decide when to expand, and when to contract, the answers. Is it better to give the short or long answer to the question? Your decision will be made on the spot and depends on the judge and the issue.

If you plunge too deeply into an issue, you risk losing the judge's interest—or worse yet, focusing on your weakness, a less persuasive strategy than focusing on your strength. However, if a judge is interested in the issue, is struggling with it, or has an expertise in the area, a more extensive discussion is advisable.

The topic involved also informs the time you must spend on the answer. The more dependent your argument is on the point, the more time must be spent. The weakness or strength of your argument also factors into the coverage you give. If you are sure to win an argument, you may want to spend more time answering the question on those "iffier" arguments you can win. On the other hand, if your point is particularly weak and not germane, then politely, concisely, and briefly respond to the point before quickly turning to your strengths. Overall, the amount of time you devote to a question depends on the judge's interest, concern, and struggle, along with the strength and centrality of the point to your argument.

7.1.6 *Step Six: Transition Back to Your Argument and Your Strengths*

Once you have explained your answer to the judge's question, transition back to your argument. The question is generally on a weakness in your position. Do not dwell on the weakness; rather, move back to your strengths. If you remain in defensive mode, focusing on your vulnerabilities, your argument will be weaker than offensively showcasing your strengths. Segue to your main themes, subthemes, and your affirmative points to keep on the offensive.

Think back to Chicago Burger:

Judge: Isn't a restaurant responsible for providing a minimum of safety to its patrons?

Counsel: Yes, Your Honor. And Chicago Burger did provide more than the minimum. *This points to a hole in the plaintiffs' case*: they cannot show that Chicago Burger reasonably could have foreseen Kenneth Levy's reckless conduct.

Note in this example, the judge's concern is based on a weakness in the lawyer's case. Counsel acknowledged the judge's struggle by answering using the judge's words and then pivoting to her strength, allowing the argument to proceed, at least for a while, to the attorney's advantage. Without the segue, counsel could have been caught up defending her weakness for much of the argument. The transition step is the most important and difficult part of answering questions. A common mistake in an argument is for counsel to answer a question and then pause waiting for the next question. Remember that the goal of the argument is not only to help the judge with her concerns, but to make your two or three affirmative points. Weave into the argument your strengths when you have the chance. You make those chances with transitional lines, such as:

TRANSITIONAL LINES	
"And . . ."	"Because of that, . . ."
"This is exactly why . . ."	"That supports our position."
"Let's turn to . . ."	"With respect to . . ."
"This issue is similar to . . ."	"Let's unpack that."
"To summarize, . . ."	"Bottom line, . . ."
"This is symptomatic of a deeper issue."	"That brings us to the next point."
"That points to a hole in [insert party name]'s case."	"I share Your Honor's concern because . . ."

Using transitional lines after answering a question, will naturally result in a more offensive than defensive argument.

7.2   Common Problems to Avoid

Two common problems occur during the questioning stage: biting back when the judge cuts you off and using weak language. Cutting off the judge is taboo. Besides being impolite, it shows the judge you do not respect him. The judge may interrupt you—immediately stop speaking when you see the judge's lips move. That means mid-sentence. You may be asking why you may not interrupt the judge, but he may interrupt you. The answer is simple: he is the judge and decides your client's fate. In defense of judges, time is usually of the essence in a hearing, and if the judge thinks your answer is going in a direction that is not productive to his resolution of the issue, he will stop you and veer you to a more productive avenue. Follow his lead.

Another common problem is using weak or qualifying language. Answers that begin with "I think . . ." or "I believe . . ." undermine the strength of an argument.[6] The argument becomes interwoven with the personal credibility of the attorney. Instead of saying, "I think the law requires excusable neglect to set aside a default judgment," simply state, "The law says excusable neglect is required on the part of the defendant to set aside a default judgment." Examples of other credibility busters appear in the table below. These feeble phrases are usually wind-ups to avoid the discomfort of silence in a courtroom. Avoid the tendency to fill the silence by taking a breath, inserting a pause, and contemplating your answer.

WHAT NOT TO SAY		
"I believe that . . ."	"I think . . ."	"I really feel like . . ."
"I really believe that . . ."	"I'm not an expert but . . ."	"Just a thought."
"Take it for what it's worth."	"If I could just say a few words about . . ."	"Just as long as we're throwing things out here, . . ."
"I'll get to that later."	"You know . . ."	"With all due respect, . . ."
"I had sort of an idea about . . ."	"Go on, finish what you were saying."	"Well, judge . . . "

As a review of the steps, for every question: Listen to the question until it is finished, pause, ask clarifying questions if necessary, answer the direct question first, explain your answer, and then transition back to your strengths. Now let's turn to a menu of question types.

---

6. Current speaking trends of Millennials have an abnormally large number of qualifiers (such as *like, kind of, sort of, you know, just*). Law school professors, partners, and supervisors should encourage young lawyers to shed qualifiers when answering questions while practicing direct-answering techniques.

CHAPTER EIGHT

A PERIODIC TABLE OF QUESTIONS

Questions are like chemicals; learn how to handle them safely. Some are harmless; some are potentially explosive. Certain general rules must be followed to manage both, but each type of question, like each kind of chemical, has various degrees of volatility requiring special precautions. There is a universe of possible questions a judge can ask at a hearing. In this chapter, we characterize those questions, name them, and give suggestions as to how to respond to each. We will use a short case file revolving around a fairytale: Humpty Dumpty. In this invented case, *Humpty Dumpty v. The King*, the King petitions to set aside a default judgment. Using our hypothetical, we illustrate how to answer various types of questions. The principles demonstrated in the motion hearing apply with equal force to an appellate setting unless otherwise indicated. However, we devote the next chapter to additional special considerations for multi-judge panels. But first, we introduce our fairytale case, which will help us to demonstrate our points.

8.1 *Humpty Dumpty v. The King*

The trial court entered a default judgment against the King on the civil complaint that Humpty Dumpty filed against him for negligence.[1] Counsel represents the King in a hearing before the same court to set aside the default judgment. Prior counsel had his head cut off by order of the King.

The facts are that Humpty Dumpty climbed the wall surrounding the King's castle. He was able to climb to the top because embedded in the wall were pieces of rebar that formed a makeshift ladder. From Mr. Dumpty's vantage point, he peered inside the King's chambers. We all know what happened from there, after which Mr. Dumpty filed his negligence lawsuit against the King.

The King's men accepted service for the King and promptly brought the complaint and summons to the King's attention. The King set the summons aside and forgot about it. A scullery maid found the complaint under the pillow on the King's throne and that same day the King's men delivered it to the Imperial Law Firm—the firm

---

1. Judge Nancy Vaidik originally created this fact scenario as a teaching tool for lectures in the National Institute for Trial Advocacy's custom motion practice course.

who routinely handled the King's legal matters. The firm's administrative assistants left the paperwork on the desk of the senior partner, Joseph Emperor, who had been the King's personal attorney for years. Unfortunately, two days earlier Mr. Emperor had a mental breakdown, ran through the kingdom naked, and proclaimed he had new clothes. Mr. Emperor's family committed him after the incident. The complaint was not answered. One week after the law firm received Mr. Dumpty's complaint, the Imperial Law Firm found the paperwork on Mr. Emperor's desk. By that time, Mr. Dumpty's attorney had moved for a default judgment against the King, which the court granted. Two months later, the Imperial Law Firm moved to set aside the default judgment.

At the hearing to set aside the default judgment, Mr. Dumpty submitted an affidavit claiming that he scaled the wall to see the Holy Grail, which was inside the King's chamber.

The pertinent legal authority in the kingdom is Trial Rule 60(b), *Everystate v. Big Bad Wolf, Old Witch v. Hansel and Gretel, The Prince v. Rapunzel, and Jack and the Beanstalk.* TR 60(b) allows a court to set aside a default judgment *only* upon a showing of excusable neglect *and* a meritorious defense. The concept of excusable neglect was examined by the court of appeals in *Everystate v. Big Bad Wolf.* There, the insurance company, Everystate, filed a declaratory judgment action against its insured, the Big Bad Wolf, claiming that it was not liable for the intentional acts of the Big Bad Wolf in blowing down the houses of the three pigs. The declaratory judgment was granted by default because Wolf's counsel, Jack and Jill LLP, did not answer Everystate's complaint. Jack and Jill claimed that they could not do so because of injuries they themselves had sustained near the time of service. The appellate court affirmed the trial court's decision to set aside the default judgment against Wolf.

As to a meritorious defense, Mr. Dumpty claims that the King has none because he created an attractive nuisance. In *Old Witch v. Hansel and Gretel*, the appellate court sustained a jury's finding that the Old Witch had created an attractive nuisance, luring Hansel and Gretel into her house. Likewise, in *The Prince v. Rapunzel*, the court found that Rapunzel had created an attractive nuisance by letting her hair fall from the tower so the Prince could climb up to save her. However, in *Jack and the Beanstalk v. Giant*, the court affirmed a jury verdict for the Giant finding that the Giant had not created an attractive nuisance. None of the cases address the potential malpractice claim against the defaulting law firm.

Assume that counsel argues for the default judgment to be set aside.

With this case in mind, let's start to examine specific types of questions you will encounter.

8.2   Open versus Closed Questions

We begin with two broad categories of questions—the open question and the closed question. The open question begins with words such as "tell me about," "explain," "describe,"or "how." When you hear the open question, the judge is inviting you to speak. Your answer should be an average of one to two minutes. Begin your answer with a summary, indicate where you are going, then follow one of the pathways we discussed in Chapter Seven to explain your answer. End by recapping your answer and transitioning back to your theme.

Closed questions require a "yes," "no," "maybe," or a "choice." Questions such as: "Does your client prefer [x] or [y]?" "Are you saying . . . ?," "Does [x] case control?" are typical closed questions. Many of these closed questions may sound like the hostile judge question we describe below. Do not read too much into a closed question. The judge simply needs an answer, and often asks a series of closed questions to help her reason to the right conclusion. Directly answer the question, and then briefly explain if necessary. *Science:* Keep your answers to thirty seconds or less. The judge wants a quick response.

Now let's classify some categories of questions. As you hear a judge's question, classifying the type of question during your baseline pause will help you answer the question more completely and responsively, and can help you deliver your answer with the right tone. You need to know where the bullets are coming from.

8.3   The Kickoff Question

Often, a judge kicks off a hearing with confrontational questions. Do not assume the judge is angry with you; the judge wants you to quickly get to your point and not waste her time.

Be ready to bound cleanly into a legal argument without confusing the judge, while simultaneously proving the need for the judge to hear your argument. Appeal to the judge's desire to have you help her decide the case and, if in a trial court, her desire to resolve the case without the necessity of a trial. Speak your answer clearly and confidently, stand your ground with no movement of your body, and signal with slow, long, and calming gestures. Here are some common questions along with our suggested answers:

Judge: Counselor, what can you tell me today that isn't already in your papers?

Counsel: I can answer your questions and underscore arguments we made.

Judge: You aren't here to tell me things you failed to argue in your papers, are you?

Counsel:	No, Your Honor. I'm here to highlight issues and answer your concerns.

Or in a motion hearing you may hear:

Judge:	Why are we having this hearing?
Counsel:	We stand by our written motion, but I'm here to discuss the motion with you, Your Honor.
Judge:	Can't I make a ruling off your written pleadings?
Counsel:	It depends; we would like to tell you facts that have developed since we wrote the papers which might impact your decision.

Or:

Judge:	Why do you want to argue this today?
Counsel:	I want to discuss the concerns you raised on our last phone conference. Those concerns are valid, and they are in line with our request today.

Or:

Judge:	Why did you need an hour of the court's time?
Counsel:	Your decision today will help both parties settle this matter, and we wanted sufficient time to discuss the issues with you.

THE KICKOFF	
General	The initial question asked by a court. Be ready to leap right away.
Words	"Your Honor, I'm here to highlight issues and answer your concerns." "I can tell you facts that have developed since we wrote the papers." "Let me bring you up to speed since the last time we spoke, Your Honor."
Voice	Clear, projected
Body Language	Home base,[2] calm gestures
Tone	Warm and engaging

8.4 The "Blank Out"

At some point in the argument, you may momentarily forget information that you know you know. Perhaps it is the name of a case or a pertinent fact. This "blank out" instills fear in the most experienced advocate. Keep your face calm.

---

2. For a discussion of home bases, *see* section 13.2.2.

Avoid the deer-in-the-headlights look. Have in your arsenal a standard-rescue line to give you a moment to calm yourself and find the missing information in your brain or your papers. Pause. Say, "May I have one moment, please." That will give you the time to calm down or look in your well-prepared notes for the answer. Notice that we suggest asking for a moment and not a minute. Most judges will be happy to give you a moment, but some may be reticent to give an entire minute.

THE BLANK-OUT RESPONSE	
General	The momentary lapse of memory.
Words	"Your Honor, may I have a moment." "Just one second, please." "It's right here at my fingertips."
Voice	Clear, projected
Body Language	Home base, calm gestures
Tone	Warm and engaging

8.5 The "I Don't Know" Question

One of the most terrifying questions is the one to which you really do not know the answer. Of course, the best way to avoid this question is to anticipate it before the hearing. But sometimes, even most times, no matter the preparation, you cannot predict every question. If you do not know the answer, usually the best course of action is to admit that you do not know.

Judges have a good ear as to when counsel is dodging a question. The more the advocate squirms and avoids answering the question, the easier it is for the judge to spot the fudge.

There are many ways to say, "I don't know."

WAYS TO SAY "I DON'T KNOW"
"I had not considered that . . . ."
"I'm not sure, but I do know . . . ."
"I'm not familiar with that. "
"I was not aware of that."
"That does not seem to be what we have here."
"I'm unclear on the details."
"That is not in the record. "
"I'm not certain and do not want to tell you anything that is inaccurate."

(Continued)

WAYS TO SAY "I DON'T KNOW"
"I do not have that at my fingertips. If you give me a moment, my colleague can provide that cite."
"That case does not appear in any of the papers filed."
"I'm not certain I can help you with this, but I will be happy later to provide the answer."

After saying you do not know, offer a reason why you do not have an answer. If you have a plausible solution, then offer it. If the question pertains to a court case, then you may feel confident enough in the area of law to ask the court to briefly provide you with details of the case to trigger your memory. If you recall, you will have avoided calamity. If not, candidly admit that nothing was sparked in your memory. Offer a solution, such as submitting supplemental briefing on the issue within twenty-four hours. After offering to provide supplemental papers, try to engage the court in a discussion to determine the nature of the problem. For instance, "Is the court bothered with [fill in the blank]?" The fill-in-the-blank pertains to whatever topic you were discussing before the question was asked. You may be able to clear up the difficulty without the need to file additional papers.

Example: *Humpty Dumpty v. The King*

Judge: How about the Little Red Riding Hood case?

Counsel: I am not familiar with the case *[admission]*, Your Honor. It was not cited in any of the briefs *(reason)*. I would be happy to brief it and provide supplemental papers in twenty-four hours *(solution)*. Is the court concerned with the assumption of risk *[find the problem]*?

Science: Do not wither when responding to a question to which you do not know the answer. Avoid looking shocked or surprised. Show interest in the judge's question. Stand upright, no slumped shoulders. In a clear, understandable voice, respond that you do not know the answer but will get back to the court. While answering, be careful not to lift your inflection as if you are asking the court a question.

You may answer that you do not know only once or twice in a long motion hearing before you lose your credibility, but probably only once in an appellate court as judges there expect more perfection. *Science:* Your best defense against the question you cannot answer is always preparation.

Exercise

Practice in front of a mirror the "I don't know" response.

- Is your posture confident?
- Are you slumping your shoulders?
- Have you practiced the words "I don't know" enough so you do not stumble over them?
- Are you maintaining the volume of your voice?
- Are you avoiding the upward inflection of your voice, so you do not sound like you are asking a question?
- Do you look and sound confident?

Practice this exercise until your responses are automatic and you look comfortable with saying you do not know.

8.6 The "Outside the Record" Question

Sometimes the judge asks a question where the answer requires a response with information not in the record. If you do not know the answer, then tell the court you cannot answer. *Science:* However, if you know the answer, but the answer is not found in the record submitted, tell the judge that the information is not part of the record. Then ask her if you should answer the question. If she says you should, then do so.

Appellate judges detest when counsel refer to evidence not in the record unless counsel is specifically asked to do so. The appellate record is complete; judges are not to consider anything outside the record. To talk about non-admitted evidence is cheating. Your credibility will take a hit not only for the case at hand but for future cases.

Example: *Humpty Dumpty v. The King*

Judge: Is the Holy Grail located in such a position in the King's chambers that someone who scaled the wall could see it?

Counsel: The answer to the question is not in the court's record. Would you like me to answer it anyway?

Judge: Yes.

Counsel: No, the Holy Grail is not visible from the window, but it does sit on the King's bedstand sometimes emitting a light that is visible from the window. Humpty does not claim in his affidavit that he saw any light when he scaled the wall. In any event, the issue of whether the Holy Grail is an attractive nuisance is a question for the jury to decide.

8.7 The Softball Question

The softball is the easy question—the one you cannot wait to answer. With a multi-judge panel, the judge favorable to your position may be speaking to another judge on the bench through her questions to you. More on that later in the multi-judge chapter.

The first step is to recognize the softball. It may be delivered in an angry tone, so the judge does not show her cards to the opposing counsel. The angry tone may throw you off. Do not let it. Instead, take advantage of the softball and hit it out of the park. Take the opportunity to give your sixty-second elevator speech on the issue.

Softball questions go to the essence of why you should win. For example, in a summary judgment hearing the softball may be, "What are the material facts at issue here?" Or in a discovery hearing, "Tell me how this request is relevant to your case" or generally, in any argument, "I see no alternative but to . . . ." If the judge does tip her hand in the question, lean into the answer and take the opportunity to side with the judge. *Art:* Use the softball question to cement your themes and affirmative points.

THE SOFTBALL QUESTION
"Absolutely, Your Honor."
"That's precisely why it matters."
"Yes, Your Honor."
"I absolutely agree."
"Yes, that's correct."
"Yes, we see this the same way."

As soon as you recognize the softball, you may nod your head in agreement with the judge, but not obnoxiously so. Try taking a step back from counsel table in order to give the judge the floor. Answer in a warm and pleasant manner. Deliver your points that align with the court in a slower-paced rhythm. Do not become arrogant, or the judge may change her mind. No one likes a know-it-all. Be gracious in your win.

Example: *Humpty Dumpty v. The King*

Judge: Doesn't *Everystate v. Big Bad Wolf* completely resolve this case?

Counsel: Yes, it absolutely does, Your Honor. *Big Bad Wolf* stands for the fundamental proposition that everyone deserves his day in court. The King deserves his day in court.

8.8 The Genuine Inquiry

The genuine inquiry is a little different from the softball question. Unlike the softball, with the genuine inquiry the judge is not leaning toward your position. The judge is sincerely asking you to teach her the law and/or the facts. Basically, she is admitting that she does not know, but wants you to explain it to her. Recognize the bravery of the judge to ask this question. Many judges would never ask for fear of appearing stupid.

Educate the judge with your response. Be the best teacher you know how to be. Your response should be helpful. Go deeper into the issue. Do not respond with the obsequious, "That is a good question, Your Honor." Neither should you point out the deficiency of the judge's knowledge with, "Many misunderstand that holding." Nor should you tell the judge that "it is complicated," implying that it is too difficult for her to understand. Be patient, not belittling. Use the opportunity for a moment to clarify and explain. Assume the senior law clerk position. Do not lecture. Keep an even volume, measured-pace voice, with the range narrowed. Speak as if you were talking to your favorite college professor. Most of all, be excited because the questions do not get better than this. It is a rare opportunity to have a bonding moment with the judge who is asking you to teach her. Mastering the tone of this encounter is critical to seize the moment. This is your chance to connect with the judge, and to convince her of your point of view.

THE GENUINE INQUIRY
"I'd be happy to, Your Honor."
"That brings us deeper into the issue of . . . ."
"I would be glad to elaborate."
Note: You can also use the judge's words to begin your answer.

Genuine inquiry questions give you a further chance to connect with the judge by using her very words in your answer. By doing so, you let the judge know that you are listening to and understanding her struggle—and you are there to help.

If you notice a judge continually asking about an issue or fact, do not ignore it. Do not interpret that questioning as an assault. The judge is telling you that she needs help with that issue. Help her.

Example: *Humpty Dumpty v. The King*

Judge: Was Mr. Emperor so ill such that there is excusable neglect?

Counsel: Yes, he was ill. Extremely ill. So ill that he was wandering the streets of the kingdom naked. The King did all he could to answer the complaint by giving it to Mr. Emperor, and, but for the illness of Mr. Emperor, it would have been answered. This is classic excusable neglect, and neither side would be prejudiced by setting aside the default.

The genuine inquiry is handled a bit differently with a multi-judge panel. One judge may have a better grasp on the law than the questioning judge. We talked about handling various levels of comprehension among the judges in Chapter Six: The Law.

8.9   The Hostile Question and the Insistent Judge

Sometimes, a judge will ask a question that you think from its tone and content is hostile to your position. Often, the question starts with something like, "You are not saying . . . ?" And that is exactly what you are saying. Or the court will ask a yes or no leading question such as, "There is no excusable neglect, right?" Or the court will ask a series of questions seemingly favorable to your opponent. Do not automatically assume that the judge is not buying what you are selling. The judge may be putting you to the test to be sure that the judge would be right in joining you. Alternatively, the judge may be having a bad day or that may be the judge's personality. Do not misinterpret formality for hostility. Some advocates recoil when a formal judge asks questions. Because the attorney mistakes the judge's formality for impatience, he foregoes a chance to connect with the judge.

To address a judge's hostility, an advocate needs to remember that he has a wide range of emotions under that business suit. Frustration, anger, and rudeness are not the only option. Being an emotional one-hit wonder does not work in any relationship. If you realize that arguing with your spouse is not working, the successful move is to adjust and try a different tactic. Court is no different. When arguing a point in a certain tone does not work, change your approach. Knowing how to adjust is key. Each attorney has a toolbox of presentation techniques waiting to be sharpened: vocal expression, pacing, volume, pause pattern, operative word stress, pitch, vocal range, home bases, gesticulation pattern, eye contact, facial expression, etc. All can be adjusted and calibrated to fit the situation.

Before you answer the unfriendly question, listen for the nuances in the judge's reasoning behind the inquiry. Calling out the distinctions may make the judge less extreme in her position. Test the waters looking for subtleties in the judge's view. For example, suppose you represent the government in an action requesting that the car used to transport illegal drugs be forfeited to the state. During the questioning, the judge makes clear her distain for forfeitures but in doing so mentions the Eighth Amendment's prohibition against excessive fines. Understanding the nuance may give you a path to agreement with the judge. In this example, you may speak to the inapplicability of the Eighth Amendment to your case. Even if you cannot come to a consensus with the judge, she will appreciate that you understand the complexity of her thinking and may even soften her hardline view.

When accord becomes hopeless, do not beg or preach. Politely hold your position. As you stand your ground, do not appear aggressive. The judge's hostile question is often delivered at a higher volume and faster pace. Do not mimic her delivery. Instead, lower the pitch of your voice, lower your volume, and slow your pace. Now is *not* the time to take a fighter's stance in the courtroom. Instead, place your palms upward and take a step back, so as not to appear aggressive. Make sure your facial expressions reflect concern, and not annoyance. No grimacing. Do not name the emotion. Do not say, "I understand that you are angry." Instead, at this stage you may say something like, "I understand that you are having difficulty with this point, if you can give me some leeway, I think my point may become clearer." Or "I hear your great concern about . . . ."

If the judge persists in the hostile questioning, do not wrestle—disengage. When to disengage is a matter of judgment. If it is clear that the court is not budging, do not fight back. You never win cases by fighting with the judge. When it becomes clear that you will not convince the judge on a point, it is time to change directions. Either pull out one of the other independent arguments you prepared or turn the court's attention to another aspect of this issue. This is where preparing alternative arguments pays off. You need to let the court know that there is nothing more you can say on the contentious point and you would like to move on. Agree to disagree. Otherwise, all your time can be chewed up arguing this losing point.

Example: *Humpty Dumpty v. The King*

Judge:	This case is completely resolved by *Old Witch v. Hansel and Gretel*. The King created an attractive nuisance here, just as the Old Witch did. The King has no meritorious defense. Tell me why this is not so?
Counsel:	The facts of this case are very dissimilar to *Old Witch*. In *Old Witch*—
Judge:	I just cannot agree with you, counsel. In *Old Witch*, candy was dripping from the cottage, and here, Mr. Dumpty could see into the King's chambers.
Counsel:	True, but like *Old Witch*, the jury should decide whether there is an attractive nuisance.
Judge:	I disagree with you, counsel.
Counsel:	It seems we have a different understanding of *Old Witch*. If I could turn the court's attention to another example of attractive nuisance with *Jack and the Beanstalk* . . . .

When all else fails, here are some suggested transitional phrases to lob you back to your affirmative argument.

HOSTILE QUESTIONS FROM AN INSISTENT JUDGE
"There is nothing more I can add to this discussion. May I move on?"
"Sadly, we must agree to disagree on this point, but we still win because . . . ."
"I'm disappointed we do not agree on this point, Judge. May I move to my next point?"
"It sounds to me like we will have to agree to disagree, but I am hoping you'll agree with me on . . . ."
"If I may turn the court's attention to another case on this issue . . . ."
"May I have some leeway here to better explain my point?"

The most important lesson here is, do not let the court shake you. Keep calm. Stay true to your integrity and personality.

Sometimes, a judge is insistent because she has what she believes is the perfect compromise to resolve the dispute. In your preparation, you have likely considered this compromise and talked to your client about the possibility of accepting it. If you have your client's approval, accept the fallback position offered by the judge. If you do not have your client's approval, then shift the court in another direction.

8.10 The Hypothetical Question

A hypothetical question is a "what if" question. What if the facts were tweaked in one respect or another, would the result be the same? Hypothetical questions are common for two reasons. One, because the "what if" scenario may come before the court in the future and the court wants to be consistent. Or two, the judge enjoys the intellectual banter because it reminds her of the Socratic discussions of law school. In either case, the hypothetical question is difficult to prepare for, as it is difficult to anticipate every future factual situation.

Your inclination is to immediately point out that the hypothetical question does not reflect the facts of your case. Do not say "That is not this case." Resist the temptation. Of course, the facts are different. Judges become frustrated when you restate the obvious.

Because hypotheticals can be confusing, you may need to begin your answer by confirming and clarifying the details. Fully engage with the judge so you may identify what is driving the judge to ask the question. Say to the judge, "If I understand your hypothetical correctly, the situation you describe involves . . . ."

 Science: After you fully understand the specific question, answer with "Yes, the result would be the same," "No, it wouldn't," "It depends," or "I am not sure." If you do not, the judge will think that you are hedging because of the weakness of your argument.

Understandably, many attorneys who appear before the same court on the same type of cases, such as prosecutors or other government attorneys, are reticent to answer definitively one way or another for fear they will be bound to their answer if the theoretical comes true in a future case. In that event, balance the likelihood of the hypothetical occurring against the impact the equivocation might have on the result of the case at hand. An "It depends" or "I am not sure" answer, with an explanation, may be the best course of action for this concern.

Science: After answering the direct question, explain your answer. During the explanation, distinguish the facts of the hypothetical from the facts of your case. Acknowledge that differing facts might create a different result or analysis. Let the court know that in her ruling she does not need to go as far as the hypothetical takes her.

Art: An elegant twist at the end of your answer is to present a clean analogy of your facts that is more perfect than the judge's. We have done that below in our second response to the example from *Humpty*. Those perfect analogies require preparation by you before the argument. Seldom does the ideal comparison spontaneously come to you mid-hearing.

Example: *Humpty Dumpty v. The King*

Judge: Would it have made any difference if a carnival was inside the King's wall at the time Mr. Dumpty scaled the wall?

Counsel: Yes, if there were a carnival inside the King's wall, then it would be more likely an attractive nuisance [*direct answer*]. With a carnival, there would be rides, music, children's laughter, and the smell of popcorn. But here there was none of that excitement. Here, there was rebar and stone walls [*differentiation*]. Even so, whether an attractive nuisance exists is a question for a trier of fact. The King deserves his day in court.

Or

Counsel: No [*direct answer*]. Of course, a carnival inside the walls would be more enticing—the smell of popcorn, children's laughter, rollercoasters, music—but even so, the trier of fact would decide whether the King created an attractive nuisance [*differentiation*]. The facts here are more like a Peeping Tom peering into Sleeping Beauty's dressing room [*analogy*]. The King deserves his privacy, and, like anyone else, should be afforded the opportunity to have a jury decide this issue.

Possible introductory lines to answering hypothetical questions:

THE HYPOTHETICAL QUESTION
"As I understand it . . . ."
"In your hypothetical, the facts are . . . ."
"Yes, under those circumstances, the court would dismiss the matter . . . ."
"It depends."
"No, Your Honor. That would not change the decision."
"It may, but one major difference with the scenario is . . . ."
"Your Honor, the court does not need to go that far. All we are asking for is . . . ."

When answering the hypothetical, have a sporting attitude, not one of dread. Your tone and facial expressions should be welcoming. Enjoy the intellectual exercise. If you have pre-planned analogies to compare with the court's, the hypothetical question can be an amazing intellectual exchange with the judge.

8.11   The Rabbit Hole

When a judge asks questions that stray off your themes and often into the weeds of opposing counsel's counterarguments, it is necessary to back out of the rabbit hole and bring the court back to your main themes. Sometimes, the rabbit-hole question does not help the court decide, but the judge is genuinely interested in the detour. As a result, it is easy to be lulled into the rabbit hole because you want to help the court. Do not get diverted. Listen to the court's musings, but do not feel compelled to follow the judge down an intellectual path that is ultimately irrelevant to the issue at hand. *Science:* Affirm the concern, if you can briefly answer the question do so, if not, explain why it is insignificant, and shift back to a major theme. Rabbit holes chew up your time, so escape as fast as you can.

Be bold in leading the judge in the right direction. Do not be brash. Increase the volume of your voice to show you know what you are talking about.

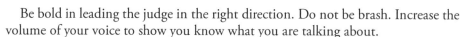

THE RABBIT HOLE QUESTION
[Answer quickly and directly, then pivot to your point.] ". . . but that makes no difference here because . . . ."
"I share your concern with fairness, and right now, the issue that faces us *is* ultimately about fairness."
"That discussion sends us on a detour, which I'm happy to briefly discuss." [Answer quickly and pivot to your affirmative point.]
Answer the question briefly and pivot back to your strengths. The answer is, "Yes, Your Honor," and then pivot to your argument.

Example: *Humpty Dumpty v. The King*

Judge: Does the King have an established procedure for receiving service? If so, did the King and his men deviate from the process and how?

Counsel: Yes, there is an established procedure. The King's men, who guard at the main gate, receive the summons and hand it to the Master of the Coin, who hands it to the King. Here the procedure was followed. Although the King sat on the complaint for a while, the excusable neglect occurred because of Mr. Emperor's illness, not because the procedure was not followed. (*Counsel briefly answers rabbit hole question, then moves on.*)

Or

Judge: Does the King have an established procedure for receiving service? If so, did the King and his men deviate from the process?

Counsel: Yes, there is an established procedure, which was followed, and it makes no difference to the outcome that the procedure was followed. Our claim of excusable neglect arises from Mr. Emperor's illness. (*Counsel does not answer the rabbit hole question.*)

8.12   The Confused Judge

The confused judge is just that: confused. She may be confused about what case is before her. She may be puzzled about the history of the case. She may not understand the nature of the proceedings.

In defense of the befuddled judge, argument days can be hectic. Patiently bring the confused judge back to your case.

Avoid the look of shock, surprise, or disgust. Lead the judge back with a relaxed posture, expanded gestures to help explain the substance, and a slowed pace of voice. Be careful not to slow your pace so slow that you imply the judge is a dimwit.

Example: *Humpty Dumpty v. The King*

Judge: Are we here today for summary judgment?

Counsel: No, we are here to ask the court to set aside the default judgment.

Here are some diplomatic opening lines to a judge who is confused:

THE CONFUSED JUDGE
"Your Honor, today's argument focuses on . . . ."
"I understand your concern, but today we're here to . . . ."
"The point is . . . ."
"This case concerns . . . ."

8.13 The Misinformed Judge

The misinformed judge is a subset of the confused judge. This judge mistakes the facts or the law. You are ethically bound to correct her even if her misunderstanding favors your position. In the long run, your credibility will be enhanced. But be diplomatic. Do not say, "No, you are wrong, Your Honor," or "With all due respect, Your Honor, ..." Either way the court knows you think she is thick. Instead, "Counsel for the other side is right about *X*, but we win anyway because . . . ." If appropriate, take the blame for the misunderstanding. Return to your theme to help refocus the judge's attention.

Here are some starting lines to answer the misinformed judge:

THE MISINFORMED JUDGE
"Counsel is correct in this, but we win anyway because . . . ."
"The holding in *X* was not . . . but it does not make a difference because . . . ."
"Just to set the record straight, the facts here are . . . ."
"Perhaps I have not been clear."

8.14 The Suspicious Judge

There is a natural suspicion in judges. They will rarely be open and friendly from the start. You must earn it. Do not take it personally; rather, use the opportunity to win the judge's trust. Return any coldness or distance with warmth and professionalism.

Sometimes, you know ahead of time, or through the course of the hearing, that the judge does not like or trust you or your client. Recognize that her distrust may not be personal against you. She may distrust the client, your co-counsel, or a previous counsel on the matter.

When answering the suspicious judge's questions, maintain longer-than-usual eye contact to show your sincerity. Slow down the pace of your voice. Do not mirror the tone of the question. Stay calm and professional. Keep your palms up when gesturing to underscore your openness. Be careful not to exaggerate or overstate. Use exhibits, if possible, to corroborate the veracity of your statements.

Example: *Humpty Dumpty v. The King*

Judge: You did not file your request to set aside the default judgment until two months after the judgment was entered?

Counsel: I think not, Your Honor. If you would take a look at the file stamp on the judgment and then look at the file stamp on the motion to set it aside, you will see it was actually a little less than two months. I have copies of those two documents if you would like me to approach.

8.15 The "Let's Make a Deal" Discussion

During a hearing, opportunities may arise to negotiate a resolution of the case with opposing counsel through the nudging of the court. Negotiations during appellate arguments are few, but during motion hearings are quite ordinary. Listen for the judge's cues. *Art:* Recognize that underneath the chatter, bargaining is occurring. Use the occasion to find win-win solutions.

"Why haven't you settled?" may be the most asked question by any trial court judge at a motion hearing. Be prepared with an answer. Do not disparage your opponent by responding that this case should have settled but for the unreasonableness of the other side. Doing so will provoke a counterattack, muddying both of you. Instead, let the court know that both parties have tried to settle, but are not there yet. Then use the inquiry to show the court that resolution of this motion, in your favor, will go a long way toward ending the case.

When asked the question, show the court that you would also like to settle the case by nodding your head in agreement. You may be thinking that the court is trying to avoid its responsibility to decide the case, but do not show your annoyance. Keep a poker face. Here are some responses to the "Why haven't you settled?" question:

"WHY HAVEN'T YOU SETTLED?"
"We have tried to find a solution and may still, but we are not there yet."
"We share your desire for resolution, and your decision on this motion will help to settle this case [or, if the motion is dispositive, will end the case]."
"A ruling will help move the parties in the right direction. Let me show you how."
"We need your guidance, Your Honor, and a ruling on this motion will give us the direction we need."

Sometimes the court initiates negotiations by expressing its concerns and offering proposed solutions. Seldom does the court outright tell you that it will rule one way if you concede a point. Often, you must read between the lines. Consider this exchange:

Example: *Humpty Dumpty v. The King*

Judge: I may be inclined to set aside the default judgment, but this may be a long, arduous, and costly process for the King.

Counsel: I understand your concern, Your Honor. [Pause.] May we have a recess so opposing counsel and I may speak to one another?

Notice that the court did not expressly indicate it was negotiating, but counsel got the message and made a judgment call. The call was not likely made on the spot. Before the hearing, counsel anticipated this discussion and had talked with his client.

Sometimes the court does not offer a solution; rather, you or opposing counsel propose solutions based on the court's concerns. These discussions are often the turning point of a hearing. Below, counsel offers a solution which may cause the court to set aside the default judgment.

Example: *Humpty Dumpty v. The King*

Judge: Counselor, by setting aside this default judgment, I will be prolonging the case to the detriment of the plaintiff. Isn't that true?

Counsel: We are willing to fast-track this case to avoid that problem.

Do not be too quick to accept a compromised solution. Stand your ground for a while until you reach the point where the court will not budge. When it is apparent that the court is not convinced with your strong position, then is the time to soften it to something your client can live with.

Example: *Humpty Dumpty v. The King*

Judge: In his pleadings, counsel for Humpty has asked the King to pay his attorney fees for responding to this motion. Should the King pay the costs incurred by Humpty to defend the motion? What do you think counsel?

Counsel: Humpty's counsel knew that Mr. Emperor has always been the King's attorney, yet did not give a copy of the summons to Mr. Emperor. The King should not be penalized for Humpty's carelessness.

Later in the opening argument of the King's counsel:

Judge: If I grant the default judgment, should the King pay Humpty for the costs of defending this motion?

Counsel: I think not, Your Honor. Humpty was a trespasser on the King's property. Further Humpty's counsel did not serve Mr. Emperor's firm despite common knowledge that Mr. Emperor had represented the King for twenty years.

Finally, during the rebuttal, counsel for the King realizes the court will not bend on the issue. And not backing down could interfere with the judge's ruling on setting aside the judgment.

Judge: I think it is only fair if I set aside the judgment that the King should pay Humpty's attorney fees to defend the motion. Both parties will be back to square one. Do you agree?

Counsel: Yes.

A common error is the attorney folding too quickly. Knowing when to fold is an art not a science. Stand firm yet professional until it becomes obvious that capitulating will give your client more advantage than disadvantage.

Even if the conversations do not resolve the case or motion at the moment, listen to opposing counsel's positions. Try to discern what matters most to the opposing party and his counsel. This information will help facilitate and inform future settlement negotiations.

During these in-court bargaining sessions, never show annoyance. Show the court that you are a partner with it in trying to find a solution. If you are not able to accept the solutions offered, explain why you cannot.

"LET'S MAKE A DEAL" (WHEN YOU CAN'T ACCEPT THE PROPOSAL)
"I cannot go as far as you want, but I can . . . ."
"I am having trouble with this one small aspect of your request . . . ."
"I need to consult with my client to get approval."
"I regret that we are too far down the road to accept this proposal."

8.16 Concessions

Concessions can be dangerous territory. Often a judge will ask you to concede certain factual or legal points that become the underpinnings of the ruling. The judge may want to clarify the nature of your request or limit the issues she must decide. Alternatively, the judge may want to decrease her risk of being reversed on appeal. Suppose, for example, that the parties argue opposing summary judgment motions. Both sides claim that the facts support summary judgment for their client. The court asks both sides whether there are any material facts in issue. Each counsel concedes there are none. With these questions, the court has reduced its chances of reversal by eliminating a key argument on appeal.

First, decide if you can concede. Think through the logical long-term and short-term consequences of conceding. The judge may be asking for a concession that will produce a domino effect, lulling you into a cascade of concessions.

 Science: Concede when it does not hurt your client and only if your client approves. Show you are elated to make this allowance. If you refuse to concede when there is no downside of doing so, you will be perceived as unreasonable—the gladiator attorney who fights for the fight alone. Once you take such a stance, prepare to engage in combat with the judge. The judge will repeatedly and incredulously ask you why you refuse to concede, thereby wasting valuable time, angering the judge, and hurting your credibility.

 Science: On the other hand, if you cannot concede because it will hurt your client's case to do so, *hold your ground*. Be firm. Depending on the circumstances, be disappointed that you cannot concede. But do not blame the lack of a concession on your client. If you need time to prepare a response, it is all right to say that you need time to talk to your client, but if after you have talked you are still unable to concede, do not blame it on your client. Explain to the court the reason, in fairness, you cannot give in on the point.

If you find yourself in a situation where you believe it may hurt the case to concede but the upside outweighs the downside, you must talk to your client before you can yield. To not do so may cause you ethical issues.

Example: *Humpty Dumpty v. The King*

Judge: Aren't there other attorneys in Mr. Emperor's firm who could have handled this case?

Counsel: Yes, there are, Your Honor, but no one had the relationship with the King that Mr. Emperor had. And that's because Mr. Emperor had personally represented the King for twenty-three years, and as a result it was excusable for no other attorney at Mr. Emperor's law firm to answer the complaint.

Or

Counsel: No; only Mr. Emperor had the knowledge, background, and relationship with the client to handle this case. It was excusable for the King to rely on Mr. Emperor.

Below are tables of typical responses when you can and cannot concede:

WHEN YOU CAN CONCEDE
"Yes, Your Honor, my client can agree to that."
"We are happy to stipulate to that, and we ask the court to . . . ."
"That is correct, Your Honor, and it does not affect the ultimate result because . . . ."

WHEN YOU CANNOT CONCEDE
"I have to talk to my client before we can agree to that."
"Your Honor, that is not going to work in this situation."
"We cannot waive that, Your Honor."
"There are far greater consequences that prevent me from agreeing."
"We cannot concede that, and the reason is . . . ."

8.17   Engaging the Disengaged Judge

What do you do when the judge does not engage with you at all? Perhaps she makes no eye contact; perhaps she says nothing; perhaps she is checking her phone; perhaps she is obviously flipping through your brief for the first time. You have no clue what she is thinking about your case. This is the time when your short script that you prepared before the hearing comes in handy.[3] Before you resort to only giving your short script, however, try to find ways to capture the judge's attention.

Art: Change the pace or volume of your speech. Increase the speed to show passion or excitement—or noticeably slow down your speech. Increase the volume of your voice—or decrease the volume to almost a whisper to make an important point. Maybe the change—fast or slow pace, low or high volume—will attract the judge's interest.

Silence can also act as an attention grabber. Use a long, three-second pause while you search through your notes for an extra moment of silence in hopes of alerting the judge. Or try clearing your throat.

Use an exhibit. If you are in a trial court, have an extra copy of a pertinent case, ask to approach the bench to hand the case to the judge, and point out a passage particularly relevant from the case. Highlight and cite to a deposition excerpt. During a hearing on a 12(b)(6) motion to dismiss, refer the court to a portion of the complaint to highlight that there are no facts upon which relief can be granted. Or use a slideshow or a poster board that you have prepared ahead of time. Utilizing a demonstrative or visual aid, at worst, requires some court participation and, at best, may spur a discussion.

---

3. We cover long and short scripting techniques in Chapter Eleven.

If you are in an appellate court, exhibits are less common. The appellate judges are not accustomed to receiving exhibits. Many appellate courts have rules discouraging exhibits. If exhibits are allowed, most courts require the attorney to notify the court and opposing counsel before the hearing. To gain the attention of the appellate court judges using paper, you may refer to testimony in the transcript, an exhibit in the appendix, or a phrase or two from a case cited. Allow time for the judges to find the spot in the record you are referring to before you proceed forward with your argument. If the court seems inclined to take from you a copy of a case or a part of the record, go ahead and hand it to the presiding judge. Have copies for all the judges and opposing counsel. If you are arguing your case remotely, alert the court staff and opposing counsel ahead of time and either provide a copy to the staff for screen sharing or get permission to share your own screen.

Example: *Humpty Dumpty v. The King*

Counsel: If I could draw your attention to page 15, lines 14 to 18, of the deposition of the managing partner of the Imperial Law Firm. [*Silence to allow the court time to find the citation. Once the judge has indicated she has found the citation and read the passage, counsel continues.*] This is the testimony indicating the condition of Mr. Emperor at the time the King was served the complaint. You will see that Mr. Emperor was very sick and unable to attend to the legal needs of the King. Illness is a well-recognized reason to excuse failing to respond to a complaint.

If these strategies do not work, the court is likely just going through the motions—pun intended—of a hearing. Revert to your short script that you prepared before the hearing. Your short script reflects your best-crafted and most concise arguments. The court will also appreciate your brevity.

8.18   The Guillotine

Unfortunately, there comes a time when you know that you have lost, based on the judge's question. For instance, "I have made my decision against your position, counselor, do you have anything else to add?" Cheerfully exit. Avoid pouting or lashing out at the judge. Do not threaten the judge with an appeal. Judges, like anyone else, do not cower at a threat. If anything, your attempt at intimidation may make the judge work harder to reverse-proof her order or opinion. Neither should you thank a judge when you have been defeated. The judge may misconstrue your thanks as sarcasm.

Science: Instead, exit gracefully. Be polite and professional. This will not be the last time you are before the judge. If you need to make a record for appeal, do so, but do not whine and repeat what you have already said.

Usually, you should not ask the court to reconsider its decision during the hearing. The prospect of the judge changing her mind on the spot is limited. If you do have new arguments that you think may sway the judge, then ask for reconsideration based on the other reasons. Otherwise, if you think the court may change its mind after reflection, file papers asking for correction.

Example: *Humpty Dumpty v. The King*

Judge: Counsel, I see no reason to set aside this default judgment. Judicial economy supports my decision.

Counsel: I understand your concern. I do have a point that we have not discussed, namely, judicial economy may not be served by upholding this judgment. If the judgment remains, the King will have a malpractice claim against the Imperial Law Firm. So, one way or another, the court will have to resolve the merits of this claim. The King deserves his day in court.

When the guillotine comes crashing down, here are some responses.

THE GUILLOTINE
"I would like to make the record clear that . . . ."
"Your Honor, I do need to make a record that . . . ."
"I understand the Court's position, although obviously I disagree for the reasons I have stated."
"I would ask the court to reconsider because [*new reasons*]."
"I do have one more argument I would ask the court to consider."

8.19   The Win

There may come a time when you know you have won. Stop talking immediately. When opposing counsel has dug himself into a deep hole and the judge says, "There is nothing more you can add, is there, counsel?" politely say no and sit down. Do not snatch defeat from the jaws of victory.

8.20   When You Sit Down

Whatever the last question, after you sit down, do not ruminate about how you could have answered the questions better. The water is under the bridge. You will have time to evaluate your performance. Instead, listen to the other side argue. If you have another chance to speak, use the information you learn. Hear the judge's problems and speak to them. Integrate the judge's words into your rebuttal. Focus your argument on what troubles the judge.

8.21 Oh, Yeah, and . . .

Provide the judge with your undivided attention. No "multi-tasking" or "rapid refocus."

Your time should be spent discussing the issues with the judge, not your co-counsel. Do not chat with co-counsel during the hearing. If the judge asks you for a citation, page number, or case name you do not have handy, ask the judge if she wants you or your co-counsel to find the cite. If the judge asks a question to which your co-counsel knows the answer better than you, respond accordingly: "Your Honor, my colleague Mr. Rodriguez can give you more detail about the technology behind this section of the patent." If the judge directly asks your co-counsel a question, let him answer it.[4]

 Also, do not speak directly to opposing counsel during the hearing. *Science:* Argue to the judge, not to the opposing attorney.

Do not minimize or trivialize the judge's question or confusion. When you take this approach, you miss out on a huge opportunity. Instead of using belittling transition lines—"Your Honor, the *real* issue is . . ."—rejoice. The right approach is to affirm and address the issue—and be thrilled to discover the concern of the court. That is why you are there.

 Art: Observe the emotions behind the words. Notice if the judge is cheerful, interested, angry, nervous, frustrated, or resentful. Respond to the emotion as well as the words. Observe all verbal and nonverbal cues, including tone, facial expressions, and other body language. It takes repetition and exposure to read any judge.

Enjoy the repartee of the questioning. You will find that the questions make your presentation more convincing. While initially you may think that the discussion is difficult, soon you will see that the monologue is more difficult because you have no idea whether your words are making any impact. With questioning, you meet the judge precisely where she is in her thinking. Make those arguments that are most convincing to her, and you are seen as a problem-solving partner.

We have covered many topics in this chapter and recalling them all can be daunting. To keep them readily at your fingertips, we have summarized a periodic table of questions in the appendix.

Let's now talk about the special concerns when you are before a multi-judge court.

---

4. For arguments scheduled for an hour or less, assign one lawyer to argue. Do not divide the time with a colleague. If, however, you have a long appearance scheduled with a court (more than an hour), changing speakers can be refreshing for the court.

CHAPTER NINE

QUESTIONS FROM THE MULTI-JUDGE COURT

It was February 29, 2016. He may have asked those questions because it was a Leap Year Day. It may have been because his close friend and philosophical twin, Justice Antonin Scalia, died earlier that month and he wanted to keep Justice Scalia's aggressive-questioning legacy alive. Or he simply wanted to end his streak of ten years and one week of not a single question—a record he had long shattered. At the time of the questioning, it had been forty-five years since any other member of the court had gone even a single term without asking a question.[1]

Whatever the motivation, Clarence Thomas fired a barrage of seven questions at the government's attorney. Attorney Ilana Eisenstein had competently argued for the government that the Federal Domestic Violence Gun Ban extends to those convicted of reckless, as opposed to intentional, domestic battery. She closed her argument with the common, "If there are no further questions," undoubtedly hoping she could sit down after a job well done. But in his baritone voice, Justice Thomas asked his first question, "Can you give me another area where a misdemeanor violation suspends a constitutional right?" The questions did not get easier from there.[2]

Always expect the unexpected during an appellate argument—even difficult questions from the usually silent judge.[3] Judges love the intellectual repartee of oral argument, especially on matters dear to them. The trick for the advocate is not all the justices have the same interests or opinions.

Learning how to successfully navigate an argument with a multi-judge panel—whether an appellate court, multiple judges in a multi-district litigation, or a judge

---

1. *See* Adam Liptak, *It's Been 10 Years. Would Clarence Thomas Like to Add Anything?* N.Y. TIMES, Feb. 1, 2016. ("It has been at least 45 years since any other member of the court went even a single term without asking a question.") Since the U.S. Supreme Court has been holding remote arguments, Justice Thomas has become a regular questioner. For an insightful article examining Justice Thomas's questioning history, *see* Timothy R. Johnson et al, *Covid-19 and Supreme Court Oral Argument: The Curious Case of Justice Clarence Thomas*, 21:1 J. APP. PRAC. & PROCESS, 113–162 (Winter 2021).
2. Voisine v. United States, 136 S.Ct. 2272 (2016). Actually, we believe that Justice Thomas asked these questions because of his passion for the Second Amendment and no other justice had questioned the attorneys on this issue.
3. Justice Thomas did not ask another question until March 2019. *Clarence Thomas Breaks a Three-Year Silence at Supreme Court*, N.Y. TIMES, Mar. 20, 2019.

and his magistrate—requires skills in addition to those set out in the last chapter. Here, we demonstrate the skills while providing examples based on the *Humpty Dumpty* case file. For purposes of the examples in this chapter, assume that the trial court refused to set aside the default judgment. The King now appeals to the Royal Appeals Court.

9.1   Who Is in Charge Here?

To the extent you are able, discover whose opinion counts for more on the panel. Sometimes, no judge dominates the decision making—sometimes, one does. If you are confident that one judge's opinion is given more weight in the panel, then tailor your argument to that judge. Be careful though; if you are wrong, you run the risk of perturbing the other judges. Even if you think one judge is dominant, do not give that judge more eye contact. Judges notice if they are being ignored. Do not risk alienating anyone. Female judges are particularly sensitive to an advocate who only has eye contact with the male judges. A male judge in Indiana in the early 1980s was renowned for telling male lawyers, "Quit looking at me. I didn't ask the question. She did."[4]

Also, whenever you call one judge by his name (Judge Albert) on a multi-panel court, you must be consistent and call all the judges by their names. When you do say a judge's name, pronounce it correctly and make sure you have the right judge. In the *Bush v. Gore* oral argument, counsel kept referring to Justice Souter as "Justice Breyer." Justice Souter finally asked counsel to "cut it out." *Science:* Always call all the judges by their actual names, using correct pronunciation.

9.2   Eye Contact

Listen with your eyes when a judge asks you a question, maintaining complete eye contact with that judge during his question. When you answer the question, spend the first fifteen seconds focused on the judge who asked the question. Then expand your eye contact and body language to include all the judges. Make sure you switch eye contact after completing a thought with each judge (three to four seconds each). Return to the original judge to conclude your answer, locking eyes again and watching for non-verbal clues that confirm you answered the question.

9.3   The "I Don't Know" Question

Pause an additional second or two if you do not know the answer. This allows time for a judge favorable to your position to rescue you if he is so inclined. If there is no lifeboat floated your way, there is no downside to the pause. Judges on appellate

---

4. Judge Patrick Sullivan of the Indiana Court of Appeals.

courts expect fewer flaws than a trial court does. You may be able to get away with not knowing the answer to one question to an appellate court, but only one. Robert Stein, an accomplished New Hampshire lawyer, recalls an argument that he had before the New Hampshire Supreme Court when Justice Souter was on the bench. Stein did not know the answer to one of Justice Souter's questions and had to admit he did not know. Halfway through the argument, Stein had a *voila* moment. He turned to Justice Souter and said, "Now back to you" and answered the difficult question.[5] Do not be afraid to answer a question when the answer comes to you, even when it comes belatedly.

But if the answer to the question does not come to you, the best path forward is to simply admit that you do not know. Feigning knowledgeability is a sure-fire way to eliminate any credibility you have with a judge. Consider a real-world example, extracted from *Bennis v. Michigan,*[6] of an attorney who should have simply said "I do not know," but decided to fake an answer. Here is counsel's exchange with Justice O'Connor:

Example: *Bennis v. Michigan*

Justice Sandra Day O'Connor: Will you tell us what the record shows was the nature of the ownership in the automobile in question?

Counsel: The record shows that the vehicle was co-owned. That is, it was co-titled . . .

Justice O'Connor: What kind of ownership under State law, joint with right of survivorship, co-tenants, what was it?

Counsel: Your Honor, I . . .

Justice O'Connor: Do we know?

Counsel: It's a heavily regulated area and I attempted to ascertain which common law joint property interest this most closely resembled. [*Counsel is dancing.*] I found nothing definitive on that, but I believe . . . [*argh, the credibility busting "I believe."*]

Justice O'Connor: You can't tell us? [*Justice O'Connor knows.*]

Counsel: I believe it's close to a tenant in common.

Justice O'Connor: How was the automobile titled?

---

5. Justice Souter smiled and said, "How about another question?" Stein responded, "I would like to quit while I am ahead."
6. Bennis v. Michigan, 516 U.S. 442 (1996).

> Counsel: The automobile was titled in their name, but there's no—
>
> Justice O'Connor: In both names . . .
>
> Counsel: Yes.
>
> Justice O'Connor: or one name?
>
> Counsel: In both names.
>
> Justice O'Connor: In Michigan law, can one co-owner dispose of good title to the automobile?
>
> Counsel: I believe that that is true, Your Honor, that . . . not for the entire automobile. [*And the hole gets deeper. If you do not know an answer, just say so.*]

9.4 The Softball Question

Continue eye contact with the judge who asks the softball until the question is finished. Recognize, though, that the asking judge wants you to convince his colleagues. So, spend the majority of your answer time connecting with the non-questioning judges. Watching the non-questioning judges is imperative because you want to see if they agree with the softball-questioning judge. If they do not, you fall in the trap of having only one vote when you need a majority. Do not be quick to agree full-throatedly with the softball. Tread lightly. Determine if you need to fully agree with the softball question in order to win. It may be that you do not have to accept the full import of the question.

> **Example: *Humpty Dumpty v. The King***
>
> Justice James: It is clear that the Holy Grail was not an attractive nuisance. Do you agree, counsel?
>
> Counsel: [*Noticing that Justice George does not seem to be buying the premise.*] Yes, we do, but ultimately the decision is a decision for a jury and the King should be afforded the opportunity to make his case.

9.5 Concessions

Concessions of the law are dangerous in an appellate argument. Factual concessions are generally not so treacherous; the facts may be cast in stone in the record or the trial court's findings. Concession questions usually begin with, "Do you agree . . . ?"

or "Do you admit . . . ?" Think about the consequences of conceding. Often, the judge hopes you agree to the first question so he may follow with a series of questions that you must inevitably concede until you have finally conceded your case. These rapid-fire questions are usually closed questions.

Concessions make an appellate judge's job easier. Often concessions at oral arguments are cited in the written opinions because those admissions simplify opinion writing, allowing the narrowest possible opinion. Think of a common beginning of an appellate opinion, "The appellant has raised seven issues, but we need only deal with one." Your concessions are gold for the judge looking for an easy write. Concessions are also gifts to the trial court or intermediate court of appeals judge who does not want to be reversed on appeal.

While you need to be cautious about concessions, you need to be equally cautious of not conceding when you ought. *Science:* If the concession does not hurt your case—concede. Many advocates waste time arguing with a judge about something that does not make any difference to the opinion. Every moment wasted is a moment you lose arguing your strengths.

Example: *Humpty Dumpty v. The King*

Judge: Do you concede that light coming from the Holy Grail lured Mr. Dumpty to the top of the wall?

Counsel: We cannot. That question is for the jury to decide.

Compare the above example, where counsel is unable to concede versus the below example where counsel should concede but does not.

Bad Example: *Humpty Dumpty v. The King*

Judge: Do you concede that there was light coming from the Holy Grail, which Mr. Dumpty could have seen as he walked by the King's castle?

Counsel: No, your honor, we cannot concede that.

Judge: The Holy Grail does emit light does it not?

Counsel: Sometimes, but we deny that Mr. Dumpty saw the light.

Judge: My question was could Mr. Dumpty have seen the light?

Counsel: I understand. We cannot concede that.

Judge: The record does reflect that the Holy Grail was on the King's bed-stand, right?

Counsel:	Yes. It was, but—
Judge:	And the bedstand is five feet from the window nearest the wall?
Counsel:	Yes, but we will not concede that Mr. Dumpty could have seen the light.
Judge:	When Humpty walked by the wall, wasn't that a time the Holy Grail always emanated light?
Counsel:	I believe that is what the record shows.
Judge:	And at the time Mr. Dumpty walked past, the curtain to that window was open, correct?
Counsel:	Well, yes.
Judge:	So, I ask you one more time counsel, Mr. Dumpty could have seen the light from the Holy Grail as he passed by?
Counsel:	W-well I-I guess . . . .

In this example, counsel should have immediately conceded that Humpty *could have* seen the light. But ultimately it was for the jury to decide whether he did see it. Instead, counsel wasted precious time, and irritated the court by refusing to concede on a point that did not hurt her client. Irritating a judge is not a successful technique for victory.

9.6 The Hostile Question from a Hijacking Judge

This hijacking judge wants to convince his colleagues through his question to you. Treat him as we explained in the last chapter as an insistent and/or hostile judge until you reach impasse. When you reach the brick wall, this judge will continue to insist, and there is nothing else you can say. You are really talking to the other judges. If the judge continues to interrupt and insist, then agree to disagree and move on. Try not to get offended when a judge turns hostile, especially in front of the other observing judges. They often see the abusive judge as the aggressor if you resist the urge to fight back. If you engage and fight the judge, the listening judges will side with their colleague to your detriment. Stay calm with a warm and professional tone. As the hostile judge increases the volume and speed of his voice, decrease your volume and reduce your speed. *Art:* Do not collapse—hold your ground calmly and with poise.

Example: *Humpty Dumpty v. The King*

Judge Hostility: (*angry tone delivering a rapid-fire question*) You expect us to buy the argument that the *Big Bad Wolf* case is like this case?

Counsel: (*calm and slow pace*) Yes, I do, Your Honor. Attorneys Jack and Jill were injured and could not answer the—

Judge Hostility: (*interrupting*) This case is similar to *Cinderella v. The Prince* where Cinderella sued the Prince for her injury, and the flabbergasted Prince did not give the summons to his attorney. There, the default judgment was not set aside.

Counsel: The facts here are different, and they matter. If you can give me some leeway, I think my point will become clearer.

Judge Hostility: (*sarcastically*) Doubtful.

Counsel: (*speaking primarily to the other judges but initiating his gaze at Judge Hostility so as not to offend him*) In *Cinderella*, the prince did not give the summons to his attorney until after he was defaulted.

Judge Hostility: (*again interrupting*) But the King knew or should have known that Mr. Emperor was ill when his men gave the law firm his summons.

Counsel: I am not aware of what the King knew. The facts are not clear on that point. May I move on?

9.7 The Crossfire Question

Often, the judges are asking questions, but they are talking to one another. They are in a debate. Your best technique is to watch and listen, unless the debate sways against you. Without interrupting any judge, insert clarifications or reorient the discussion if the debate starts turning against your position.

Example: *Humpty Dumpty v. The King*

Justice George: I am disturbed that the King sat on the summons and complaint for such a long time. This does not seem to be excusable neglect.

Justice Ann: The King sat on the complaint for less than a month.

(*Continued*)

> Justice George: True, but Mr. Emperor was not sick during that month and
> could have filed an answer.
>
> Justice Ann: I see your point.
>
> Counsel: *(who up to this point has enjoyed the discussion but realizes that it is going south)* Let me remind the court that the King did give the summons to the law firm before the default judgment was granted. During that time, Mr. Emperor could have filed an answer but for his serious illness.

9.8 The "Let's Make a Deal" Discussion

Seldom does negotiation occur in an appellate argument, but it has been known to happen. In this case, you are negotiating with the panel of judges about one sticking point that you may be willing to concede. Be careful negotiating with one judge on the panel. If the judge is not the decision maker, you may be giving up something unnecessarily because the majority of the panel is with you. When it becomes clear, though, that all judges are drawn to the deal and you and your client can live with it, then negotiate away.

As an example, suppose you are defending a $3 million verdict. One judge seems particularly concerned about a portion of the damages amounting to $100,000. You argue that fraction of the judgment is proper. Another judge is skeptical of your reasoning on this point and intimates it might impact the overall judgment. The last judge of the panel agrees. You may concede, or in reality "settle," with the judges, admitting the argument on the $100,000 is thin.

Another example is where you are advocating for a particular rule of law, but the court seems interested in limiting the scope of the rule. If, with the narrower rule, your client still wins? Accept the offer.

9.9 The Interrupting Judge

The interrupting judge asks a question immediately after his colleague asked a question, and you do not know which question to answer. Generally, answer the questions in the order they were asked. At times, the second question will be asking about a nuance to the first question and comes with the consent of the first judge. *Art:* If so, find a common thread to both questions and answer them in the same response.

Example: *Humpty Dumpty v. The King*

Justice Albert: Explain to me why the Holy Grail is not the Holy Grail of attractive nuisances.

Counsel: Becau—

Justice George: And when you answer Justice Albert's question, could you kindly include the fact that the Holy Grail emits a light that may escape the King's bed chambers?

Counsel: The Holy Grail is not an attractive nuisance because it could not be seen from outside the King's wall. It is true that at times, a light from the Holy Grail emanated beyond the chambers, but Humpty did not claim he had seen the light. In any case, the issue of an attractive nuisance is for the jury to decide.

Another type of interrupting judge is one who interrupts your answer to the first judge's question before you have an opportunity to fully explain your answer. Answer the second question, and then transition back to your full response to the first judge. Say something like, "that point goes to Justice Albert's (the first judge's) question." Then complete your response. The first judge knows it is not your fault for failing to completely answer his question and will forgive you for the interruption. When transitioning, do not say, "and let me now get back to Justice Albert's question," implying you were rudely interrupted by the second judge, which of course you were. Here are a couple examples of ways to handle this type of scenario.

Example #1: *Humpty Dumpty v. The King*

Justice Albert: Explain to me why the Holy Grail is not an attractive nuisance.

Counsel: It is not an attractive nuisance because—

Justice George: *(cutting off counsel)* Does it make a difference that Georgy Porgy also climbed the wall?

Counsel: In answer to Justice George's question, it depends. It may make a difference to the jury. In answer to Justice Albert's question, it is not an attractive nuisance because . . .

Example #2: *Humpty Dumpty v. The King*

Justice Albert: Explain to me why the Holy Grail is not an attractive nuisance.

Counsel: It is not an attractive nuisance because—

Justice George: *(cutting off counsel)* Does it make a difference that Georgy Porgy also climbed the wall?

Counsel: It depends on the evidence admitted at the trial and how the jury sees it. The important point is that the King deserves a trial. As to Justice Albert's question, the Holy Grail is not an attractive nuisance because . . .

9.10   The Consistency Question

Judges want to be consistent with their previous opinions and decisions. This is particularly so when those decisions are written and published. A judge may ask a question about one of his cases. You must reconcile that case with your case.

Example: *Humpty Dumpty v. The King*

Judge Victoria: How do you distinguish the *Jack and the Beanstalk* case?

Counsel: As you know, Judge Victoria, you authored the opinion. This case is very similar to *Jack and the Beanstalk,* and as in the *Jack* case, there is no attractive nuisance here. If anything, the facts in Jack are more likely to have been an attractive nuisance than here. The beanstalk Jack climbed belonged to him, whereas Humpty did not own the wall.

You are very safe in acknowledging that a judge authored an opinion when he himself asks the question about his own opinion. But outside of this circumstance, be careful about naming judges as authoring judges. If you name a specific judge, the judge whose name you used will probably be pleased that you recognized him, but you risk alienating the other two judges and appearing obsequious. *Art:* Referencing an opinion authored by one of the judge's you are standing before is discretionary.

9.11   Common Questions from an Appellate Bench

Be prepared to answer these common questions from an appellate bench*:*

- What is the standard of review?

- What relief are you asking for? What is the legal support for your position? Is there case law supporting your position?

- Are you proposing a new rule of law?

- Have any other courts addressed this issue?

- What rule of law are you proposing?

- Has your argument been preserved, or have you waived it?

- Does the rule expand or contract existing law? Is this a natural progression of the law?

- What does history tell us?

- Tell us exactly what the rule you propose is? If we were to write the rule what would it look like?

- How will the rule work?

- How far will the rule go? (*Prepare here for hypothetical questions.*)

- What is the limiting principle you advocate?

- What are the real-world consequences of the rule you propose?

- What policy considerations affect the rule of law you are advancing?

- How is fact *x* congruent with your legal theory?

- Is there anything in the record that supports such a conclusion?

- Where is that in the record?

- Explain how the plain words of the statute support your legal theory?

- How does *x*, the leading case in this area of law, (*fill in the case*) impact our decision?

- How do you distinguish *x* case?

- Why is your case similar to *x* case?

- What is the flashpoint between you and your opponent's arguments?

- Are your arguments independent of one another? Does your entire argument depend on one of your points?

- If your arguments are not dependent on one another, what is your strongest argument?

- Will you concede *x* point? If so, what is left of your argument?

9.12 Visual Table

Here is a visual representation of the information discussed in this chapter:

	The Consistency Question	The Interrupting Judge	The Crossfire
General	Be prepared to answer questions about opinions written by a member of the panel on the issue presented. If the authoring judge asks the question, recognize him as the author.	If one judge interrupts another during questioning, answer the questions in the order asked. Or find a common thread between both questions.	When two judges are debating an issue, listen. Interject only if the conversation is going south for your client.
Words	As you know Judge X, you wrote the opinion you ask about	As to the first question . . . , as to the second . . . . Both questions share the same concern which is	Let me remind the court that Client X did give the summons to the law firm before the default judgment was granted.
Voice	Raise pitch slightly and keep an even pace.	Extend baseline pause to avoid speaking over. the interrupting judge, and stop speaking the moment you hear the judge's voice.	When you interject, slightly raise volume and pitch.
Body	Expand gesture box and use descriptive gestures to show connections.	Reduce gestures and remain relaxed and still.	Try stepping back from the podium slightly to allow the judges to discuss, then step forward to interject.
Emotion	Show enthusiasm.	Express no frustration when interrupted, and instead welcome the conversation.	Stay engaged during the judges' discussion, and show enthusiasm when interjecting.

	The Hostile Judge	Concessions	"Let's Make a Deal"
General	Hold your position. Explain it. When the judge will not budge, ask to be able to move on.	Concede if it will not hurt your client. Be careful conceding legal issues.	Negotiation seldom occurs in an appellate argument, but when the opportunity comes, only proceed if a clear majority of the judges are attracted to the deal.

(Continued)

	The Hostile Judge	**Concessions**	**"Let's Make a Deal"**
Words	"We may have to agree to disagree, may I move on?" "I think I have not been clear, may I have some leeway in answering your question."	"We cannot concede that point. That question is for the jury to decide." "Yes, Your Honor, we concede that Person X could have . . . "	"Your Honor, I see your point."
Voice	Slow down your speech. Lower your volume.	Use an even vocal pace and tone.	Slightly lift the pitch of your voice if you can agree with the judge or find a way to negotiate.
Body	Take a step back. Have your palms upward. Look initially at the questioner and then send your eye contact to the other members of the panel.	Use descriptive hand gestures to showcase how you are trying to reach agreement.	Use descriptive hand gestures to showcase how you are trying to reach agreement.
Emotion	Do not argue back with the judge. Remain professional; if not, the other judges will side with their colleague.	Avoid appearing defeated, and instead showcase a grateful tone.	If you can agree, be pleased. If not, stay neutral.

	The Softball Question	**The "I Don't Know" Question**
General	Maintain eye contact with the judge asking the question, but then spend the majority of your time convincing the other judges of your position.	Pause. Attempt to find an answer. If an answer is not apparent, simply admit you do not know. Do not pretend to know. Faking it is not an option.
Words	"Yes, Your Honor, I agree. Ultimately, the question rests on whether . . . ." "I agree with that premise. Let me flesh out the reasoning behind . . . ."	"Your Honor, I am unclear on that point. I can come back to you with an answer at a later time, but right now I do not know."
Voice	Use an even vocal pace and tone.	Use an even vocal pace and tone.
Body	Stay consistent with your established body language.	Stay consistent with your established body language.
Emotion	Appear enthusiastic and seek agreement.	Avoid appearing defeated.

Let's turn from questioning to the final component of an argument—appealing to the concerns of the court.

Chapter Ten

Appeals to the Concern of the Judge

On a hot August day, with the Lincoln Memorial as his backdrop, Martin Luther King Jr. belted out his iconic "I Have a Dream" speech to a crowd of 250,000. At the close, he roared "and when we allow freedom to ring, when we let it ring from every village and every hamlet, from every state and city, we will be able to speed up that day when all God's children, black men and white men, Jews and Gentiles, Protestants and Catholics, will be able to join hands and sing the words of the Old Negro spiritual—'Free at last. Free at last. Thank God Almighty, we are free at last.'" After the speech, James Baldwin described the effect of the words on the audience: "We stood on a height, and could see our inheritance; perhaps we could make the kingdom real."

Political speeches, television ads, and literature use the power of what Aristotle called pathos. Pathos is a persuasive technique that stirs the emotions of the listener; it is a call to action. While logos appeals to the logic and rationality of the listener, pathos speaks to her passion, her duty, her obligation, her concerns.

Pathos can also be an effective persuasive device to use in your arguments. To be sure, judges were trained—as all attorneys are—to think logically and follow the law. Your argument should appeal to the judge's analytical mind, as discussed in Chapter Six. Logic and law are an important part of a decision, but often, the law is flexible enough to allow the judge to rule for either party. This is particularly so at a trial court level, where the judge is the sole determiner of the facts and has broad discretion. However, law is more than logic; it is about people, right and wrong, good and bad; it is about consistent application, predictability, and resolution.

At the end of your argument in chief to the court, add a simple, short, powerful appeal to the judge's concerns. The lessons you learned in Chapter Two about discovering the motivating concerns of the judge are incorporated here in this section of the argument. The concern may be a particularized concern with an issue in the case or a generalized concern motivated by a sense of fairness, a desire not to be reversed, a concern for consistency, an interest not to confuse the law, and a wish for resolution.

Using these pleas comes with rules. If you do not follow these rules, your plea will not be heard and may even backfire.

Rule One:

Do not argue pathos until *after* your logical argument. Timing is everything. If you argue the pathos of your argument before the logos, you risk the judge thinking you have nothing to argue but emotions. Naked appeals to emotions, before laying a logical foundation, generally flop because a judge views a sound decision as a reasoned one, not an emotional one. Earn the right to preach an emotional point. Waiting for the right facts, the right moment, is key to finding a sweet spot where emotion can really appeal to the judge.

Rule Two:

Exercise stealth persuasion when venturing into pathos. Do not be too obvious. The blatancy of the appeal depends on the judge and the facts of the case. Some judges are more amenable to these pleas than others. Deliver your pleas without jury theatrics. Use an even tone. Be serious, convicted, but not dramatic.

Rule Three:

Earn the right to speak emotionally by avoiding hyperbole. You are more likely to be believed that "all interrogatories are lacking" if you have previously avoided using "always," "never," "all," and "completely" for emphasis. Over-exaggeration is a dangerous way to cry wolf. It makes it hard to deliver a believable emotional argument when you have over-inflated most points along the way.

Rule Four:

Be brief and focused in your plea. Choose one, maybe two, of these interests to appeal to, not all of them.

Now let's turn to typical concerns of the judge you can appeal to in the final moments of your argument.

10.1   Fairness

Judges became lawyers and judges to serve justice. Use your parting shot to win the soul of the judge. Take her from the monotony of your case to a higher purpose. Make the judge proud of her decision and give her the courage to make the right, just, and fair decision. Show you have confidence in your position. After all, your ask is only the fair result.

Appeals to fairness work in motion hearings and Supreme Court arguments. During the many training sessions we have done, we have received pushback on this advice from attorneys handling motion hearings to advocates in appellate courts. The trial attorney's comment that it may work for big and consequential questions before a higher court, but not for the routine motion matters. Appellate attorneys say that appellate court judges are swayed only by logic and not emotions; better to use these pleas for motions practice. It works for both. Consider some Supreme

Court arguments. In *Miller v. Alabama*, Bryan Stevenson, founder of Equal Justice Initiative and author of *Just Mercy*,[1] argued that giving life without parole sentences to juvenile offenders violated the Eighth Amendment's prohibition against cruel and unusual punishment. Some of his final words:

> But what this court has said is that children are uniquely more than their worst act. They are quintessentially children in a way that the Constitution requires that we respect their child status. And our argument is simple. It would be unusual to recognize that in virtually every area of the law but when a crime is committed, to simply abandon it, to simply ignore it. *Roper* and *Graham* teach us that we can't do that consistently with our Eight Amendment prohibitions. And so, for that reason, it is unusual, and it's our judgment that it would be cruel to declare these children fit only to die in prison given what we know about their status, about their development, and about their potential.[2]

Mary Bonauto, representing the petitioners in *Obergefell v. Hodges*, ended her argument as follows:

> My friends say they care about people staying together and providing a long term, stable situation for children. This interest applies in full force here because denying marriage to same sex couples denies protection not only for the adults but for the children by denying them the protection that comes from having married parents.[3]

Both cases were won.

Appeals to fairness also are effective in motion practice. When arguing to set aside a default judgment, point out to the judge that litigants deserve their day in court—to be heard by an impartial tribunal that will solve their dispute. In a simple continuance hearing, discuss the injustice to your client of going forward without adequately prepared counsel. In a discovery dispute, describe the unfairness of not receiving the documents that will reveal the truth.

10.2   Reversal

When appealing to a court's concern for being reversed on appeal, no matter what, do not say, "I am going to take you up on appeal if you rule against me."[4] Statements like this only make the judge more resolute in her conviction. Do you imagine after

---

1. Stevenson, Bryan, JUST MERCY: A STORY OF JUSTICE AND REDEMPTION (Speigel & Grau 2014).
2. Miller v. Alabama, 567 U.S. 460 (2012).
3. Obergefell v. Hodges, 576 U.S. 644 (2015).
4. Every experienced trial lawyer has one story how threatening an appeal worked on a judge. The operative word here is "one." With years of experience and credibility to back it up, the threat may succeed for the veteran who delivers the message with style and elegance.

threatening appeal a judge will say, "Oh, I now see the light. You're right. I'll reverse my position"? The odds are highly unlikely. With a challenge like this, the judge usually says, "Go ahead." When you alert a trial court judge of your intention to appeal, she is usually more careful with her written findings. Remember, a trial judge is the sole decider of credibility, and your threat may have inspired the judge to find facts unfavorable to your position, making a successful appeal difficult. Threats of appealing are not only unsuccessful, they also reduce your chances of a reversal on appeal. An appellate court that sees a record showing you threatened the trial court judge with appeal will not look kindly on that slight to their fellow-judge-in-arms.

How, then, do you appeal to a judge's sensitivity to reversal? If the law is on your side, wrap yourself around precedent. Glue yourself to it. Identify quotes of well-respected jurists who support your position. Identify the author of the quote, who may be the judge you are before. Explain that the case before her is squarely on all fours with another case that supports your argument. Although state supreme court justices are rarely swayed by threats of reversal, they often wish to preserve the status quo and not overrule precedential cases from their court.

To a trial court, argue the standard of review, but again with a soft touch. Attorneys seldom think in terms of the standard of review on appeal because so few cases are appealed; but judges know the drill. If the appellate court engages in a *de novo* review, a judge is much more likely to be reversed than if the higher court reviews for an abuse of discretion. Argue that what you are asking is within the broad discretion of the judge. Empower the judge, appeal to her pride and discretion. However, if you are pushing the limits of the law, argue that the relief you request is in line with the natural progression of the law or gives the judge a golden opportunity to be a pioneer.

On the other hand, if opposing counsel is asking for relief that may be legally weak, tell the court the relief the other side asks for is without precedent. Explain that no reported case has provided such broad relief. You can discourage the judge from being a trailblazer by casting the move in a risky light. Try these alternatives:

SENSITIVITY TO REVERSAL	
"Our case is on all fours with *Smith*."	"A long line of cases hold that . . ."
"There is nothing new here; the case of . . ."	"Judge Learned Hand said of this . . ."
"The leading case in this area . . ."	"This is within your discretion, Your Honor."
"The relief the other side asks for is unprecedented."	"No reported case has ever provided such broad relief."

10.3 Desire for Consistency

Consistency in the application of the law is an important virtue. A consistent judge is taken seriously; you can rely on her for predictable rulings. Lawyers can predict what a judge is likely to do, which saves time and money and encourages settlement. Judges know this.

Argue that a ruling for your client will be consistent with the way the judge has ruled in a similar case and therefore gives predictability to the attorneys who appear before her. Also, you may argue that the case is a typical case that should result in a typical ruling—one she has decided in the same manner many times before.

Of course, sometimes judges made mistakes in previous rulings. It takes a courageous and secure judge to admit error. You will find plenty of these brave judges. If your case is before such a self-assured judge and you honestly believe a mistake was made, argue against consistency. Tread lightly though. First, show logically why the case was wrongly decided. Then explain that mistakes are made, and there has never been the perfect case from either the lawyer's or judge's perspective. Better to clean it up now because it will eventually be necessary. Alternatively, if you do not want the court to follow a normal course, argue how atypical this case is based on the facts.

CONSISTENCY/INCONSISTENCY	
"Our case is similar to the case of *Smith v. Jones* which you authored."	"We all make mistakes; this was a mistake because . . . "
"There is nothing new here; the case is a typical (fill in the blank) case. . ."	"This case is not your typical case because . . ."
"There is a distinction in the case, but the distinction does not make a difference because . . . "	"This case differs from *Smith v. Jones* because . . . "
"We can arrive at the same place when we consider . . . "	"Better to take care of this mistake now than later; it will save everyone time."

10.4   Concern for Time and an Overloaded Docket—In a Motion Hearing

Even if the motion is not dispositive, show the trial court judge how to use a motion to encourage the parties to settle. Indicate to the court how a ruling in your favor will facilitate settlement. Or show the court that ruling for your opponent will likely result in future headaches for the judge. If you doubt you will prevail on the motion, encourage the court to take a ruling under advisement pending negotiations.

CONCERN FOR TIME AND AN OVERLOADED DOCKET	
"Ruling in my client's favor on this motion will go a long way toward settling this case because . . . ."	"This motion is dispositive of this case."
"Granting the request of opposing counsel will cause the court many hours of its time because . . . ."	"Grant this motion and the case is over."

10.5   The Parade of Horribles

In a parade of horribles argument, the attorney argues the real-world consequences of a ruling against his client. He lists the undesirable results that will follow from an adverse ruling. The power of a parade of horribles argument is the emotional impact of the predictions. Either a party will suffer, justice will not prevail, or it will start an avalanche of negative consequences for a case. On an appellate level, additionally, the law will be turned upside down; longstanding procedures and practices will be upended; the court will be to blame; another court must straighten out the mess.

Effective parade of horrible arguments paint with word pictures the consequences of decisions. Give the details of what will likely occur. Let the judges visually see the catastrophe ahead. Do not tell the court how horrible the result will be; show the court.

In *Ramos v. Louisiana*, Elizabeth Murrill, for the state, argued to uphold the law permitting non-unanimous jury verdicts in criminal cases. She ended her argument with the parade of horribles. She argued:

> And we do have fifty years of reliance, which is why I emphasize that we have 32,000 people who are incarcerated right now at hard labor for serious crimes, and every one of them would be subject—would be able to file an appeal.[5]

Justice Alito envisioned those appeals from prisoners incarcerated for serious crimes when he wrote in dissent: "States face a potential *tsunami of litigation* on the jury-unanimity issue."[6]

Likewise, Patrick Strawbridge invoked the parade of horribles in his closing on *Trump v. Mazars USA*,[7] when he argued for limited congressional subpoena powers for a president's personal records:

> There is no reason under his theory why the President and his family and his grandchildren could not be declared useful case studies and, therefore, Congress could send out a subpoena for their medical records. For that matter, the President eats and drinks like everybody else and Congress naturally has the ability to regulate food safety. But that does not mean that Congress can subpoena medical records or even the President's DNA . . . .[8]

---

5. Ramos v. Louisiana Oral Argument, October 7, 2019. Audio clip and transcript available at https://www.c-span.org/video/?c4833881/user-clip-32000-people-incarcerated (last visited January 29, 2021).

6. Ramos v. Louisiana, 140 S. Ct. 1390, 1406 (2020).

7. Trump v. Mazars USA, LLP, 140 S. Ct. 2019 (2020).

8. Trump v. Mazars Oral Argument, May 12, 2020. Audio clip and transcript available at https://www.oyez.org/cases/2019/19-715 (last visited January 29, 2021).

In other words, Strawbridge argued that before you know it Congress will be subpoenaing even the president's DNA, annihilating the separation of powers. Judges are sensitive to messing up the law. To show how powerful Strawbridge's parade of horribles argument was, here is a portion of Chief Justice Roberts' majority opinion:

> Far from accounting for separation of powers concerns, the House's approach aggravates them by leaving essentially no limits on the congressional power to subpoena the President's personal records. Any personal paper possessed by a President could potentially "relate to" a conceivable subject of legislation, for Congress has broad legislative powers that touch a vast number of subjects. The President's financial records could relate to economic reform, medical records to health reform, school transcripts to education reform, and so on. Indeed, at argument, the House was unable to identify any type of information that lacks some relation to potential legislation.[9]

To contest the parade of horribles argument, first identify it for the court for what it is—a prediction—nothing more. Show how the prediction is unlikely to occur. If the test you propose swoops up too many contingencies, propose a narrower test. As you can see above, the House's counsel's test was too sweeping in *Mazars*, and the Chief Justice's opinion called him out.

Alternatively, admit to the parade of horribles but argue the benefit outweighs the harm. Justice Gorsuch addressed in the majority opinion the argument made in *Ramos* that granting a right to a unanimous verdict would create havoc. He wrote:

> Taken at its word, the dissent would have us discard a Sixth Amendment right in perpetuity rather than ask two States to retry a slice of their prior criminal cases. Whether that slice turns out to be large or small, it cannot outweigh the interest we all share in the preservation of our constitutionally promised liberties.[10]

Finally, another option is to argue that the parade of horribles will come no matter what the court rules. In other words, whatever the court rules, there will be problems. As the maxim goes, "Do not let the perfect become the enemy of the good."

---

9. *Trump*, 140 S. Ct. at 2034. This case also illustrates how dangerous it is for an advocate to fail to pre-plan a fallback position before the argument. The government attorney in this case had no limits or suggestions of where to limit Congress's subpoena powers, and he lost.
10. *Ramos*, 140 S. Ct. at 1408.

ARGUING FOR AND DEFENDING AGAINST THE PARADE OF HORRIBLES	
"The state would face a tsunami of litigation if the court rules . . . "	"The sky won't fall if the court rules in favor of my client because . . . "
"Broadening Congress's subpoenaing power would annihilate the separation of powers because . . . "	"Either way you rule, Judge, there are potential negative consequences ahead because . . . "
"Consider the searing effects, Judge, of a decision like this on . . . "	"While there is a possibility that the negative consequences described by my colleague will occur, there is a greater chance of positive consequences because . . . "
"Your Honor, a ruling in favor of my client would avoid an overt attempt to circumscribe the civil liberties of . . . "	"This argument is nothing more than the 'parade of horribles' hyperbole."

10.6 Tailoring the Argument to the Trial Judge for a Motion Hearing

To see how to pull all of the elements we have discussed thus far into a rhetorical strategy for addressing the trial court judge you will appear before, consider the hypothetical case *State v. Weaver* below.

Connor Weaver has been charged with aggravated battery. He faces a 10-year sentence. The facts leading up to Weaver's arrest are that Bess Green, a sophomore in college, was attacked on campus at approximately 12:30 a.m. on September 24. The description she gave of her attacker was that of a male, 6'2" tall and approximately 190 pounds wearing a black hoodie, black jogging pants with white stripes on the sides, and a black ski mask. Because it was dark, she was unable to provide any further description.

Before the assault, Bess had been at a fraternity kegger. At about 12:15 a.m. and after she drank three beers, and as she described, was a little tipsy, she left the party alone to walk back to her dorm. Five minutes into her walk, her attacker approached her, hit her on her lower abdomen with a baseball bat, forcing her to her back. As she laid on her back, the assailant crouched over her, three feet away, looked her directly in the eyes and said, "You may not deserve this, but someone does." It was at that moment that Bess was able to catch an image of the eyes of her mugger with her cell phone application *Eye-Squared*. The assailant then ran north on College Avenue and out of sight. Nothing was taken from Bess. No witnesses saw the attack.

Bess reported the crime to the campus police and provided her cell phone to the investigators so they could access the *Eye-Squared* application. *Eye-Squared* uses iris detection technology to allow secure access to software by multiple users on a single device. A police investigation ensued, and an investigator talked to a student who saw Connor Weaver leaving the same party shortly after Bess left. No one remembered what Weaver was wearing. Weaver is 6'4" tall and 220 pounds. A further investigation revealed that Weaver had been arrested two months before the assault by Bess's father, who was a police officer in the college town, for consuming alcohol as a minor. Immediately after his arrest, Weaver told two friends that, "the officer who messed up my life will be sorry one day." Weaver's trial for consuming alcohol as a minor is scheduled, and Officer Green is expected to testify.

Two days after the attack on Bess Green and after the preliminary investigation, police acquired a warrant to search Weaver's apartment. The police found a black hoodie, black jogging pants with white stripes down the sides, and a baseball bat in his room. No ski mask was found. Weaver's apartment was located five blocks north and two blocks east of the attack.

After subpoenaing Weaver's iris images from a local airport security provider and securing the image taken by Bess Green of the eyes of her attacker, an iris detection specialist, Michael Barnes, compared the two pictures. Barnes noted that Bess's image did not depict the entire irises of the attacker, nor was it perfectly clear. Although iris detection is generally done with a static UV reader and subject, producing a clear and complete image, Barnes determined that Bess Green's image was sufficient for analysis. By using ocular biometric identification, Barnes opines that the irises in the images taken by Bess were Weaver's.

If you are representing the State, you want this evidence to convict Weaver. If you are defending Weaver, you move to exclude Mr. Barnes' opinion on two grounds. First, his testimony is based on insufficient facts or data, is not the product of reliable scientific methods, and thus, is not admissible under Nita Rules of Evidence, N.R.E. 702, and *Daubert v. Merrell Dow Pharmaceuticals*.[11] The standard of review for the evidentiary issue is an abuse of discretion. No case in the jurisdiction has allowed any type of iris detection evidence, let alone evidence taken from a cell phone application. Second, you argue that by failing to obtain a warrant for the images possessed by the security company, the state violated Weaver's Fourth Amendment right to privacy.

The judge who will hear your case is a former solo practitioner who was appointed to the bench by the governor three years ago and stands for election next year. She is sensitive to being reversed, especially with the election looming. She is fair and wants to get the right result. She has experience in the law of evidence and the Fourth Amendment, reads everything, and is known to be thorough and hardworking. The judge has no law clerk. She has developed a reputation for having a keen legal mind and actively questions the attorneys. She efficiently disposes of cases, but not at the expense of fairness, justice, and victims' rights. The judge does not know either attorney; she is generally known to be politically liberal. The judge runs her courtroom in a formal manner, is a stickler for rules, and moderately deadpan. Her daughter is a freshman on the same campus where Bess Green was attacked.

---

11. Daubert v. Merrell Dow Pharmaceuticals, Inc., 509 U.S. 579 (1993).

Your motion is set for a one-hour hearing.

A spectrum graph of the judge, her concerns, interests, and proclivities would look like the following:

THE JUDGE

Concern for law	Concern for fairness and justice
Sensitive to reversal	Oblivious to reversal
Concerned with case load	Unconcerned with case load
Dispositive	Not dispositive
Formal courtroom	Informal courtroom
Time certain	Cattle call
Relies on law clerk	No law clerks
Active questions	Does not ask questions
Stickler for rules	Easygoing
Serious	Fun-loving
Prepared	Not prepared
Expert in area of law	Novice in area of law
Developed judicial philosophy in area of law	Neutral philosophy in area of law
Concerned about consistency	Unconcerned about consistency
Conservative	Liberal
Elected	Appointed
Close alignment with opposing attorneys	Not aligned with opposing attorneys

Let's take a look at the strategies for both the attorneys based on the judge's proclivities listed above.

Both Attorneys:

Recognize the judge's proclivities toward formality, somberness, and active questioning. Follow all court protocol. Display the seriousness of this motion. Prepare for many questions. Know the facts and the law. Because the hearing is set for a time certain, you should have this judge's attention.

Defense:

Remind the judge that you must only win one of the two arguments to suppress the evidence. Begin with the strongest argument—the *Daubert* issue. Because the judge is thorough, talk in detail about the problems with the method used to take the Bess photo. Go back to Nita Rule of Evidence 702 and its demand that the testimony must be the product of reliable scientific principles and methods. Highlight the facts of the photo—not the facts of the assault. Cite cases where the court has explained reliable scientific methodology. Argue the facts of those cases. Get into the weeds of the law. Appeal to her concern of reversal by stressing that no court has admitted this type of evidence.

Turn secondarily to your Fourth Amendment argument as it is the weaker of the two. Compare and contrast precedent to the facts of this case. With this judge you cannot afford to ignore the law. Bring the legal discussion to the platitude of an individual's right to privacy and the limited demands of requiring a warrant. In the rebuttal, analogize this case to DNA genealogy services where there is no expectation of the information ever being released to the government and surely not without a warrant.

Make no mention of her election or the fact that her daughter lives on campus, but recognize that this is a tough case and although the sympathies lie with the victim, the law requires a result for Weaver. Give the judge the courage to do her duty to apply the law.

A preparation worksheet for the defense may look like the following:

TAILORING YOUR PRESENTATION	
Judge's focus on detail: deep	Emphasize the problem with the method used to take the "Bess" photo.
Judge's concern with the law: strong	Discuss the Nita Rule of Evidence 702: testimony must be the product of reliable scientific principles.
Judge's attitude toward reversal: sensitive to reversal	Stress that no court has admitted this type of evidence.
Judge's level of formality: strong	Be serious, formal, and follow protocol to the letter.

(Continued)

TAILORING YOUR PRESENTATION	
Judge's personal sympathies: lie with the victim	Do not mention the fact her daughter lives on campus; focus on highlighting the necessity of following the law.
Judge's style: active questioner	Argue the facts of particular cases; be prepared to dive into the details of the law.
Strongest argument: *Daubert*	Focus on the strongest argument—*Daubert*. Remind the judge you must only win one of the two arguments to suppress evidence.
Weakest argument: Fourth Amendment	Focus on the platitude of an individual's right to privacy and the limited demands of requiring a warrant.
Judge's election status: up for election	Make no mention of her election.
Judge's alignment with opposing attorney: neutral	No need to worry about the judge having a familiarity with the opposing attorney.

State:

Begin with the best of the two arguments: the privacy issue. Stress that Weaver voluntarily turned over his iris images to a private security company for the sole purpose of clearing airport security more quickly. Liken the facts to cases holding no privacy issues when a person voluntarily turns his information over to another. Without vocalizing citations, tick off case names where no warrant was necessary. Show the judge that precedent is on your side; she will not be reversed.

Next, turn to the expert issue. Stress the history and policy behind *Daubert*—to liberalize the admission of expert testimony. Discuss Barnes's expert qualifications and the general reliability of iris detection evidence. Talk the big picture first instead of the method used to obtain Bess's photo and its clarity. Advise the court not to second-guess the expert's opinion. Remind her that her decision will be reviewed only for an abuse of discretion. Evidentiary calls are primarily within the purview of the trial court judge.

End with an appeal to justice for the victim and safety for the college community. Do not harp on these as this judge is more apt to be convinced with the law. She will get the point that this may affect her election and possibly her daughter's safety. If you are too overt, this judge will resent you and your implication.

A worksheet for the state as they prepare for arguments may look like the following:

TAILORING YOUR PRESENTATION	
Judge's focus on detail: strong	Try to avoid spending too much time on the method in which the information was obtained. Focus on the big picture instead.
Judge's concern with law: strong	Try to liberalize the admission of expert testimony. Liken the facts of the case to the cases where there are no privacy issues when a person voluntarily turns information over to another.
Judge's attitude toward reversal: sensitive to reversal	Show the judge that precedent is on your side; she will not be reversed.
Judge's level of formality: strong	Be serious, formal, and follow protocol to the letter.
Judge's personal sympathies: lie with the victim	Appeal to justice for the victim and safety for the college community.
Judge's style: active questioner	Get ready for a detailed dive into the facts; tick off case names where no warrant was necessary.
Strongest argument: the privacy issue	Stress Weaver voluntarily turned over his iris images to a private security company, losing his right to privacy in the process.
Weakest argument: *Daubert*	Liberalize the admission of evidence. Discuss the expert qualifications of Barnes.
Judge's election status: up for reelection	Subtly highlight the fact that a ruling in your favor would garner public approval. [Ex]: "Allowing such evidence will keep kids safe on campuses, especially since most students carry their phones at all times. The cell phone becomes a built-in defense system."
Judge's alignment with opposing counsel: neutral	No need to worry about the judge having a familiarity with the opposing attorney.

Exercise

Plan your next motion hearing. Fill out the spectrum graph and table. Decide how to tailor your argument to the judge.

THE JUDGE

Concern for law	Concern for fairness and justice
Sensitive to reversal	Oblivious to reversal
Concerned with case load	Unconcerned with case load
Dispositive	Not dispositive
Formal courtroom	Informal courtroom
Time certain	Cattle call
Relies on law clerk	No law clerks
Active questions	Does not ask questions
Stickler for rules	Easygoing
Serious	Fun-loving
Prepared	Not prepared
Expert in area of law	Novice in area of law
Developed judicial philosphy in area of law	Neutral philosphy in area of law
Concerned about consistency	Unconcerned about consistency
Conservative	Liberal
Elected	Appointed
Close alignment with opposing attorneys	Not aligned with opposing attorneys

10.7 Tailoring the Argument to the Appellate Bench

Suppose that the trial court judge admitted the expert evidence. No interlocutory appeal was filed, and a jury found Mr. Weaver guilty of aggravated battery, a level 2 felony. Weaver now appeals the trial court's admission of the iris recognition evidence to the intermediate court of appeals. You know your panelists well in advance of the argument. Your research of the judges reveals that:

> Judge 1 was a female prosecutor for fifteen years before taking the appellate bench. She started the first victims program in the state, is conservative, and believes in law and order. She knows good police work from shoddy work and has no patience with the latter. She is an expert in evidence and has written extensively on *Daubert* issues. Judge 1 does not want to be reversed. She has ruled on privacy issues but is not a warrior for them. She is easy going and known to joke from the bench. She likes to ask questions of the attorneys.

> Judge 2 is a liberal judge who has been on the bench for five years. Before becoming an appellate judge, he was a law school professor teaching criminal law. He is neither a novice nor expert in evidence but is very concerned with privacy issues. He is concerned about reversal but not overly so. A fair ruling is very important to him. He actively questions attorneys, often on specific cases.

> Judge 3 is male and has been on the bench for thirty years. Before he was an appeals court judge, he was a trial court judge and tends to give trial court judges the benefit of the doubt. Throughout his career he has made big statements. He wants to be viewed as the judge who has made a difference in the law. He has no interest in any particular area of the law. He relies on his clerks extensively. He has little or no concern about being reversed. He is very creative. He talks more to his fellow panelists through his questions than expecting answers from the attorneys. He hates to reverse a jury verdict.

Both attorneys:

Know this will be a spirited argument. Expect many questions and know the law and facts cold. Judge 1 may inject a little humor into the argument. Keep your formality even though you will be smiling at Judge 1's jokes. Be prepared to let Judge 3 make his speeches to the other judges. Do not be eager to agree with him. Let him talk to the other judges and agree with the part of his questions that supports your position. Dive into the law with Judges 1 and 2, but come up to the theme occasionally to keep Judge 3's attention.

Let's find common threads among these judges. Use the threads to craft convincing arguments that will speak to all panelists. Below we analyze various potential arguments identifying the thrust of the arguments to each judge.

Weaver:

Weaver's thread #1—Weaver's right to privacy was violated when the police subpoenaed records from a private company.

Judge 1: It is not too much to ask the police to get a warrant.

Judge 2: Privacy is an important concern especially in our era of technology.

Judge 3: Finding a right to privacy here will have immense implications for future cases since our whole world is becoming digitalized.

Weaver's thread #2—The procedure Bess used to take Weaver's image was not scientifically reliable.

Judge 1: The procedure does not meet the standards of *Daubert* and N.R.E. 702.

Judge 2: This is not a good case to make precedence on privacy—the pivotal issue in this case involves using a scientifically sound principle—iris detection—in a scientifically unsound manner—on a phone app. Save the privacy issue for a case where the technology is likely to come into evidence under *Daubert.*

Judge 3: No court has ever ruled on iris detection evidence, either obtained with a cell phone or with a static iris scope. This is a case of first impression.

State:
The State's thread #1—Admission of this evidence satisfies Daubert and N.R.E. 702.

Judge 1: *Daubert* was meant to liberalize the admission of expert testimony; too often courts use it in a way not intended—to exclude expert testimony. Barnes was a well-qualified expert, and he should be relied upon.

Judge 2: Barnes was qualified; he is the expert, not the court.

Judge 3: The trial court got it right. She heard the expert's testimony; she weighed his credibility. The court should not disturb the trial court's judgment.

The State's thread #2—There was no Fourth Amendment violation of privacy here.

Judge 1: Case law provides that no warrant is required when an individual voluntarily gives over information to a private company.

Judge 2: Intermediate appellate court judges must follow Supreme Court precedent. Not following it risks a judge losing future credibility on a case where it matters.

Judge 3: This is harmless error anyway as there is other ample evidence to convict Weaver. Let the jury verdict stand.

When giving the customized arguments to each judge, make eye contact with the judge you are trying to reach. Of course, multiple threads may convince more than the targeted judge. Just be careful not to throw out an argument that will repel the majority of judges.

Now that we have studied in depth the component parts of an argument—the theme, facts, law, questions, and appeal to concerns of the judge—let's give the argument some structure.

CHAPTER ELEVEN

STRUCTURE AND NOTE PREPARATION SYSTEMS

One of America's great authors, Mark Twain, was also one of America's great performers. When he could not pay the costs of his extravagant lifestyle, he went on the lecture circuit, drawing huge audiences to hear his musings. Kurt Vonnegut commented, "Twain was so good with crowds that he became, in competition with singers and dancers and acrobats, one of the most popular performers of his time."

Among the many secrets to Twain's speaking success was the "counterfeit impromptu." He opined that "the best and most telling speech is not the actual impromptu one but the counterfeit of it." Twain admitted that it "Usually it takes me more than three weeks to prepare an impromptu speech."

To be sure, preparing a lecture differs from preparing an oral argument. Giving a speech is less likely to provide as many moments of spontaneity as your argument to the court. The occasional taunts or questions of an audience pale in comparison to the interjections of an active court. Nonetheless, both settings require you to be flexible—and flexibility flourishes with a plan.

For example, before entering the courtroom—whether physically or electronically—you may have had a terrific plan to present your strongest argument, deal with your weakest, and win over the judge. Sadly, you were interrupted before you even had an opportunity to say your name. By the time your argument was over, you were sinking in a whirlpool not of your own making, but nevertheless one you could not escape. You never reached the stage of discussing the strengths of your case. Your argument was simply hijacked.

In this chapter, we will help you avoid this trap using Twain's prepared "counterfeit impromptu." It begins with structure—a blueprint. Structure reminds you where you need to go and what to include in your argument. Structure will assist you in transitioning back from the unexpected to your perfect arguments—those concise and memorable lines you created in the weeks before the hearing.

We wed the organizational structure with note preparation because your structure will determine what your notes will look like. When all else fails, your notes will provide a lifeline back to the impromptu conversation you spent hours planning.

11.1   The Architecture of an Oral Argument

Below is a schematic explaining the organization of an argument-in-chief. We break down the beginning, middle, and end below.

11.1.1   *The Beginning*

The beginning constitutes the portion of the argument that the judge will remember most, so put your best material in this section. Think of the beginning as being so strong that it could stand alone and carry the day for you. Imagine the judge saying, "Counselor, I am short on time, so please limit your remarks to ninety seconds." A lot of ground must be covered in the opening section of your argument. Begin clearly and concisely. In the words of Winston Churchill, "It is slothful not to compress your thoughts." Every word should be considered and practiced by you during your preparation sessions. Here is the list of four "must haves" in your beginning ninety seconds.

11.1.1.1   Greet the Court

"Good morning, Your Honor. My name is Jane Doe, here representing XYZ."
You may think the introduction does not matter. It does. The introduction leaves the first impression with the court. If you sound like the court is the last place you want to be, the court gets the message. The judge will know immediately this is the last place he wants to be for the next thirty minutes. Introduce yourself professionally with warmth, sincerity, and energy.

National Institute for Trial Advocacy

11.1.1.2 State Your Theme and Why It Matters to the Court

Here is where all your work writing and rewriting your theme pays off. *Science:* Start strongly with your theme that captures why you win and why it should matter to the court. Themes, synonymous themes, and sub-themes for the King in *Humpty* include:

- "Every person deserves his day in court, even the King."

- "The King's case ought to be heard."

- "The King should not be penalized for the inaction of his attorney."

- "The King's attorney dropped the ball."

Follow your attention-grabbing theme with a short recitation of the crucial facts. If you have filed a brief before the argument which the judge has likely read, this condensed presentation may be the bulk of your discussion of the facts unless you integrate them into your analysis. Generally, the court has little patience for the story of the case it already knows.

"Humpty was a trespasser; he assumed the risk of his own misconduct."

After stating your theme clearly, be specific and simple in your requested relief. "We ask the court . . . ," "We are here today . . . ," "Today we ask this court . . . ." If you are speaking to an appellate court, tell the court the rule of law you are advocating.

Example

Every person deserves his day in court—even the King. The King was denied his day in court because his attorney, Mr. Emperor, was too sick to answer the complaint filed against him by Humpty Dumpty, an egg who injured himself while trespassing on the King's property. We ask that the default judgment be set aside.

11.1.1.3 The Road Map

Use as your road map the two or three points you prepared for the argument. You may enumerate each of the important points you wish to make, saying "I have three points. One, ... Two, ... Three, ..." or simply tell the court where you are heading. If you have a theme using the rule of three such as: "Text, history, and tradition all make clear that New York City's restrictive premises gun license is unconstitutional," you can use the three points of your theme as your organization.[1]

---

1. New York State Rifle & Pistol Association Inc. v. City of New York, New York, 140 S. Ct. 1525 (2020).

Your road map reminds you of where you are going and is easily remembered by the judges. *Science:* Use language different from the language in your brief or the court will lose attention, believing you are just reiterating your brief and wasting the court's time. If you can, have a different spin than you had in your brief. Look at the argument from a different perspective. The judge will be relieved that you will not regurgitate your brief.

You will often see the judge writing down your points for his use when writing the decision. Also, at the end of an argument the judge may remind you that you promised three points and ask for the point not discussed. Always welcome the prompt.

Make sure the road map delineates your affirmative points, not your weaknesses. For the King in *Humpty*, you may discuss that:

1. The King never had a chance to defend the case because of the excusable neglect of his counsel;

2. Humpty assumed the risk when scaling the wall.

Do not start off defensively with, "Humpty's counsel will say that the King created an attractive nuisance."

Because you will not cover everything in your pleadings, tell the court where you wish to rest on your pleadings. Simply say, "I will focus on x and y today."

Let's look at an example of a good *Beginning*, complete with the *Introduction*, the *Ask*, and the *Road map.*

Example

Good morning, Your Honor. My name is Daniel Smith, and I represent Mr. Sebastian. *Miranda* warnings are not merely suggestions from the courts. The police arrested Mr. Sebastian without Mirandizing him, and we ask this court to exclude the confession obtained during the arrest. This morning, I will discuss the *Miranda* standard and why the police failed to meet it.

Exercise

Practice the beginning of your argument. Time yourself. Begin with a three-minute opening, gradually reducing it to ninety seconds then thirty seconds.

National Institute for Trial Advocacy

11.1.1.4 The Appellee's/Respondent's Beginning

Because you argue after the movant or appellant, you must decide where to begin your argument. If the other side scores a compelling point with a judge during her argument to the court, go right to that point. You cannot wait to respond. Begin with a defensive plan. You must tackle the argument before the court will entertain your side. Do not respond to every point raised by the other side; pick the strongest argument—the one that captured the judge's attention. You can contest the other points during your argument but in an affirmative way showing strength and not weakness. After you have briefly spoken to the problematic point, work your plan. Go back to your theme and road map.

Art: On the other hand, if your opponent's argument is not capturing the court, then beginning on the defense only gives it credence. The line is subtle and can be made only by assessing, on the spot, the judge and the relative grip the argument has on him.

11.1.2 *The Middle*

In the middle, discuss the facts of your case and the law, then apply the law to the facts so it supports your desired result. Much needs to be included in the middle. *Science:* You must analyze the law and facts in your case, answer the court's questions, cover your affirmative arguments, bury yet deal with your weaknesses, attend to the judge's needs, and possibly negotiate with the court and opposing counsel.

The middle of your argument is the olly-olly-oxen-free section of the argument. During a children's hiding game, when someone yells olly-olly-oxen-free, pandemonium breaks out as all the children still hiding come out in the open yelling, running around in circles, and waving their arms. Likewise, chaos can occur in the middle section of your argument. Judges want their questions answered; you want to make your affirmative points. Put your game-face on and prepare your structure well so you have your objectives clear and mapped out to manage the middle.

The competing goals of the judge and the advocates are never more apparent. The judge often comes into the argument with a view about how to resolve the case. The judge tests his theory with questions designed to support or negate it. You have your own hypotheses.

With a panel of seven judges, there may be seven working solutions being tested. You must either kill the preliminary view or change the perspective. You may spend so much of your time fighting off each judge's theory that you miss persuading with your affirmative arguments. If you do not have an organizational system in mind, the court may drag you into a quagmire of potential solutions but never present *your* solution. *Science:* Your road map will focus the thread of the strong arguments stitched throughout your entire presentation.

11.1.2.1 Sketch Out Essential Points You Must Make in the Middle

Your road map highlights the two or three strongest points you will make. Order your points so your strongest is first. The beginning might be the only chance to discuss your best argument. Place your second compelling argument next, understanding you may never get to the third one.

Within each of your points, determine what the court needs to know to rule for your client. If you do not have an overarching theme covering all the points, develop a theme for each. Decide on the critical law and facts the court must know to hold for your client.

Determine if you will have a dedicated fact section, will blend the facts with the law, or emphasize the law. Consider whether 1) the facts and law are equally balanced between both sides, 2) the facts are predominantly on your side, or 3) the law is predominantly on your side. When the facts and law are equally balanced, you can choose methods of dealing with them:

- **Issue-based:** blend the facts and the law together to cover a legal issue, weaving in the relevant facts. Move from one issue to another.

- **Sandwich approach:** develop the legal principle, present the facts, then finish with the law applied in the current situation.

- **Facts, principle, law:** present facts, then explain how the facts fit the public policy or legislative intent behind the law, which you cover last. This requires a patient judge or a law that is well-known to the court.

When the law is weak for you but the facts are in your favor, prepare an undisputed facts section and rely on the judge's sense of fairness to rule in your favor. Highlight the equities. When the law is on your side, lead with a simple presentation of the law and, if needed, use analogous fact patterns that prove your point and lead the judge away from the bad facts at hand. The tables below outline these various approaches:

FACTS AND LAW EQUALLY BALANCED		
	Description	**Benefit**
Issue-based organization	Law and facts blended.	Useful to sequentially lay out one or more issues. Familiar pattern for judge accustomed to reading briefs.
Sandwich approach	Legal principle, facts presented, then law applied.	Less likely to be interrupted than if you begin with facts.
Facts, principle, law	Contextualized facts, public policy or legislative intent, law.	Use when there is law that everyone knows or that is court specific (discovery motions, preliminary injunctions).

FACTS ONLY ON YOUR SIDE		
	Description	**Benefit**
Through-line story	Facts-heavy delivery	The equities are highlighted rather than the law.

LAW ONLY ON YOUR SIDE		
	Description	**Benefit**
Leading with the law either through analogous case study or using facts of other cases	• Law and public policy • Facts • Three strongest points • Address anything damaging	Use when the law is on your side but the facts are not. Emphasis is on the law.

11.1.2.2 Other Organizational Systems to Make Your Affirmative Points

Within each issue, decide on an organizational system. When you are in the heat of questioning, you will answer the question but then revert to the place in your argument you were before the question was asked. Memorizing your structure will ensure that you make your essential points. You may use the issue-based sandwich, or facts/principle/law approaches described above, or use the easier to remember thematic, "what, so what, now what," or primacy/recency systems described below—or combine the approaches.

11.1.2.2.1 *Thematic*

Organize each point by its theme. Return to your themes at every opportunity. Paul Clement often presents thematically. His affirmative points are never missed. In the first Affordable Care Act case, *National Federation of Independent Business v. Sebelius,*[2] Clement argued against the constitutionality of the law. His theme was Congress has the power to regulate existing commerce but does not have the power to compel people to enter commerce just so Congress can regulate it.

After he answered each question of the justices, he revisited his theme or synonymous themes.[3] Here are examples he used to repeat his theme:

> "Congress wanted to capture those people [people who did not want to buy insurance]. These people are essentially the golden geese that pay for the entire lowering of premiums."

> "The whole problem is that everybody is not in the market, and they want to make everybody get into the market."

---

2. National Federation of Independent Business v. Sebelius, 567 U.S. 519 (2012).
3. National Federation of Independent Business v. Sebelius oral argument. Available at https://www.oyez.org/cases/2011/11-393 (last visited February 2, 2021).

"And if we tried to solve it [the problem] through incentives, we wouldn't be here; but, it's trying to solve it in a way that nobody has ever tried to solve an economic problem before, which is saying, you know, it would be so much more efficient if you were just in this market . . . ."

"And in the same way, I think if the framers had understood the commerce clause to include the power to compel people to engage in commerce, then . . . ."

Clement made his point. The art of the thematic method is to say the theme a little differently each time, so it doesn't become an annoying drumbeat.

11.1.2.2.2   *What, So What, Now What*

Like attorneys, improvisational actors prepare for spontaneity. They, too, wish to avoid cognitive overload. It is hard to speak contemporaneously without a structure. One improvisation technique used to create a scene is "what, so what, now what." The scene begins with the "what," meaning what event will unfold before the audience or what event occurred before the scene. The actors shift to "so what" that it happened. "So what" in this scenario means "what are the consequences?" The "so what" is not necessarily inconsequential; it can be catastrophic. The scene closes with "now what."

For the petitioner/movant, for each issue, explain what happened, show why it was wrong and why it matters—the "so what"—and end with the "now what"— what the court should do. Maybe you did not timely receive discovery, or a trade secret was stolen, or the lower court let in inadmissible evidence. End with the relief you request.

For the respondent, explain your version of what happened. The "so what" is just that—a big "so what?" Explain why what happened fully followed the law and is meaningless. "Yes, Your Honor, Mr. Jones didn't give Mr. Smith his tax returns because Mr. Smith was not entitled to them." Conclude with "now what"—your ask. "Now, we ask that you order Mr. Smith to pay for the costs of this hearing."

This approach can be blended with the lessons learned above about the strength of your facts and law. When the facts are on your side, "the what" and "so what" will emphasize the facts; when the law is on your side, the law is emphasized, and when they are equally balanced, the law and facts are blended.

11.1.2.2.3   *Primacy and Recency*

Just as you want to start and end strong in your overall argument, start strong and end strong within each issue. It is empirically proven that people remember more and give more significance to information heard first and last. Use this principle to your advantage. Take your weaknesses and place them in a position of less prominence—the middle. Begin and end each issue with a bang. Tuck the shortcomings between your strengths.

Certain arguments will naturally fit into one of the aforementioned structures. Pick the best one, or combine them and let the structure create a foundation for your argument, which gives you a place to return as you begin answering the court's questions.

11.1.2.3   Questioning

When the questioning begins in the middle, not only do you need to go back to your structure after each question, but you must manage the questions to get across your vital facts and law. Here are a couple suggestions during questioning.

11.1.2.4   Dolphining: Gluing Theme, Facts, and Law Together

Whatever organizational structure you use for each of your points, include "dolphining" when questioned. *Art*: Swim up to your theme, through your simple and concise argument,[4] then dive down to the detailed facts and law. Move seamlessly through these elements, cycling between the theme, best argument, law, and facts.

Just as dolphining works to speak to a panel of judges with various degrees of expertise and preparation, it also reduces the cognitive load of a single judge by bringing him up for air occasionally, up to your theme. Dolphining melds your crucial points of fact and law during the questioning.

Think of dolphining pictorially as the shape of a mountain. The peak is where your theme hovers, then stack your strongest two or three arguments, and the details of the facts and law will create the base of the mountain. The size depicted of each subsection of the mountain does not necessarily reflect the time you will spend on each. For the judge who is experienced in the law of your case, you may spend more time on the detail of fact and law; for the judge who is a novice, you may spend your time lingering over the best arguments and your theme.

---

4. Use the simple, concise arguments you created in your preparation. *See* Chapter Three, in particular 3.5.1 and 3.5.2.

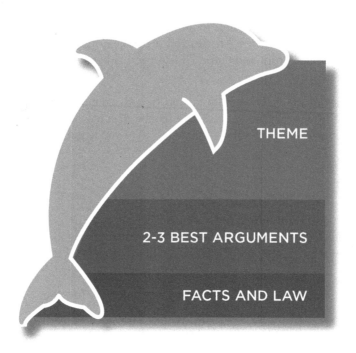

To illustrate this concept of "dolphining," let's look at *Bostock v. Clayton County.*[5] Pamela Karlan argued that Title VII of the Civil Rights Act of 1964 encompasses discrimination based on an individual's sexual orientation. One of her themes was that it is acceptable for the law to treat sexes differently, but not where it causes injury.

Karlan: So, for example, in Johnson against Santa Clara County Transportation Agency, everyone recognized Paul Johnson was denied the job because of his sex, but because it was a permissible affirmative action program, that was okay.

In Dothard against Rawlinson, this Court said Ms. Rawlinson is discriminated against because of sex, but there's a BFOQ. (Bona Fide Occupational Qualification) So if Congress writes an exemption into the statute, that's one thing [*deep dive into the law*].

But this Court really shouldn't be writing in an exemption for those purposes.

Justice Sotomayor: Do you think we need exemptions for those BFOQs? It's not just the—physical fitness standards for different sports,

---

5. Oral argument available at https://www.oyez.org/cases/2019/17-1618 (last visited February 2, 2021).

but the big issue right now raging the country is bathroom usage. Same-sex bathroom usage. How are those cases going to be dealt with absent a congressional exemption?

Karlan: Well, I think the way that they get dealt with is everybody agrees if you have men's bathrooms and women's bathrooms, that's because of sex.

It treats men one way; it says go to this bathroom.

It treats women another way; it says go to this bathroom. Then the question becomes is that permissible to do? And if I could just begin with an example that I think will show why this is so.

When I got up, the Chief Justice said to me, "Ms." Karlan. I am willing to bet any amount of money I have that when Mr. Harris gets up, he is going to say "Mr." Harris. He has treated us differently because of sex [*she argues one of her main arguments*].

But that's not discriminatory because neither of us has been subjected to a disadvantage [*up for air with the theme*].

And as this Court said in Burlington White against North— Burlington Northern against White, what the statute means when it says "discriminate against" is to cause an injury and requiring people generally to use separate bathrooms is not an injury [*down to the nitty gritty of the law*].

Justice Gorsuch: How would you deal with those, given that—that at least those affected might think that they're suffering a harm?

Karlan: So, there's no categorical rule about these.

For example, the fact that all of the men sitting at counsel table knew that they had to wear ties today and I was free not to didn't cause an injury (*back up for air to theme*).

This is an example of good dolphining. Coming up from the details to the theme and then back down into the details while swimming through your best arguments. It is an extremely effective technique for gluing theme, facts, and law together and getting your points across during questioning.

11.1.2.5 The Respondent's and Appellee's Middle

If you are the second or third to argue, listen to the questions the judges ask your opponent. If you have a multi-judge panel, note who asked the question. Record the questions that your opponent stumbled over. Generally, judges ask both counsel about the weaknesses of their cases. So, the questions asked to opposing counsel are generally your strengths. When it is your turn, remind the judge of the question and use that question to launch the argument about your strength. In a perfect world, the judge will take your idea as his own. If not, you still have an effective transition to one of your strengths.

11.1.3   The Ending

The ending, much like your beginning, has a defined structure and must be kept brief—no more than two minutes. The ending is where you go when you see your time is over, when the court is clearly agreeing with you, or when the court asks you to "wrap it up." The ending should act like the final paragraph of a superb essay: it advances the original thesis. The finale is not just a repetition of the beginning; it pushes the argument one step further. It haunts the judge with a lingering thought by plunging directly into the judge's concerns. Because the argument may reveal a concern of the judge you did not predict, develop the ability to nimbly adapt your ending. What you planned may not end with the judge's top concern, so spontaneously react and edit the ending on the spot.

The "must-have" list for the ending includes:

11.1.3.1   Appeal to the Motivating Concerns of the Judge

Go to the gut of the judge—the emotional rather than the rational. Use the advice from the last chapter to appeal to the judge's concern for fairness, resolution, consistency, parade of horribles, and desire not to be reversed.

11.1.3.2   A Return to Your Theme

If possible, merge your theme into your appeal to the concern of the judge. Consider this sample ending that appeals to the judge's concern for consistency while integrating the theme of limiting government's power:

Example

Counsel: The courts repeatedly stress the need for Mirandizing citizens under arrest. This keeps the government power in check. There is not confusion in case law about the exceptions, and the government does not assert a valid exception today. Your Honor has written extensively on the issue of Miranda. The police are well trained in how to issue proper Miranda warnings, and the police cannot pick and choose when they Mirandize a citizen under arrest. Miranda warnings are not merely suggestions from the courts. The police cannot ignore the courts' clear direction. We ask for the confession of Mr. Sebastian to be excluded from evidence because the police failed to provide even a basic Miranda warning to my client.

Merging your theme into the ending need not take a long time. Sometimes the ending should be short and sweet. An ending could be as short as: "Your Honor, this case is exactly like *Johnson v. Jones*, and that's why the defendant deserves his day in court."

Exercise

Think about an upcoming hearing you have. Why is it fair for your client to win? Draft and deliver a one-minute argument on why the fair result is a ruling for your client.

Apply the same appealing to the court's interest to clean his docket. Why would a ruling for your client lead to a quicker resolution of the case?

11.1.3.3   The Ask

Science: End with your prayer for relief and how to get there. Help the court write its order. Present a short and concise statement as to why you win. Do not end with, "I want justice for my client!" or, "If there are no further questions, I will sit down." End with a specific request for relief and the reason the relief is appropriate. "Judge, we ask that you deny my opponent's request for summary judgment and grant one for us because there are no material facts in dispute."

These last lines are your exit lines. They will be remembered. *Science:* Prepare your last words ahead of time and practice delivering them. Stay connected to the judge through eye contact and display a confident posture. Do not move to sit down until you have finished speaking. The conviction with which you deliver the lines may be enough to convince the court you must be right.

11.1.3.4   The Movant/Appellant's End

If you argue first and are confident that you will be allowed a rebuttal argument, you may want to save the appeals to the concerns of the judge and the *ask* for the end of your rebuttal. In doing so, the last words uttered by you to the court will be powerful.

11.2   Long Script

Once you sketch your beginning, middle, and end, create a long script for your argument. A long script has enough text within it to cover your entire allotted time. The long script is used to help you practice your entire presentation and is eventually reduced into talking points for use during questions from the bench. The long script clarifies thinking, builds confidence, and keeps long-winded or detailed-averse advocates on the right track.

The long script will rarely be read to the court. The exception is motions where preserving the record is the only goal. Here, you deliver your long script only to lay the seeds for an appeal. Except for this and other rare circumstances, it is even dangerous to take your long script to the podium with you. The temptation is to read the long script instead of delivering the argument in a confident, connected fashion. There are real dangers to reading or memorizing a text. Your voice will be flat, you will abandon nonverbal expression, and you will lose the connection to the judge. If you forget one word, you will crash because the memorized semantics will trip you. A long script also tends to create overall slow or fast delivery. If you absolutely must bring your long script to the podium, take it with you, turn it upside down, and let it serve as a security blanket.

Use your outline to create your long script. How would you convince your colleague, in seven to ten minutes, that you should win? If you are arguing a motion, some advocates draft their long script as if they were putting everything on the record. The long script needs to be well-organized and efficiently written. If nerves completely paralyze you during questions, the written words of a long script can rescue you from the foggy brain or forgetfulness that strikes when adrenaline runs high. Remembering or referring to the section of the long script usually snaps an attorney out of the haze and allows him to reconnect with the judge.

A word of caution: there are stages of preparedness. The first stage is complete unpreparedness. Next, a basic framework of organization (often useful for attorneys with fast-moving cases and rapid-fire motions with little prep time), then onto shaky memorization of phrasing and order, to a mastery of the substance, and finally to complete readiness, where you can add stylistic direction to your delivery.

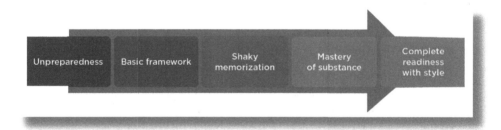

Complete readiness occurs when you have true control of the text—able to float in and out of it when necessary, yet you have spontaneity when needed to transition in and out of sections. Your delivery is natural and convincing. If you stop after the memorization phase, you will look robotic.

Take the example of an actor on stage. Once the actor memorizes the lines of a play or movie, he can appear robotic if he does not have complete mental mastery over the lines and cannot focus on the delivery style. This balance of focus on the present moment and connecting with a listener while delivering substantive information happens in stages. Keep preparing through the memorization phase and you will appear natural and confident, able to deliver the finely crafted magic phrases that help win the day.

One way to break out of sounding mechanical is to practice phrasing your points in different ways. This allows you to test whether you are too locked into the specific syntax in your long script. Should you need it, the long script is there to rescue you. But it should not be delivered as a stale, memorized piece to the judge. The hearing is supposed to be a discussion, an interaction, a chance to connect with the judge and discover whether he is, or is not, seeing it your way.

Example: *Humpty Dumpty v. The King*

Long Script for the King's Counsel: Seven-Minute Delivery Default Judgment Hearing

All people deserve their day in court, whether the litigant is a pauper or a king. [*Theme that resolves the suit and appeals to the judge's sense of fairness.*] Through no fault of his own, the King did not have his opportunity to be heard, and so we are asking you to set aside the default judgment entered for Humpty Dumpty and against the King. [*The upfront ask.*] The King asks that the judgment be set aside because his counsel's failure to answer the complaint resulted from understandable excusable neglect, and he has a meritorious defense: Humpty Dumpty assumed the risk of his injury. [*Road map using magic words.*]

Humpty Dumpty climbed up on the wall surrounding the King's castle. [*Facts: pertinent facts only in a story fashion.*] We may never know why he did so, but we know that from his vantage point he peered into the King's private chambers, where the Holy Grail was stored. The King's wall was an eight-foot brick wall, with rebar attached that formed a type of ladder. Mr. Dumpty climbed onto the makeshift ladder. From there, he had a great fall, and as we know, all the King's horses or men could not put Mr. Dumpty together again. Mr. Dumpty sued the King, timely serving him at the castle. One of the King's men promptly gave the summons to the Imperial Law Firm and attorney Emperor, who routinely represented the King.

Days later, Mr. Emperor had a nervous breakdown. He was found on the street naked, but claiming he was wearing his new clothes.

Mr. Emperor was so ill, he simply forgot to answer the complaint. Mr. Dumpty's attorney then sought default. This court entered a default judgment, and two months later, the King's law firm moved to have the judgment set aside.

(Continued)

[If there has been a brief filed and the court has read it, you likely cannot give this quick factual recitation; the court will interrupt you. You will need to integrate the facts into the law section.]

[Intersection of facts and law, citing and distinguishing cases.] Failing to timely respond was excusable neglect by the law firm. This case is very similar to the recent case of *Everystate v. Big Bad Wolf.* Everystate had filed a declaratory judgment action requesting the court find that Everystate's policy did not cover the intentional acts of the Big Bad Wolf in blowing down the home of the three little pigs. The Big Bad Wolf gave his summons to his law firm, Jack & Jill LLP, just as the King did here. It was the attorneys' illness—Jack fell down and broke his crown and Jill came tumbling after—that caused the default judgment. In *Everystate v. Big Bad Wolf*, our appellate court affirmed the trial court's order setting aside the judgment, as even the Big Bad Wolf deserved his day in court. Likewise, because the King's conduct did not cause the default, he should not be penalized for the acts of his law firm. Even the King deserves his day in court. *[Back to theme.]*

The King also has a meritorious defense. *[Your second issue from your road map.]* Mr. Dumpty assumed the risk when he climbed the wall, and therefore the King has no liability here. Assuming the risk is a complete defense and the King will be denied the chance to assert that defense if this default judgment is not set aside.

[Deal with your weaknesses.] Now Mr. Dumpty's attorneys claim that the King does not have a meritorious defense. They claim that the wall is an attractive nuisance and this case is similar to *Old Witch v. Hansel and Gretel. [Distinguishing cases.]* It is not. In *Old Witch*, the attractive nuisance was a sugarcoated cottage dripping with icing, chocolate, and peppermint sticks; here the King has a brick wall and embedded rebar. The Old Witch induced starving Hansel and Gretel into her home; here the King had a guard to keep Mr. Dumpty out. In *Old Witch* the enticement was favorite children's treats; here the alleged enticement was an old cup. These cases are not alike. More importantly, Your Honor, in *Old Witch*, even the Old Witch had an opportunity to have her day in court. The King deserves nothing less.

Our system of justice is premised on the concept that every person, a pauper or a king, big or small, young or old, should be given the opportunity to have their case heard by a fair and impartial judge or jury. *[Appeal to sense of justice.]* The King ought to have his day in court, just as Big Bad Wolf and old witch did. *[Theme.]*

(Continued)

There would be no prejudice to the plaintiff. While this case has been slowed down because of counsel's illness, we will agree to have the case fast-tracked to mitigate the delay. [*Negotiate with the court.*] Maybe a jury or a judge will ultimately find that the King is liable. But to deny him his day in court undermines confidence in the judicial process. The King deserves his opportunity for justice; he has done what he needed to do to be heard. His attorney dropped the ball, but that mistake should not result in this drastic denial of his right to a trial. He should not be punished for the actions of his attorney. He has a meritorious defense: that Mr. Dumpty assumed the risk of his own conduct.

[*The Ask.*] We ask that you set aside the default judgment, allow discovery to ensue, and set this matter for a pretrial conference because we have shown excusable neglect and a meritorious defense. [*Specific request for relief.*]

11.3   Short Script

Once you have written your long script, you are ready to prepare your short script. The short script is a two- or three-minute speech concisely explaining why you win. It should begin with your theme, continue with an organized middle giving the strongest reasons why you win, and end with a specific prayer for relief. Use the short script when 1) you have only minutes to give your argument or 2) you have only limited time to set out your case between the questions of an inquisitive judge. The short script requires you to focus on what really matters.

To create your short script, review your long script section by section and decide how you would summarize each one. Highlight specific lines that can resonate with the judge and reverberate in his mind after you sit down—these will be your magic words. What is memorable about this section? What is critical to say? Can this section be dealt with in questions if the judge shows interest, but discarded altogether as part of the short script?

The short script keeps the court's attention as you get right to the point with bite-sized chunks of information. Also, with the short script, you know you have missed no important points. But as with the long script, do not read it to the court or memorize it. An additional danger with the short script is that you leave out critical information that the court needs to know to understand your argument. In an effort to be concise, do not be tempted to start in the middle of the argument instead of the beginning. This will leave the court puzzled.

Example: *Humpty Dumpty v. The King*

Short Script for the King's Counsel: Three-Minute Delivery Default Judgment Hearing

All people deserve their day in court, whether the litigant is a pauper or a King. The King was denied his day in court because his attorney, Mr. Emperor, was too sick to answer the complaint filed against him by Humpty Dumpty, an egg who injured himself while trespassing on the King's property. The court should set aside the default judgment because the default was entered because of excusable neglect, and the King has a meritorious defense.

After Mr. Dumpty fell off the King's wall, he served the King with a complaint. The King eventually gave the complaint to his attorney. His attorney, Mr. Emperor, was ill and was running around the kingdom without his clothes. The attorney was not in his right mind. It was because of the attorney's illness that Mr. Dumpty's complaint was not timely answered.

Failing to timely answer the complaint was excusable.

The King should not be punished for his attorney's illness.

The King, like everyone, deserves his day in court.

The facts are similar to what happened in *Everystate v. Big Bad Wolf*. In *Big Bad Wolf*, the Wolf did not timely answer the complaint of *Everystate* because his attorneys were ill. The appellate court determined that the Wolf's failure to answer the complaint was excusable. Even Big Bad Wolf deserved his day in court.

Likewise, the King's failure to answer the complaint was excusable.

The King should not be punished for his attorney's illness.

The King has a meritorious defense. Humpty Dumpty climbed on the King's wall of his own accord. Mr. Dumpty's actions caused his own injury, not the King's. The King will prevail at trial. The King did not create an attractive nuisance. The wall itself was a clear sign notifying all to stay out of the King's grounds. This is unlike the case of *Old Witch v. Hansel and Gretel*. There, the Old Witch enticed the starving Hansel and Gretel with candy, while here, at best, the King's wall had a makeshift ladder made of rebar. Whether an attractive nuisance causes an injury is for a jury to decide.

And let me add there is no harm to Humpty Dumpty if the court sets aside the default judgment. While this case has been slowed down because of Mr. Emperor's illness, we will agree to have the case fast-tracked to mitigate the delay. Fairness requires that the case be heard on the merits because:

(Continued)

> - There is excusable neglect.
>
> - The King should not be punished for his attorney's illness.
>
> - There is a meritorious defense.
>
> - The King deserves his day in court.
>
> We ask that you set aside the default judgment, allow discovery to ensue, and set this matter for a pretrial conference.

11.4 Note Preparation for Flexibility

We now turn to a menu of preparation systems available for you to use, either alone or with one another, that will help you remain flexible, yet persuasive and thorough, and able to adapt to the challenges you will face in court. Some of these techniques should be a staple for all arguments; others depend on the skills of the advocate and the substance. To figure out what works for you, set aside enough time to try all the methods. As you try a new note preparation system, practice out loud and record yourself. Notice as you deliver whether the system of preparation:

1. made things easier for you to have fluid thoughts and nimble responses;

2. became too cumbersome and hindered your ability to effectively deliver; or

3. provided an unsuccessful return.

Keep track of which system works and which wastes your time. To successfully litigate, you must develop an individualized, efficient process that includes a combination of these techniques.

Just as every hearing is different, every advocate is different. Some attorneys struggle with questions, others with closing remarks, while others with remembering the details of case law. Your personal preparation system—a pattern of preparation that can be adjusted for a specific judge, argument, or opponent—should account for your particular strengths and weaknesses. So too should your preparation system account for the organizational structures you decide on. Either alone or in combination, the menu of systems provides rescues for the uncertainties of an argument.

11.4.1 Bullet Points (with Transitions)

No matter what system you use, inevitably your short script should be turned into bullet points. A bullet point system gives you confidence and a conversational style. The bullet points should be large enough for you to see at a quick glance. Make the font size at least 18 to 22 points. Usually, in the intensity of a hearing, you cannot read notes containing full sentences. If you need to search for your points on the page, your notes will be useless. Keep the detail down. The bullet points should have enough content to spark your memory on the broad topics you wish to cover, and on those smaller points you always seem to forget. Each issue may have a separate page—one page, no more. Or alternatively, in their book, *The Articulate Advocate*, communication experts Brian K. Johnson and Marsha Hunter suggest creating horizontal notes. Their technique recommends making notes easier to read by using the horizontal view instead of the vertical orientation. Your notes will flow like a timeline of your topics, and it will be easier to glance down to find your place.[6]

With your presentation organized and reduced to bullet points, you will find it easy to fill in the details of each point during the hearing. However, many advocates find the transitions between points more difficult. For seamlessly navigating between points, consider writing out your transitional phrases.

BULLET POINTS (WITH TRANSITIONS)		
Opening line (Argument 1)	Opening line (Argument 2)	Ending/Back to theme
Theme, headline	Theme, headline	Appeal to interest
Bullet points	Bullet points	Ask
Rescue/transition line	Rescue/transition line	
Theme, headline	Theme, headline	
Bullet points	Bullet points	
Rescue, transition line	Rescue, transition line	
Theme, headline	Theme, headline	
Closing	Closing	

BULLET POINTS (WITH TRANSITIONS)		
All people deserve their day in court. (Issue 1)	There is a meritorious defense. (Issue 2)	King deserves his day in court. (Ending)
The King's failure was excusable.	Humpty was a trespasser.	• Justice • Fast track? • No resolution with malpractice case
• Complaint to Emperor • Emperor sick • No one else could handle • Jack and Jill	• Wall • Climbed wall • Guard • Jack and the Beanstalk	Attorney dropped the ball.

(Continued)

6. Marsha Hunter & Brian K. Johnson, The Articulate Advocate: Persuasive Skills for Lawyers in Trials, Appeals, Arbitrations, and Motions (Crown King Books, 2d ed. 2016).

BULLET POINTS (WITH TRANSITIONS)		
The King should not be punished for his attorney's mistake. (theme)	No attractive nuisance • Old Witch: candy, starving kids • Stone wall (picture) Humpty caused his own problems.	Ask • Set aside • Allow discovery • PTC
Which leads me to . . . (transition)	To sum it up . . . (transition)	

11.4.2 Law-Driven System

For the law-intensive case, where the law is your strength, consider a law-centric preparation. It works well for those whose mind cannot hold and remember the specifics of each case and law. Use the law-driven preparation system for the judge who is an expert in the area of law and is known to be an active questioner. This system may not be very helpful for the big-picture judge who prefers not to become bogged down in argument with the specifics of cases.

For each issue, create a separate page that summarizes the cases, statutes, or rules relevant to that issue. Too much information will be difficult to access during the heat of the argument. Although many fine attorneys include the citation to the case in their notes, do not give the citations to the case unless asked. Have enough information to remind you of each case.

For cases, your notes should look like this:

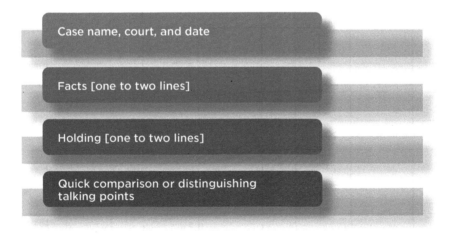

For statutes and rules, this format should be helpful:

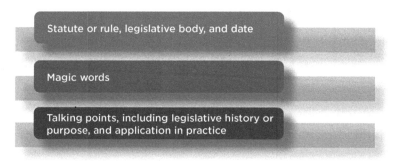

At the back of your three-ring binder, make separate tabs for each case, rule, or statute so you can access the details easily. If you would rather use a folder system, either electronic or paper, create a separate folder for each authority. Chances are that you will never reach for the full case or statute, but having them near you will give you confidence.

11.4.3 A Fact-Based System

For a fact-intensive case, where the court may ask you the record cite of a certain fact, create a fact-crib sheet. Place the facts by issue so you can quickly find them. Tab the sheet in your three-ring binder or have a separate file folder for it.

ISSUE 1			ISSUE 2			ISSUE 3		
FACT	DOCUMENT	LOCATION	FACT	DOCUMENT	LOCATION	FACT	DOCUMENT	LOCATION

(Continued)

Excusable Neglect			Meritorious Defense					
Facts	Document	Location	Facts	Document	Location	Facts	Document	Location
Emperor sick	Emperor Depo	p. 36, line 30	Humpty climbs wall	Guard Depo	p. 11, line 12	Wall	King's Aff	line 36
Emperor naked	King's Men Depo	p. 45, line 2–3	Humpty an egg	Humpty's Depo	p. 5, line 7	Rebar	Guard Depo	p. 18, lines 3–6
King's man gave summons	King's Men Depo	p. 15, line 4–5	Avoids guard	Humpty's Depo	p. 15, line 7	Guard present	Guard Depo Humpty's Depo	p. 36, line 3–4 pp. 10–15
King sat on summons	King's Aff	p. 4, line 5				Holy Grail position	Maid Depo	p. 10, line 7–10
Default after summons delivered	King's Men depo	p. 45, line 9–15						
No ask for another atty by King	King Aff	p. 12, line 8–20						

11.4.4 Question-Driven System

For those who fear questions, anticipate them and plan your answers. Formulate transitions back to your main points. Bullet-point the likely questions in the first column, the answers in the second column, and your transitions in the third column. Again, your main notes should not be over three pages and the questions should be separated by issue.

RULE 60(B), EXCUSABLE NEGLECT		
LIKELY QUESTIONS	**ANSWERS**	**TRANSITIONS**
Why couldn't another attorney in the Imperial Law Firm handle this?	"Because of the intimate relationship between the King and Mr. Emperor."	"Mr. Emperor's illness should not damage the King's opportunity to be heard."
Doesn't Everystate v. Big Bad Wolf *completely resolve the case?*	"Yes, it absolutely does, Your Honor. It stands for the proposition that everyone deserves his day in court."	"Just as the King deserves his day in court."
You did not file your request to set aside the default judgment until two months after the judgment was entered?	"Yes, we did, Your Honor. If you would look at the file stamp on the judgment and then look at the file stamp on the motion to set it aside, you will see it was actually a little less than two months."	"I have copies of those two documents, if you would like me to approach." (Tab 7) The King acted promptly; he should not be punished for the Emperor's illness."

Or if you feel comfortable with your answers, but the transitional lines always stump you, try these:

TRANSITIONAL LINES	
"And . . ."	"Because of that, . . ."
"This is exactly why . . ."	"That supports our position."
"Let's turn to . . ."	"With respect to . . ."
"This issue is similar to . . ."	"Let's unpack that."
"To summarize, . . ."	"Bottom line, . . ."
"This is symptomatic of a deeper issue."	"That brings us to the next point."
"That points to a hole in [insert party name]'s case."	"I share Your Honor's concern because . . ."

11.4.5   Point/Counterpoint

Identify your opponent's main arguments. Reduce them to a few words, listed on the left side of a page. On the right side, bullet-point your response to her argument. Again, each issue should have its own separate page. As you listen to your opponent, you can highlight those points made and cross off those not covered. This system works well for respondents, appellees, and for rebuttal arguments. During the argument, you can cross off points not covered. The danger with this method is that it may make you too defensive.

HUMPTY'S ARGUMENTS	RESPONSE
There is no meritorious defense because there was an attractive nuisance.	*Old Witch v. Hansel and Gretel*—peppermint, icing, candy, starving children (Tab 3) Rebar, ladder, stone wall (Exhibit 17, picture of King's wall) (Tab 6)
Mr. Dumpty could not have predicted the severity of his injuries.	Mr. Dumpty scaled the wall (King's Man Depo, p. 3) (Tab 5) Mr. Dumpty is an egg (Dumpty's Depo, p. 5) (Tab 8)

11.4.6   Theme

Write out your themes and sub-themes for each issue. This system works if you organize your middle thematically. Write out a variety of ways to say each theme so you do not sound scripted and you keep the judge's interest. After every question or main thought, go back to your theme or its variation. This serves as a bold reminder to constantly transition back to a winning theme. Don't forget to argue the details when using this note style.

THEMES		
There is excusable neglect.	There is a meritorious defense.	The King deserves his day in court.
Failing to answer the complaint was excusable.	Humpty climbed the wall on his own accord.	If the Big Bad Wolf deserves his day in court, so does the King.
Mr. Emperor was the problem.	Humpty is a trespasser.	

11.4.7 Deliver It from Your Hand

This system is for the attorney with little time to prepare for a simple motion hearing. In complex cases, this method can also be used by the fully prepared, skilled advocate with a quick memory and loads of confidence. Here, the attorney has three to five points she wants to make and uses her fingers to remember the points. Find three to five points you wish to make. Boil them down to one-word reminders. Then deliver them, in order, without notes. Keep points crisp and in a logical place so you can recall them. For example, Saint Teresa of Calcutta gave the "Gospel on Five Fingers." She would say the words, "You did it to Me," as she held up each finger of her hand. She explained:

You—who was responsible

did—that action was necessary

it—what they needed to do (feed the hungry, give water to the thirsty, visit those in prison, shelter the homeless, visit the sick)

to—that the actions are in service of another

Me—why and to whom, God

Humpty Dumpty v. The King could be reduced to "RISKY":

Risk—Humpty's actions were risky

Illness—Mr. Emperor's and excusable neglect

Same—the law should treat all the same

King—how he was served and what he did with the complaint

Yucky—wall of brick with rebar, no attractive nuisance

Exercise

Take a case that you have argued, or will, and reduce it to a three- to five-word phrase. Practice arguing, using each word as a cue.

The hand system allows a spontaneous discussion with the judge while re-minding the attorney of her important points. The structure is easy for you and the judge to remember. It allows for the fullest expression of your voice and gestures and fosters a connection with the judge. For complex cases, though, it is not for amateurs.

11.5   Logistics

All these note systems, except long and short scripts, may be laid out side by side on the podium or counsel table. You need a three-ring binder on the podium, which has your short script, and tabbed sections, as described below. We do not recommend using a laptop for your notes. The screen is a physical barrier between you and the judge; it will affect your connection to the judge. In many courtrooms, you must present behind a podium and a computer hides even more of you, creating yet another obstacle to bonding with the court. Tablets laid flat work.

11.6   Preparing Your Three-Ring Binder

The opening pages should be the main outline of your argument. Begin your notes/outline on page two so when you open your binder like an open face sandwich, pages two and three of your outline will be on the left and right sides of the open binder. Print your notes with a bottom margin of three inches, and in large font (18 point or above) so your eye contact stays up and towards the judge(s) as much as possible instead of struggling to read words on the bottom of any given page. This three-inch bottom margin also allows blank space for note-taking, should you need it. Behind those pages, make tabs for copies of statutes, rules, or pertinent cases. Likewise, make tabs for depositions, exhibits, affidavits, transcripts, and other documents you will need to answer the court's factual questions. The fewer the tabs, the more likely you can find them by touch in the heat of battle. But the more tabs, the more comfortable you may feel with your information near you. You need to decide the right balance for you.

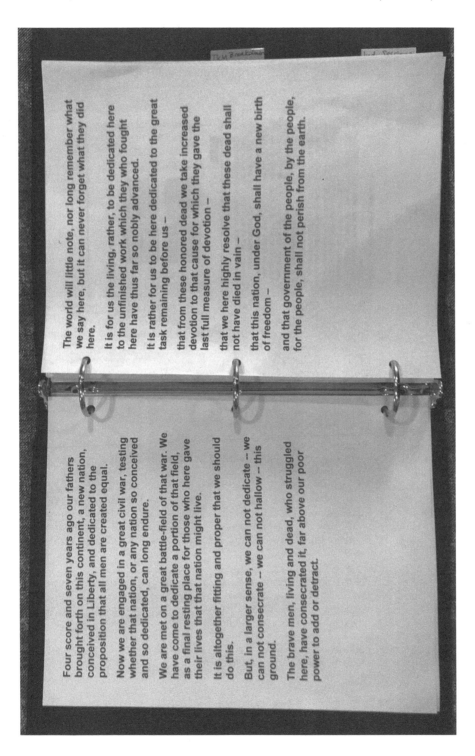

Four score and seven years ago our fathers brought forth on this continent, a new nation, conceived in Liberty, and dedicated to the proposition that all men are created equal.

Now we are engaged in a great civil war, testing whether that nation, or any nation so conceived and so dedicated, can long endure.

We are met on a great battle-field of that war. We have come to dedicate a portion of that field, as a final resting place for those who here gave their lives that that nation might live.

It is altogether fitting and proper that we should do this.

But, in a larger sense, we can not dedicate -- we can not consecrate -- we can not hallow -- this ground.

The brave men, living and dead, who struggled here, have consecrated it, far above our poor power to add or detract.

The world will little note, nor long remember what we say here, but it can never forget what they did here.

It is for us the living, rather, to be dedicated here to the unfinished work which they who fought here have thus far so nobly advanced.

It is rather for us to be here dedicated to the great task remaining before us --

that from these honored dead we take increased devotion to that cause for which they gave the last full measure of devotion --

that we here highly resolve that these dead shall not have died in vain --

that this nation, under God, shall have a new birth of freedom --

and that government of the people, by the people, for the people, shall not perish from the earth.

The following table shows advantages and disadvantages of all the preparation options discussed in this chapter.

PREPARATION SYSTEMS		
System	**Advantages**	**Disadvantages**
Long script	Confidence building; clarifies thinking. Keeps an advocate who has trouble with wordsmithing (too long winded or not detailed enough) on the right track. Tends to calm nerves.	Tough to take to the podium with you. Risk that you will fall into reading to the judge. Less eye contact. Not able to connect with judge or watch his reactions. If memorized, the tendency is to be flustered when one word or phrase is missed. Bound by words on page. Stifles expression in body language and flattens vocal delivery. Tends to create overall fast or slow delivery. Quickly sounds stale. Not recommended.
Short script	Clarifies thinking to be concise and to the point. Simplifies diffcult concepts. Develops magic phrases. Keeps attention of the court. Takes less time. Useful for rebuttal later. Easier to manipulate style changes than the long script. No fear of not making a record. Can be read for the disengaged judge.	If memorized, can be delivered flat with no connection to the court. Tendency to be flustered when one word or phrase is lost. Risk of the advocate knowing too much and starting the story in the middle.
Bullet points (with or without transitions)	Security blanket for things you always forget. Helps with organization when law and facts are merged in deliveries. Easier to talk more conversationally off bullet points than full script. Transitions give you confidence. Magic phrases are front and center.	If too detailed, difficult to see and you cannot find your points quickly enough. You can get lost in the paper. May have to shuffe multiple pages. Usually flattens gesture pattern because hands are needed to keep place on outline and mark what has been covered.
Law driven	For the law-heavy case, the case law and statutes are at your fingertips. Use when the judge is an expert in an area and wants to get into specifics. Gives you confidence you will not forget the facts, holdings, or principles of multiple cases.	If judge is a big-picture person, then case-by-case analysis is too specific. If too detailed, diffcult to use in the argument.

PREPARATION SYSTEMS		
System	**Advantages**	**Disadvantages**
Question driven	For those nervous with the prospect of answering questions. Plan transitions from questions back to your arguments or themes. Use with an active bench.	If the judge asks no questions, you will need a short script to preserve the record.
Point/ counter-point	Able to quickly respond to your opponent's arguments. Works well for rebuttal and respondent/appellee's arguments. During your opponent's argument, you can cross off those points not covered.	You have a danger of becoming too defensive and may not offensively argue your case.
Theme	Keeps you focused on your main arguments.	Lacks detail. You lose the specifics.
The hand (three to five points, cued by words within a short phrase)	To be used when there is minimal preparation time. Allows for focused and simple directed delivery. Perfect for the spontaneous discussion with the judge. Easy to remember for you and the judge. This allows for the fullest expression of your vocal instrument and your body language because there are no notes. It fosters a relationship with the judge, as if you were discussing it outside the courtroom.	Lacks detail. You may forget something crucial for the motion. It is not right for an amateur in a complex case or the judge who wants to discuss the specifics.

CHAPTER TWELVE

REBUTTALS

Rebuttals are risky. Done well, they serve as a way to briefly address your opponent's arguments and remind the court why it should find in your favor. A rebuttal should be "the finishing touch of color; there is nothing more to add."[1] Done poorly, they bore and frustrate the judge and could turn the court against you.

Often, an advocate would have been better off abandoning the rebuttal all together. Think strategically about when a rebuttal is the right move. If the court chews up your opponent's arguments and clearly sees things your way, resist the temptation to deliver a rebuttal. That is right: pass on a rebuttal when the court sees it your way. Stay seated.

Use the rebuttal when a judge is interested in or confused about an aspect of the argument. Often, your opponent made a point, and the rebuttal gives you a chance to acknowledge the point and convince the judge that your position should prevail or offers you an extra moment to clarify a point of confusion. Use the rebuttal to quickly set the record straight if the court or opposing counsel misunderstands the law or facts. Finally, use your rebuttal to drive home your best argument in a different way than you have ever said it.

A successful rebuttal requires preparation, but also flexibility and quick decisions. Because judges are impatient with rebuttals, *keep them short*. Unless the judge wants to keep talking, keep rebuttals to less than five minutes, even in a long hearing.

Always ask the court if you may set aside time for a rebuttal. Even if you do not use the time, knowing you have the last word keeps your opponent honest. Discover the court's practice. Does the court allow rebuttal? Is the court known to allow surrebuttal or continue the conversation back and forth until all parties exhaust their argument?

12.1 Ineffective Rebuttals

Certain types of rebuttals should never be spoken:

- Laundry list or checklist deliveries. Here, the attorney stands up and lists all the arguments, grievances, and counters in a checklist format. Because

---

1. Joseph Joubert, Pensées of Joubert (Nabu Press, 2010) (1896).

a listener can only remember a few points at a time in oral delivery, the laundry list approach has little impact and is remembered as a waste of time.

- Same old song replay. Argument regurgitation is an ineffective way to connect with the court. Many judges dislike rebuttals for this reason. The court hears one side, then another—and the rebuttal ends up being nothing more than a rehash of one or both. If you have delivered a memorable and full argument, a repeat is unnecessary. When the attorney uses the rebuttal to deliver the argument again, it is usually the same order and wording. Instead, treat a rebuttal like a good essay ending. Finish with a twist or fresh development on the main theme. Offering the court a way to see things from a different angle is often useful, as opposed to sounding like a broken record repeating the same thing.

- Defensive whining. A judge will shut down during a rebuttal used to complain about opposing counsel or his arguments. A defensive and whiny rebuttal sounds weak and annoying. Imagine hearing two children tattling on one other. Instead, address points without complaining. Show strength and avoid a whining tone.

- Smugness. If the judge dislikes opposing counsel's reply to your argument, there is no reason to stand up and use rebuttal time to rub it in his face. Instead, be dignified and unemotional, and do not crow over your opponent's apparent loss.

- My way or the highway. Often an attorney delivers a rebuttal without addressing issues that clearly needed to be covered. Even worse, not addressing your opponent's argument looks conceited. This will not gain you favor with the court. If the judge seems perplexed or needs information or to be brought back to your side on an issue, address it head-on. Do not treat the rebuttal as if you ignored your opponent and the judge as they discussed the argument. Listen and respond accordingly.

12.2 The Parts of an Effective Rebuttal

REBUTTAL		
First	**Second**	**Third**
Respond directly to the judge's concern or opposing counsel's winning argument.	Make corrections, clear up misunderstandings in fact or law.	Go to the heart of the judge, write the order.

12.2.1   *Part One of Your Rebuttal (Two Minutes)*

To successfully plan for the first portion of the rebuttal, think of this section as being on the defensive. Using no more than two minutes directly address a couple points where your adversary did the most damage to you. These points can be predicted ahead of time. The predetermined simple points for this section will rein you in and prevent a laundry list from leaving your mouth. Read the judge—her questions and reactions will let you know where you have to go and how much work you have to do to bring her back to your side. Deal with the problems first and get them out of the way before you go back to what you want to talk about.

The topics and talking points can be outlined ahead of time, with high predictability. Simply create bullet points that summarize the opposing counsel's predictable arguments, with corresponding rebuttal talking points. If you research the judge, you may predict her areas of concern. Listen closely during the opposing counsel's actual argument, and respond directly with the help of your pre-scripted responses.

Although you have thought ahead about your response, do not be tied to your script. *Art:* Weave the judge's words into your rebuttal. Doing so will let the judge know that you listened to her concerns, while at the same time you can use her words to align yourself with her and lead her to your view.

There are a couple of ways to organize this first section of your rebuttal. One way is to reorganize the framework and redefine the issue. In a motion for summary judgment, your opponent may seem to have made points with the court on three factual issues. You may argue in response that these factual matters do not change the outcome. "Your Honor, summary judgment is precluded only where there are no material facts at issue. Here there are no material facts. Materiality requires . . . ." What matters is the law that applies. In other words, change the framework.

Another way to reply is to argue a few key points that are determinative of the case. This is usually the section where advocates feel tempted to throw in a laundry list of "gotcha" points. When following this approach, be choosy and respond to a couple of the hot items the judge discussed with opposing counsel. If you have prepared a topic list, with responses on one page in front of you at counsel's table, you can listen closely and expand any necessary talking points.

The following example was prepared as the rebuttal to a large, multi-district litigation (MDL) motion.[2] The MDL is a class-action products liability suit.

To set the stage for you: opposing counsel just sat down after calling [Acme]'s motions petty, whiny, and hyper-technical. They attempted to shift the make-up of the class parties without leave of court.

---

2. Thank you to Mariah Brandt, a partner at Pillsbury Winthrop Shaw Pittman LLP, for permission to adapt this rebuttal.

Example

Brandt: Your Honor, nothing [Acme] has raised is technical or petty. Properly crafted claims—standing, jurisdiction—these are foundational issues. Plaintiffs call these things mere procedures. Well, procedures keep things fair and create fair dealing.

Adding Smith and his California subclass creates problems. They don't even know where he belongs. They don't know which court will welcome Smith and his subclass once this MDL is finished. We can't even properly address the jurisdictional issues until we know what action he is in.

And the *manner* in which Smith and the subclass were added, without any leave of court, creates a dangerous precedent.

Responding to the hot topics covered by your opponent takes preparation. Some advocates make the mistake of furiously taking notes to capture opposing counsel's position and the judge's response. This technique usually results in a less thoughtful and more disorganized rebuttal. Instead, prepare a manageable list of predictable and less predictable subtopics with a planned, thoughtful response. To do this, predict what opposing counsel will argue based on the briefs. *Art:* Step into opposing counsel's shoes and argue their best case, then imagine how you would rebut their points and which ones are worth spending precious rebuttal time.

Here is an example of a planned Rebuttal Checklist used during the same MDL hearing, when listening to opposing counsel's argument. It is a predicted summary of opposing counsel's best arguments. As opposing counsel delivered, Mariah Brandt could watch the judge's reaction, check the two to three items that deserved attention, and address those items during Part One of her rebuttal.

REBUTTAL CHECKLIST PREDICTING OPPONENT'S ARGUMENTS	
The court has subject-matter jurisdiction because all of the plaintiffs have suffered an injury-in-fact because of the Acme products.	☐
Smith should not be struck because it is not necessary to seek leave of court.	☐
The subclass claims should not be dismissed because notice is not required.	☐
Several plaintiffs have standing to pursue a claim.	☐
The plaintiffs have standing to seek injunctive relief.	☐
The plaintiffs' claims are valid.	☐

By creating a checklist with the predictable rebuttal points, you can spend your time listening and watching instead of furiously taking notes. This allows you to observe non-verbal reactions, especially important to observe in a multi-judge hearing when you have to watch multiple reactions at once. In an oral argument, it is impossible to simultaneously take effective notes while watching the non-verbal reactions of all the judges during opposing counsel's presentation to the court.

Exercise

Create a rebuttal checklist for your next hearing.

12.2.2   *Part Two of Your Rebuttal (One Minute)*

Use the second part of the rebuttal to set the record straight on any misunderstandings or misstatements heard during opposing counsel's argument. The judge's patience is running thin at this point, so avoid correcting a misstatement that will not make a difference in the end. For example, if opposing counsel states that the contract was signed on February 2 when the correct date is February 3, with no meaningful events in between, let it go. Avoid making distinctions without a difference. For instance, it is best not to stand up and correct opposing counsel's word choice—your client "slapped," not "smacked," the victim, as an example.

Science: Correct an interpretation of the facts or law that makes a difference to the case. This could be when you discover during opposing counsel's argument that the judge is confused on a higher court's position on the pivotal law in the case. Or that opposing attorney has misinterpreted case law. That is worth correcting, even if the truth cuts against your present win. You can use transitional language like, "Your Honor, let me correct the record," or "Just to be clear, the case law here states . . . ."

A key emotional goal here is to stay intellectual and avoid correcting opposing counsel in an accusatory fashion, as if you caught him. Remain courteous and extend opposing counsel the benefit of the doubt. The judge will determine if opposing counsel misspoke or lied. Instead, just state the correction and allow the judge to dig in with any questions that may arise. During a motion hearing, the judge may directly ask opposing counsel to chime in with a response to the correction, so this could become a true discussion. Be willing to stand back from the podium for a moment to allow opposing counsel to respond to a judge's direct question to him.

Avoid talking over opposing counsel or increasing your volume in an attempt to overpower him. The point of this second part is to set the record straight on matters of facts or law.

To prepare for this second section of the rebuttal, comb through the opposing counsel's brief and collect any inconsistencies, misstatements, or misrepresentations of facts or law. Have this list at counsel's table in a Rebuttal Checklist format, and quickly check or highlight anything that must be addressed after hearing the discussion between opposing counsel and the judge.

If it is clear, after the first two parts of rebuttal, that the judge is not buying what you are selling, now is the time to turn to your Plan B. You will hear the judge's resistance in her argumentative or sarcastic tone. You will see her resistance in her skeptical face.

Plan B is the fallback position you have agreed to with your client before the hearing. It may be that you have no fallback, but if you do have a fallback, now is the time to use it. Suggest that the court need not go as far as you or the opponent asked her to go. Recommend a middle position. Appeal to the "inner Solomon" of your judge.

Sometimes, you will skip the second part of the rebuttal. If there are no misstatements of fact or law, move directly to Part Three. Also, if you are trying to convince the more liberal judge to be brave and pioneer a new legal path, do not worry about misstatements that will make little difference to the trailblazing judge, instead go to the heart of the judge. Proceed to Part Three.

12.2.3 *Part Three of Your Rebuttal (One to Two Minutes)*

Part Three returns you to the offensive. You have done the hard work of getting the judge back to the middle; now is the time to talk about what you want to talk about. Repeat your strongest winning point, but say it in a way that you have never said it before.

Art: Your goal is to leave the judge with a deeper understanding or reason to rule for you. Often, the last gem is the public policy argument. For example, if you are asking for a default judgment to be set aside, now is the time to talk about the reasons the law prefers a decision on the merits. Tell the court that resolving a case on the merits enhances the credibility of our judicial system, while procedural maneuvering has the opposite effect.

Example

Brandt: On the face of the complaint, all of the claims fail because the plaintiffs have not alleged the correct business relationship with [Acme]. And they cannot, because [Acme] does not sell directly to consumers. The plaintiffs even concede this point.

Not only do all the plaintiffs fail to state a claim, we now know that the plaintiffs do not even have standing, based on their sworn deposition testimony. While the plaintiffs urge this court to ignore this fact, the bell cannot be un-rung.

This same exposing deposition testimony reveals there is no imminent threat of future harm and that all plaintiffs have an adequate remedy at law. The Supreme Court mandates that injunctive relief be denied.

Patrick Strawbridge, President Donald Trump's attorney in *Trump v. Mazars USA*[3] brilliantly argued public policy in his rebuttal. He repeated his theme that Congress's subpoena asked for a vast swath of documents, including tax returns, without showing a demonstrable need for them. He concluded with his public policy argument, "This is not an attempt to preserve the balance of powers. It's an attempt to eviscerate them."

Provided that you did not include an appeal to the interests of the judge in your opening argument, you may choose to place it in the end of the rebuttal. End by returning to your theme and your specific request for relief. Continuing with our Acme example from above, consider this rebuttal delivery:

Example

Brandt: The complaint is flawed. Not only does it fail to state certain claims, fail to show jurisdiction, and fail to show standing, but it includes the claim of unjust enrichment, which does not even exist in California law.

It is the epitome of judicial efficiency for this Court to determine these issues now.

This Court should grant [Acme]'s motion to strike and dismiss in its entirety.

---

3. 140 S. Ct. 2019 (2020).

12.3   Analogies and Metaphors

Rebuttal arguments are an excellent time to bring out your analogies and metaphors. Metaphors help people understand a new concept by looking at it through the prism of a familiar one. Metaphors reach people on both an intellectual and emotional level. Think of the phrase "Don't throw the baby out with the bathwater." It conveys more than the intellectual concept "not to throw away the good with the bad." Because of the connection we all have to babies, an emotional component is also communicated.[4]

When used properly, metaphors can give the judge an *aha* moment and an emotional reaction. Courts are receptive to analogies and metaphors as courts have a history of using them. Consider the fruit of the poisonous tree, a wall of separation between church and state, or shouting fire in a crowded theater. Your analogy might even make it into the opinion.

An analogy or metaphor must be bulletproof. By bulletproof, we mean that the comparison is extremely close, and the metaphor cannot be turned against you. You must test your metaphor and analogy with many critical audiences before your argument.

Analogies and metaphors can and are convincingly introduced at any time of an argument. Turning back to *Trump v. Mazars,* Patrick Strawbridge introduced early in his argument that subpoenas are weapons in the standing arsenal of Congress which will undermine the presidency. Nevertheless, launching an analogy during the rebuttal is a particularly safe time to do so because your opponent cannot respond.

But it is not completely safe, because judges have been known to fight back against an analogy. Make sure the comparisons are solid. The attorney representing the petitioner in *Drye v. United States*[5] received some judicial kickback with his analogy. After his mother's death, Drye disclaimed his interest in his mother's estate. The Internal Revenue Service claimed rights to Drye's interest because they had a valid tax lien against him. Here was the exchange:

> Counsel: For our Socratic dialogue I am armed with a borrowed Gideon and the fruit. This is . . . these aids go right to the jugular of this case, and the genesis of the case, which is Chapter 3 of Genesis. What we have here is, when the serpent extended the fruit to the offeree, free will said that the offeree had a right to accept or reject the gift. Assuming that that offeree was a tax delinquent, the Government's position is that

---

4. Analogies, similes, and metaphors differ, but for purposes of our discussion we lump them into one category.
5. 528 U.S. 49 (1999).

their 6321 Federal tax lien attached at the moment that the serpent extended the fruit.

That is not—,

Justice Kennedy: Well, of course, the IRS was not in Paradise.

[Laughter]

Counsel: I'm . . . that is where the case starts, is with the idea of free will, that people have a right to accept or reject a gift. The Government doesn't believe that. They believe that when you have the right to make that decision and grab the fruit, that their lien attached to that personal right of decision to elect … I don't believe that that's the law of this Court, as announced by this Court. I don't believe—

Justice Ginsburg: Counsel, the Government is not relying on the Good Book, but it is relying on title 26 of the Internal Revenue Code . . . .

Ouch.

Malcolm L. Stewart fared better with his sports analogy in *EPA v. EME Home City Generation.*[6] In this case, governors from downwind states urged the EPA to force upwind states to reduce smog and soot emissions from their power plants. Stewart argued that the EPA should be permitted to use a standard of "contribute significantly" when determining a state's cost-based share of transported air pollution.

Malcolm Stewart: And in terms of the language "contribute significantly," I think there are—there are various reasons to think that the EPA reasonably construed that term to include a component of difficulty of achievement.

That is, in common parlance, we might say that dunking a basketball is a more significant achievement for somebody who is 5 foot 10 than for somebody who is 6 foot 10.

We might say that a $100 charitable contribution is more significant if it's made by a person who makes $10,000 a year than a $1,000 contribution by somebody who makes $1 million a year.

Chief Justice John G. Roberts, Jr.:   That's—I was just going to say, that just is because of, in the latter case, because contribution happens to be used in both an affirmative and a negative sense.

---

6. 572 U.S. 489 (2014). Oral argument available at https://www.oyez.org/cases/2013/12-1182 (last visited February 2, 2021).

The question is, for example, whether somebody who fatally stabs somebody and someone who fatally shoots them have each significantly contributed to the bad result . . .

Stewart: I would say if—if you cause death by alternative means, then both people would have contributed as significantly.

But to include—to set out a hypothetical that involves contribution to a bad result, if you had a basketball team that lost a game by one point, and the coach was asked to pinpoint the plays that contributed significantly to the defeat, the coach would be much more likely to identify a missed layup or a turnover than the missed half-court shot at the buzzer.[7]

It's true that the missed half-court shot at the buzzer would, in one sense, contribute significantly, in that it was a but-for cause.

If the shot had been made, the outcome was—would have been different.

But if you're talking about significant contributions to a bad result, you'd more likely to focus on errors that could or—and should have been avoided, not simply the failure to accomplish something that's extraordinarily difficult.

When opposing counsel argued, the Chief Justice asked:

Chief Justice Roberts: What is—what is your answer—do you have an answer to Mr. Stewart's basketball hypothetical?

I mean, I thought that was pretty good.

Slam dunk. A 9–0 decision. That is good advocacy.

Exercise

Pick a current case. Take one of the main themes and develop a sports analogy to help a listener understand the theme.

12.4   Surrebuttal

In a motion hearing, the judge may allow surrebuttal. Often, a trial court judge will want to continue the conversation. Watch the judge to see cues. She will be looking

---

7. Notice that Attorney Stewart is responding to a hypothetical question and has in his repertoire a planned, more-perfect hypothetical than the Chief Justice's. *See* Chapter Eight: A Periodic Table of Questions.

at you, goading you to speak. If the judge is receptive to it, then speak away. Only speak to the issue in your opponent's rebuttal that troubles the judge. Stop when you are ahead. No judge likes someone who always must have the last word.

Whether you are about to deliver the beginning, middle, end, or rebuttal portion of your argument, knowing how to deliver it makes all the difference. Now that you have powerful substance well at hand, Chapter Thirteen provides presentation techniques to persuade the judge on the stylistic front.

Chapter Thirteen

"Now That I Know What to Say, How Do I Say It?"

President Barack Obama delivered the eulogy for Rev. Clementa Pinchey, killed in a tragic shooting at a Charleston, South Carolina, church. Many considered his delivery to be one of the most inspiring of his presidency, as he spontaneously led the entire church in song to "Amazing Grace." The president of the United States broke out in song during a eulogy which had a dark backdrop of tragedy. He managed to turn the nation back to hope by bravely taking a chance. Few can watch the video footage of that moving moment without being taken back by the stylistic excellence used in the president's delivery.

Some are born with a natural "gift of gab." These are the friends who you gravitate to at a party to hear them tell a tale and share a laugh. These are the lawyers in a negotiation who seem to have the board room eating out of their hands. These are the advocates who can "hold court" with the most difficult of benches and persuade.

But the skills of rhetoric can be learned, and habits can be formed that allow us to also hold the room with our stylistic excellence. Breaking down the moments right before President Obama broke out in song gives us a taste of how to learn from a great orator:

President Obama sets up the moment by talking about the "reservoir of goodness" within each of us, and of grace.

> He says, "If we can tap that grace, everything can change . . ." [three-second pause]
>
> "Amazing grace . . ." [one-second pause]
>
> "Amazing grace . . ." [eleven-second pause]
>
> "*Amazing grace, how sweet thy sound...*"[1]

And off he went, leading the congregation, the grieving, and the nation back to hope. He set it up with a sustained pause—an *eleven-second pause*, which fit the gravity of the situation.

---

1. https://www.youtube.com/watch?v=IN05jVNBs64.

In an argument, advocates have to lead the court to a logical place, and the style a lawyer uses can make or break the argument. Psychological research reveals how important the style of your delivery is to your message. Psychologist Albert Mehrabian's research[2] reveals that audiences understand oral communication in the following manner:

- Vocal—38 percent through voice quality

- Visual—55 percent through body language and appearance

- Verbal—7 percent through the message

These percentages shed light on just how important the delivery is for any oral communication. Too many attorneys focus solely on the content in an argument and neglect the manner of delivery. The judge should have received the bulk of the content through the papers. The hearing allows you to utilize the visual, vocal, and emotional components Dr. Mehrabian notes to persuade the judge. When speaking, master the substance so you can focus on your stylistic delivery.

Oral communication training gives you skills that, coupled with your expertise and experience, will help you explain a complex matter or persuade even the most difficult judge of the legitimacy of your position. Fine-tuned oral communication skills help you craft arguments that appeal to the widest possible variety of judges without sacrificing your individuality. In arguments, certain behaviors, mannerisms, and styles can offend, while others appeal to most judges. Advocates should shed the habits and inclinations that do not appeal and develop the appropriate successful techniques. Some attorneys naturally perform stylistically better than others. Some have the gift of a great voice. Some attorneys put you at ease or inspire you simply with their body language. Others win an argument because of their emotional mastery over a substantively difficult issue. If you are one of these individuals, you can become even more successful by training and developing your gifts. If you are not naturally gifted, you can learn techniques that improve your skills.

Art: To improve the delivery at a hearing, your goals should be to:

- Identify and ditch bad habits;

- Cultivate good habits so you can employ them at their peak level; and

- Enhance those good habits at which you already excel.

---

2. Mehrabian, Albert. *"Silent Messages"—A Wealth of Information about Nonverbal Communication (Body Language).* Personality & Emotion Tests & Software: Psychological Books & Articles of Popular Interest (Los Angeles, CA: self-published, 2009). Available at https://www.scribd.com/doc/98446772/Albert-Mehrabian-Silent-Messages-1971 (last visited February 2, 2021).

National Institute for Trial Advocacy

13.1   Voice

Ultimately, you want a friendly, engaging, clear vocal quality that can be heard by the judge. Vary volume, speed, pitch, range, and word stress to create interest for the judge. Blend natural variations with purposeful variations implanted for emphasis.

A judge connects to the quality or tone of the attorney's voice. Display your instrument's best quality by properly using volume, articulation, pitch, inflection, speed, and pauses. As your voice improves, you will learn its limitations and can work on techniques to compensate for those limitations. This is important to your professional advancement, and you will achieve results by paying steady attention to each element.

13.1.1   Volume

Project your voice enough for the judge to hear you clearly. The projection changes that are needed will depend on courtroom acoustics and room size. In general, project more than you think is necessary. A judge and a court reporter should not strain to hear you. The audience cannot comprehend what it cannot hear. It is far easier to turn down the volume if you notice the judge reacting poorly to your loud voice. That will likely not be the problem. Most of the time, volume problems happen because attorneys do not project enough. When the judge or the court reporter asks you to speak up, overcorrect and sustain the louder projection. When asked to "speak up, please," most lawyers project for a sentence or two, then quickly slip back into an inaudible volume.

Divide volume into two categories: projection and focus. Project enough voice or sound to create the right decibel level necessary for the courtroom. The steadier and stronger the flow of air from your lungs, the greater the decibels. To be heard, you also need to focus your voice toward the back wall behind the judge.

Often, when attorneys consult their notes too much, volume vacillates because the sound is not consistently focused on the same target. A noticeable volume change happens when the attorney looks up from the page and then speaks a line. The judge hears two different volumes because the attorney is delivering the words in two different directions. This volume vacillation is often accentuated with a podium microphone. If she turns her head toward the microphone, volume increases. If she looks away, volume decreases.

To correct volume vacillation with a microphone, do not rely on it to project your voice. If you rely on the microphone, you are likely to lean into the podium, placing your mouth too close to the microphone. This is hard to recover from—if you try to adjust and align your posture, now the judge cannot hear you. That leaves you hunched over and kissing the microphone. This is even more important during an oral argument when the lawyer must keep the voice projected consistently for all the justices, as she directs her voice to different justices.

Volume is one of the most common stylistic corrections given to an advocate by a judge. Think about how important this elemental piece of performance is—if the court cannot hear you, you might as well sit down.

Exercise

Before an argument, practice your opening out loud in a space that allows you to replicate the expected distance between you and the bench. If you struggle with projection, consider enlisting a colleague to sit in the judge's position, get their "live" feedback on volume, and adjust.

To increase volume safely, breathe with diaphragm support. When audiences cannot hear you, they will tune out. When you speak too loud, audiences will be annoyed or perceive that you are shouting at them.

Adjust volume using your diaphragm, controlling the inflow and exhale of breath that fuels your voice box. Make certain that you are using your diaphragm while breathing by placing your hand above your abdomen between your ribs. When you inhale, that area should expand; when you exhale, the area should return to normal. Practice changing and adjusting your volume; you will develop muscle memory and better regulate your volume based on the acoustical needs of the setting. Noticing when to adjust volume is critical. Watch for nonverbal cues from the court to help you know when to dial up or down. The table below outlines a few nonverbal cues to look for to know whether to turn up or down your volume. Watch for a combination of these context clues and pivot in the moment.

TURN IT UP	TURN IT DOWN
Judge asks basic questions about topics clearly covered.	Judge is reluctant to ask any questions.
Judge breaks contact completely and stops listening (checks cell phone or reads material).	Judge moves or shifts away from you.
Judge's facial expression shows frustration, confusion, strain, or boredom.	Judge's facial expression shows pain or annoyance.
Judge speaks to you in an overly projected voice.	Judge speaks to you in an overly quiet volume.

13.1.2 Articulation

Another barrier to clear comprehension for the judge is the lack of good articulation. An advocate must pronounce the words. Crisp consonants frame the vowel sounds, making them—and you—more confident and expressive. In contrast, when you mumble, the essential sound elements of the words glide together, and you appear shy, unconfident, and wavering. Enunciate clearly with crisp consonants. Practice aloud tricky words, especially names. Before your argument and out of earshot of anyone else, say each planned word of the first minute of your argument out loud over-stressing the consonants, stretching your face as you speak. This exaggeration exercise will warm up your facial and mouth muscles to speak more articulately during the argument.

Science: Avoid contractions. It is difficult sometimes to tell the difference between "can" and "can't" or "is" and "isn't," among other contractions. The judge hearing "is" rather than "isn't" may confuse him for long enough that your point is missed.

A note about accents: Accents should stay intact unless they impede the judge's ability to understand you. Clearly articulating the consonants will keep your accent in check.

13.1.3   Pitch

Singers classify themselves by voice part—soprano, mezzo, alto, tenor, baritone, and bass. To keep it simple, classify yourself as having a voice that is generally high pitched, medium pitched, or low pitched. Speak in the middle of your register. Good projection often raises the overall vocal pitch of certain speakers. If your voice creeps too high and you notice it, lower it slightly.

For the most part, judges prefer lower-pitched speaking voices, unless a voice is of such excellent quality they are drawn to listen to it. A high-pitched voice usually sounds whiny, shrieking, piercing, and diminutive.

Women generally have higher-pitched voices. Pay careful attention to overemphasizing words with a high-pitch stress. Men often speak in a low-pitched voice, subconsciously dropping into an even lower-pitched voice to sound more masculine and authoritative. The trouble with low-pitched voices is two-fold: they are harder to hear and can easily slip into a monotone drone.

An argument normally should be delivered with a tone of calm confidence. Keep your voice away from hysterical jumps that throw your voice in an unusual high pitch. Strike the right balance of keeping the interest of the court with proper stress on important syllables and avoiding sounding over-excited, nervous, or angry.

Exercise

Practice greeting the court with calm, warm confidence by finding your natural pitch.

"Good morning, Your Honors." First, say this sentence in an abnormally high pitch. Next, deliver the sentence in an abnormally low pitch. Finally, deliver it in the middle—the natural pitch of your voice.

13.1.4   Range

Range means the span of high to low notes you use when speaking. Once you know your own habitual pitch (generally high, medium, or low), notice whether you cover a wide range of pitches in a conversation or monologue. Actors use a wide range of notes—the wider the range, the more expressive a speaker sounds. A robot's "voice" would have a narrow range of notes, leaving it virtually monotone. If you find yourself bored or tired when listening to someone speak, they are probably displaying a narrow vocal range. This boring mode of speech dampens the audience's attention. A good attorney speaks with a wide range of pitches, accentuating his voice with high and low pitches as the moment demands. This pitch variation keeps the attention of the judge and helps communicate emotion.

Stretching your vocal range allows you to express emotion when you are making your presentation and helps keep the judge's interest. You may find you have a wider vocal range when standing, because most speakers take advantage of better breathing and posture in a standing position—it gives them the ability to reach higher and lower notes in their voice.

13.1.5   Inflection

Your voice should naturally stretch to different pitches, covering a range of notes. An attorney creates patterns of speech depending on when she causes her voice to fall in pitch at the end of clauses, phrases, and sentences. Imagine a "bossy voice," full of deflections in pitch at the end of each phrase. This voice barks a command with every descent in pitch. Now imagine someone who sounds insecure and uncertain about her position, questioning each phrase with an upward turn in pitch. In America, some call this repetitive pattern a "Valley girl" voice, "upspeak," or "upward inflection."

Properly used, *upward inflection* is the occasional upward tick in pitch at the end of questions or to keep attention in the midst of a series. It is imperative that you have the proper inflection and vocal descent to your voice when you end a declarative statement. There are several good reasons to raise your pitch at the end of a phrase:

1. To ask a question, even rhetorical.

2. In a series ("We requested emails, photographs, and copies of the contract." The voice should inflect in pitch at "emails" and "photographs," telling the listener that the series or list is not finished yet. The voice should fall in pitch at "contract," signaling to the judge that the series is complete.).

3. Before the conjunction of a compound sentence ("Mrs. Smith assaulted her neighbor, and then fled the scene." The voice should inflect in pitch on "neighbor.").

4. For specific emphasis.

Every speaking rule has exceptions. There are times when we purposely raise the pitch of the final syllable or word in a declarative sentence to signal irony or curiosity or frustration. ("Surely, the legislature did not intend that.")

Countless attorneys cannot properly inflect and descend in pitch. Sadly, improper upward inflection becomes a pattern for many speakers, even in court. Once it becomes a pattern, the voice lacks confidence and sounds insecure or patronizing.

Improper upward inflection patterns can be corrected by stressing the operative words in a phrase—the important words that deserve stress. You can train your voice to go up or down on syllables or entire words within and not at the end of a sentence. Put differently, for your voice to inflect confidently, inflect it up somewhere in a sentence so your voice can descend in pitch at the end of the sentence.

Exercise

Say: "I would like to go to the grocery store today." Inflect on the word *like*. Now inflect on *grocery* or *store*. Notice the difference in your inflection pattern.

13.1.6 *Speed*

Speed is where advanced advocacy takes flight. Crafting the pace of your delivery is essential to success, but balancing the fast and slow segments is an art. Shape the piece by using speed. There are several guideposts to speed that every attorney should know:

- Judges dislike super-slow speakers. First, he gets bored. Second, he feels like you are being condescending when the pace is too slow.

- Judges often get lost with fast speakers. If your pace is too fast, the judge is turned off. The rate of speech must be delivered at a digestible pace for messages to flow into the judge's mind. You also risk sounding over-rehearsed and robotic.

- Increasing your speed in a list or series makes it sound like you would have more facts to list if time permitted. Usually these faster phrases are ones that contain easy-to-understand facts, sections needing momentum, or a review section which you need to say but do not need to slow roll.

- If you have a chance to list a series of facts in your favor, speeding through them makes the judge think there are endless examples waiting in the wings. Slowly defining things makes them sound singular and finite.

- An argument should be delivered in the United States at an average of 150 to 160 words per minute.

13.1.7 Pauses

Pausing equals power. Imagine being in a courtroom with an attorney who speaks like a scared rabbit, covering time with needless fillers such as *uh, eh, ah*. Now imagine a different attorney, who projects confidence with silent moments. Pausing makes the listener wait for the speaker. It allows absorption time for the information just given. Pausing also cushions those words the attorney wants remembered. Pausing is essential.

Pauses are powerful during an argument. They allow the judge to hear more complexity because the attorney allows him to catch up. There should be natural breath breaks within any spoken delivery. In a breath mark, the attorney refuels the voice effortlessly for the next section of spoken text. Pauses can also be strategically positioned. Here are a few places where short pauses should be strategically placed:

- After you greet the court ("Good morning, Your Honor.").

- After you state your name.

- Between sections to transition.

- Before answering a question (this is your baseline pause).

- To set up a meaningful phrase or word.

13.1.8 Operative Words

Operative words are words stressed or accentuated to convey meaning. When you speak, you "make points" by stressing operative words. You can stress an important word by increasing your volume, pausing before a word, or an inflection change. Stressed words become the "operative words" in any sentence.

Exercise

Say the following sentence out loud: "Judge, Washington Bank will close the deal in October." Your voice determines the operative words in the sentence for the listener and depending on the word emphasized changes the meaning of the sentence. If timing is important, you would stress the word *October*. Say the sentence with that word stressed. If the finality of the deal is important, you could stress *close the deal*.

13.2 Body Language

Body language, used in concert with your well-crafted message and voice, is a powerful persuasion tool. Nonverbal communication includes your stance when delivering or seated posture at counsel's table. Body language nonverbally communicates

National Institute for Trial Advocacy

feeling and meaning. Body language areas covered in this book include home bases, movement, gestures, facial expression, and eye contact. Your posture, gestures, and facial animation should match the energy level of your message. Your body should appear connected to your words. The judge wants to pay attention, so do not be the speaker that makes him struggle to stay interested. Most of us know an acquaintance who acts so subdued in social situations that you wonder if they need an oxygen infusion to show some life. Keeping life injected into your delivery becomes easier when you focus on body language.

As you notice problems and set goals to correct, avoid telling yourself to simply stop the offending body language behavior. Instead, give yourself something better to do in its place. To improve body language, *replace* ineffective motion, posture, or activity instead of eliminating it. For example, if you want to stop randomly pacing back and forth, *replace* the pacing with deliberate movement at key moments at the hearing. If you want to stop an overused repetitive gesture, *replace* the gesture with specifically chosen and timed alternatives. If you want to correct an awkward brooding expression, *replace* it with an appropriate cheerful one.

We come in all shapes and sizes, with different energy levels and a variety of backgrounds. Because of this diversity, strive to feel natural in a way that is suitable for the courtroom. Here, body language needs to be professional, respectful, and polished while being yourself.

Improving body language can be hard for some advocates. Presenting a more confident appearance may feel fake or out of your comfort zone. Find the courage to stretch your comfort zone and you will see results. Research such as Amy Cuddy's inquiry into body language and the "power pose," which has been popularized by her well-known TED Talk,[3] proves that being more confident on the outside makes you actually more confident on the inside.

13.2.1   The Six Most Common Body Language Errors

CareerBuilder conducted a study using Harris Poll to survey a representative sample of hiring managers and human research personnel asking them to identify the most common body language errors during a job interview.[4] Here are the results:

---

3. Amy Cuddy, *Your Body Language Shapes Who You Are*, TED Talk, June 2012. Available at https:// www. ted.com/talks/amy_cuddy_your_body_language_shapes_who_you_are?language=en (last visited February 2, 2021). Cuddy's research was under attack after her TED talk. Since that time, she has scientifically proven that "the power pose" does make individuals feel more powerful. She now calls the phenomenon "postural feedback."

4. *The Most Unusual Interview Mistakes and Biggest Body Language Mishaps, According to Annual CareerBuilder Survey* (Career Builder study of 2,500 hiring managers), http://press.careerbuilder. com/2018-02-22-The-Most-Unusual-Interview-Mistakes-and-Biggest-Body-Language-Mishaps-According-to-Annual-CareerBuilder-Survey (last visited February 2, 2021).

- Failure to make appropriate eye contact (67 percent)

- Lack of smile (38 percent)

- Fidgeting too much (32 percent)

- Bad posture (31 percent)

- Crossing arms over chest (31 percent)

- Playing with hair or touching their face (26 percent)

- Using too many hand gestures (13 percent)

Attorneys make the same mistakes in arguments. We talk about these problems and others along with the body-language solutions below.

13.2.2 "Home Base"

Still positions taken between gestures are "home bases." Every attorney should find a few standing and seated home base positions, but first a word about posture. Good posture makes you look confident—in your argument and your client's position—and authoritative. It also increases your lung capacity, which improves the quality of your voice and sends more oxygen to your brain to concentrate and think.

Exercise

To improve your posture, stand with your back to a wall. Align ears, shoulders, hips, knees, and ankles in one straight line. Balance your weight equally on each leg. Now move from the wall, keeping the same alignment.

Now let's find some comfortable home bases. A home base is a calm posture from which gestures flow, allowing you to show passion and confidence. Notice your own home bases when you speak to friends and family. You likely have comfortable home bases already in your toolbox.

Actor's neutral (hands resting straight down on either side) and a torso hold (hands connecting at a height between belly button and belt) are staples. The others depend on your personality and body shape. A tall, imposing man may want to try a one hand in pocket home base during a discussion with the judge. A smaller-framed woman needs an elbows-wide, shoulders-back podium hold to look commanding in a courtroom.

We encourage you to always stand during your argument, but if you must sit, find a comfortable seated home base.[5]

---

5. We talk more about sitting postures in Chapter Fifteen.

> **Exercise**
>
> To find your seated home base, place both feet firmly on the floor forming a ninety-degree angle at the knees. Do not lean forward or back. Place your hands or your arms below the elbow on the table. Avoid tightly clasping your hands so there is no impediment to your gestures. Do not cross your arms at your chest.
>
> Once you find solid home bases, both standing and seated, practice transitioning in and out of each home base, eventually gesturing in and between these positions. Moving from base to base prevents you from looking like a statue.

For shorter hearings, you may notice that you only need one home base. If you plan on speaking for an extended time, a few home bases help break up the presentation for the judge and keep your body energized for the duration. Remember that audiences need a change approximately every three minutes. Sometimes a presentation will not have logical three-minute breaks in substance, but you can reset the judge's attention by changing your home base.

Below are some home bases that you should try while you read this book. You may have already incorporated some into your presentation style. Others may feel strange until you try them out. You may find that you already have a better one that suits your personality. If so, use it.

STANDING HOME BASES	
Hands resting on either side of a podium	This is formal. Have no tension in hands—do not grip the podium. Avoid looking like you are holding on for balance.
Actor's neutral	Keep body aligned, arms at side, chest lifted. Good position to reach after you have incorporated yourself into the arguments.
Hand in pocket	Personality and body-frame driven. It is generally more useful for men, because women's slacks rarely have pant pockets. This home base can purposely make you more approachable. Do not play with anything in your pocket, and use only one hand.
Hands clasped at mid-torso	Rest hands between belly button and belt. Do not clasp with tension. Keep arms relaxed.
Hand holding a prop	The prop can be a writing utensil or remote clicker/pointer. Be careful not to play with the prop or point it at the judge.
Standing to the side of a podium or table, with one hand resting on it	This is effective for a question and answer session, and/or to break up the monotony of a podium position. Some judges allow you to use this home base if you are passing documents or visuals to the bench and opposing counsel. Others allow this if you are close enough to touch the podium. Do not use this with judges who are sticklers for formality. Never use in an appellate court.

Decide on your home bases beforehand, so you know how you will stand and command the space during the hearing. Because most presentations occur behind a podium, practice the standing home base options discussed here at a podium.

Your available space at a podium is larger than you think. Imagine a triangular formation, with the tip of the triangle at the top of the podium, and the base of the triangle spanning behind you two to three feet. This is how much space you have to use in a hearing:

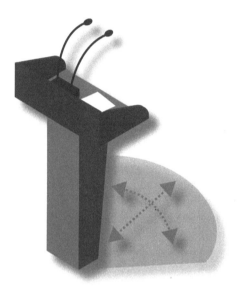

There are certain physical behaviors that should not be done in court. While there are a few exceptions to these prohibitions, do not try these in court:

- **Wonder Woman**—two hands on hips in a resting pose

- **The Angry Parent**—one hand on hips, the other with the pointer finger up, hips shifted toward the hand on the hip

- **Point**—hand gesture with pointer finger flexed forward at the judge or opposing counsel

- **Military rest**—hands behind back

- **Fig leaf**—hands clasped below beltline

- **Choir boy**—hands clasped at bust level

- **Podium avoidance**—it is not electrical, it will not shock you, interact with it at some point

- **Podium lean**—avoid lounging on and lunging at the podium

Do not confuse changing home bases with distracting movements during the hearing. Avoid swaying, rocking, and pacing.

Exercise

Choose a comfortable stance and place a piece of paper under one foot during a moot or practice session. See if the lodged paper keeps you grounded in the chosen stance and avoids the pacing habit.

Exercise

Stand up in front of a mirror. Do all the bad habits listed above, one at a time. Say goodbye to those positions. Now, find three comfortable home bases from the table provided, and practice moving in and out of all three.

Some advocates who rock back and forth find that placing feet slightly "pigeon toed" helps stabilize them. For attorneys who sway side to side, place one foot slightly in front of the other to prevent this frustrating movement.

13.2.3   Gestures

Your gestures should be fluid in court. They should match your message and intensity. They should, above all, match your personality. Gestures are a powerful tool, allowing you to bring the judge's attention to key points, move the plot forward, and leave the court with a memorable impression. Gestures also help advocates remember text. To memorize long presentations, add gestures and blocking (directions for the speaker where to move and stand) to help sear the performance in your mind.

Connect your gestures to your words. Imagine a bad actor trying to perform Shakespeare, throwing out random gestures a half-second behind the lines to be illustrated. This disconnected style is uncomfortable to watch and signals that the attorney is fearful or inexperienced.

What gestures should you use? Those that are productive and varied. Observe your natural gesticulation pattern. Notice what kinds of emphasis gestures you use, when you use them, and how wide they span in space. In a hearing, vary your gestures so they stay fresh and move the argument forward. If a judge remembers a repeated gesture (karate chopping the podium, wagging a pointed finger), you need to vary those movements. If the judge sees movements that help describe the text, the judge will understand better and remember more.

Gestures help bring the judge into the conversation. Everyone has a natural gesture size, frequency, and style. Understand your natural emphasis-gesture pattern to determine how many gestures should be added or removed from your repertoire.

A skilled advocate adds to their natural gesticulation pattern. To create a visual imprint in the judge's mind, a smart attorney uses the space in front of her to connect gestures with the substance of the delivery. There are natural and easy ways to connect gestures to the meaning.

- **Chronological.** When describing a timeline of events to the judge, use your hands to show the timeline and when certain events occurred. Keep the placement consistent. The rim of the podium offers a perfect sightline for the judge to see a horizontal timeline. This physical display of elapsed time can be a powerful way to show the court the impact of time. For example, if you are waiting for interrogatories, *showing* the judge how long you have waited while you tell him can make a huge impact.

  Tip: Show the past dates to your right, so the judge across from you sees the past on his left and the future on his right.

- **Compare and contrast.** When describing two different positions or courses of action, you can divide the space in front of you into two pieces. One position receives gestures placed on the left side, and the other position receives gestures placed on the right side.

  Tip: Once you set up a regime in space (the defendant's position discussed on the right, the plaintiff's on the left), keep all related gestures in the correct zone.

- **Enumeration.** When describing a short list of things, number the items both verbally and physically. You can number points on your hands or use the space in front of you.

  Tip: Try showing a foundational enumeration by starting low with a gesture, and showing each additional number at a higher level physically with your gestures.

- **Sensory.** Use showing gestures. Demonstrate the words you are describing. Make a small circle with your hand to show the court the *core* of your argument. Or if representing Humpty, illustrate with your hands the emanating light from the Holy Grail.

- **Problem, solution, next steps.** Some advocates take their hands and place the "problem" away from their bodies, then move the "solution" right in front of them, and finally use their fingers or hands to show an organized way to move forward. There is no one way for this system, and it will look more natural if it is not too choreographed.

Much has been written about the psychological effect of using gestures with palms facing down and gestures with palms facing up. In general, use palm-up gestures when you offer a suggestion to the court and ask for agreement. Use palm-down gestures when describing something that is not in dispute, something in the past, or something that has been decided.

Gestures signal your level of emotional control. Keep gestures smooth and completed in court. An attorney should avoid rapid-fire gestures, flailing gestures, or the huge or tiny gesture that looks out of place. Complete a gesture, hold it out there for a moment, and return to your home base. You know that your gestures are too many when the judge(s) moves backwards, shows surprise in his eyes, or exhales deeply, because the wild gestures usually put the court in an uncomfortable position. For an argument, keep your gestures within a controlled gesture box that extends from just below your chin down to the podium, and extending just beyond the width of the shoulders. When you do gesture, keep the hands heavy. Complete a gesture and return to a home base. Avoid repetitive, flailing, and super-sized gestures to be most effective.

Some hand motions, such as touching your face or eyeglasses, playing with hair, or fidgeting, become distracting for any audience, but look even more awkward in a formal court setting. To break a physical habit, you first have to be made aware of it. Before you are in front of a judge, take advantage of personal devices that allow you to record yourself mocking your argument. Try to set up your rehearsal space to mimic the courtroom, preferably with a podium and wearing courtroom attire. Watch your gesticulation patterns and see if you fidget. Ask for presentation-style feedback from trusted colleagues or friends, and specifically query whether you fidget when nervous or excited when speaking or listening. Enroll in a learning-by-doing CLE that provides coaching from professionals who can help you identify distracting habits. This feedback is invaluable.

13.2.4   Facial Expression

More and more research shows there are core universal facial expressions. Using the right facial expressions can be your most subtle and powerful way to convince a judge. Knowing how intensely you express emotion on your face will help you recognize when you need to tone down or amplify expression.

13.2.4.1   Resting Facial Expression: How to Find and Change It

Everyone has a resting facial expression. Some people maintain a grin when they are not talking or reacting to a speaker. Others maintain a perplexed look. Some settle into an aggressive expression. An attorney's resting facial expression gives the judge a first impression of the advocate. Video-recording yourself in presentation and listening modes will help you find your resting facial expression. A good friend or colleague can also shed light on your resting facial expression, so ask her.

Once detected, decide if it should be controlled or changed. If so, pick a neutral pleasant expression and continually remind your facial muscles to return to this newly identified pleasant expression. With enough muscular training, those facial muscles will respond to your newly picked resting facial expression when you speak to the judge.

13.2.4.2   Matching Facial Expression with Your Words

When you utter certain words and phrases, the facial expression needs to match the words spoken. Lead the judge with your facial expression. Do not mirror his. Your facial expression will direct the judge towards the right empathetic reaction. If you say, "My client is a respected member of his community," then you should have a proud expression on your face. If you say, "This injunction will ruin my client's business," then you should have a concerned expression on your face.

Smile during your introduction and when smiled at, to establish a connection with the judge. There are also hopeful, solution, and good-news moments in any argument when your facial expression should reflect the positive verbal message.

13.2.4.3   Poker Face and More

Sometimes, you need to hide emotion in a hearing. The judge or opposing counsel can be truly trying. Things do not always go your way. Train your facial muscles to a pleasant "poker face" to hide offensive emotions (anger, smugness, conceit, defensiveness) and/or defeat and weakness. To hide emotion, you must control not only your facial muscles, but your vocal tone and body language.

When a certain offensive emotion begins to creep into your psyche:

- Regulate your breath by taking even and effortless breaths,

- Avoid hitting high-pitch notes in your voice, and

- Keep your speed even—speaking too slowly can sound patronizing and/or seething mad, and speaking too fast can make you sound defensive, angry, or scared.

13.3   Make Genuine Eye Contact

Eye contact is powerful and moving. The judge senses when you actually look into his eyes and when you cheat, looking near or above his eyes. Keep eye contact with the judge until you complete a phrase, point, or section. Think about eye contact as a way to ensure you have explained yourself, and that the judge understands you. Glean information about your own messaging by the way the judge listens.

Eye contact needs to be handled sensitively. In general, keep eye contact with the judge 70 percent of the time. Hold eye contact with the judge for three to four seconds, or the completion of a thought. Give the judge breaks in eye contact by training yourself to look at notes or down and away instead of glancing up. Some listeners interpret an up-and-out eye pattern to mean lying or inventing information. This pattern can also make the advocate appear less intelligent. If you stare too long at the judge, you risk crossing into an uncomfortable zone. Instead, allow one another to look away, think, or let the judge take notes.

Sometimes, the judge is the one who avoids eye contact. If you cannot get the eye contact of the judge, make sure you are projecting your voice in his direction, change home base, and keep looking at the judge as if he is listening (the law clerk is probably watching).

Refining the physical performance end of your courtroom advocacy technique can be, in the beginning, overwhelming and feel a bit forced. Start slowly: choose just one stylistic habit at a time to replace or enhance. It may be awkward at first, but with repetition, these practices will soon become your new normal and feel natural. To inspire your development, take every opportunity you get to watch outstanding advocates whose courtroom performances you admire. Some advocates find it easier to learn new stylistic techniques by observing actors and politicians who often express themselves more intensely, like the excellent performance in 2015 by President Barack Obama in Charleston, South Carolina. The magnetic qualities these advocates possess combine into something we call the "It Factor," a topic we discuss in the next chapter.

Chapter Fourteen

The "It Factor"

Oprah Winfrey was born in Mississippi to a teenage mother. Because she could not support her child on her own, her mother brought little Oprah to Milwaukee and the two lived with Oprah's grandmother, Hattie Mae. While in Milwaukee, the family was so poor, young Oprah wore potato sacks to school, prompting mocking from the other children. At fourteen years of age, she moved to her father's home in Nashville, where she excelled in high school. She started her radio and television career in Nashville. She later moved to Baltimore to work for WJZ-TV where the management was unhappy with her for crying on television while reporting tragedy. They also were disappointed with her physical appearance, especially when she lost all her hair to a bad permanent.[1] She moved to Chicago and within months on AM Chicago, she garnered higher ratings than the then highest-rated Chicago show, *Donahue*. From there her rise skyrocketed. Among her many awards in her lifetime are *Time* magazine's one of the *Most Influential People of the 20th Century*, the Presidential Medal of Freedom, and the Cecil B. DeMille Golden Globe lifetime achievement award.

How does a person with such a challenging early life become arguably the best communicator alive? There is no way to explain it except she has the *It Factor*. Early in her career, *Time* magazine stated, "What she lacks in journalistic toughness, she makes up for in plainspoken curiosity, robust humor, and above all empathy."[2] *Newsday's* Les Payne said, "Oprah is wittier than Donahue, more genuine, and far better attuned to her audience . . . ." Phil Donahue said, "She makes people care because she cares."

All things being equal, certain attorneys rise to the top. They are just better. They are genuine. We trust them. We like them. We want to listen to them. The final ingredient needed to succeed is the *It Factor*. This is what separates good attorneys

---

1. George Mair, Oprah Winfrey: The Real Story, p. 46 (1995).
2. *Oprah Winfrey, Lady with a Calling*, Time (August 8, 1988).

from great attorneys. The *It Factor* can be broken down into conviction, confidence, trustworthiness, excellence, and connection. Here is how you can develop that special something.

14.1   Conviction: Believe in Your Case

Those who show conviction for their clients' causes move judges. Let the judge know that you believe in your argument. To show conviction:

- Deliver a confident introduction of yourself;

- Ask the court for relief within the first ninety seconds;

- Use a theme that allows you to show enthusiasm for your cause;

- Keep eye contact with the court; project your voice so you can be clearly heard;

- Deliver your sentences with a descent in pitch at the last syllable of the phrase, and stress the right syllables with passion;

- Stand tall and control your movement, communicating with your body that you are strong in your stance;

- Use powerful gestures, although limitedly;

- Emphasize with pausing and volume changes, the most important information the court needs to rule for your client; and

- Refrain from saying, "I believe," "I think," or "I feel." Instead say, "this is the law," or "the facts are these." Do not couch your argument in language that sounds like your opinion. Just say it.

Judges steel their resolve to rule in your favor from you. If you do not believe in your case, neither will the judges. Show you have confidence in your position; your enthusiasm will be contagious.

Conviction in the righteousness of your cause does not mean rabid zealotry. Do not appeal merely to the emotions of the case. Neither must you discount summarily the other side's argument as if it is so weak it does not deserve your attention. After arguing your strengths, consider the other side's position—and then crush it with logic.

Being real is more important than being slick. Judges connect with the technically imperfect argument from the passionate, albeit clumsy, attorney more than the silky-smooth, technically perfect attorney.

> **Exercise**
>
> Watch the ten-minute YouTube video of Oprah Winfrey's acceptance speech for the Cecil B. DeMille award in 2018 in the middle of the *MeToo* movement.[3] Whether you believe in her cause or not, ask yourself, does she believe in it? What makes you think so? What does she do to convince you of that? Notice the strength she exudes with the lack of movement of her body. Notice that her facial expressions match the content of her message; at one time she was so touched that she looked like she was about to cry. See how she connects to her audience through eye contact and stories the audience can see. Watch when she puts her left hand in a fist. Listen for her pauses, and when she slows down her speech and speeds it back up. Listen for the changes in her volume. Is her enthusiasm contagious?
>
> Now record yourself talking about a topic that you are passionate about. What techniques do you use to show your conviction? Use your insights gained with this exercise to develop your own style.

14.2   Confidence: Conquer Your Nerves

Great attorneys appear confident. Most attorneys, even the greatest, tackle nerves. When an attorney is not nervous, he does not care, and his argument suffers. A large part of appearing confident is controlling the nerves. Learn how to take charge of your nervousness.

The stress of arguing is real and crippling at times. Adrenaline generally spikes during the first minute of any public-speaking event. That minute is charged with adrenaline. The adrenaline gives the speaker energy and natural presence, but it can also be visibly inhibiting. An argument is full of high-stakes nerves. The judge will naturally feel sorry for the advocate who has severe hand shaking, or who forgets all the words in his head and is dumbstruck. But this is not the sympathy we want as attorneys. We do not want the judge to feel sorry for us. We want to persuade the judge to rule in our favor.

Each advocate should discover his personal, psychosomatic reactions to nerves, then find a technique to control, mask, and, at times, combat it. Most of us need to focus on controlling these "nervous tells" for the first sixty seconds of an adrenaline rush. Certainly, nervous tells can creep into a presentation midstream, but most advocates can sense this happening and control it.

---

3. https://www.youtube.com/watch?v=TTyiq-JpM-0.

The ending of a presentation is different. Many attorneys reach the end of their presentation and begin a relentless attack of self-doubt. To finish quickly, the attorney ends up throwing away the impact of the ending, rushes through the final remarks, and quickly sits down. Use techniques listed below for the nerves that hit at the beginning, but also at the end if the editor in your mind hinders your ability to finish strong. Once you know your nervous tells, you can overcome them with proper techniques.

Most attorneys have a place where their tension resides. Many contract their jaw muscles or hands, for example. Video-record yourself giving your ninety-second beginning and look for your tension areas. Once you identify them, work on relaxing those areas when you speak. If you notice that you hold tension in your jaw, massage your jaw joint and facial muscles before presenting. If your hands show nerves, stretch them before and during a communication. Use a video-recorder to see if this works. Keep "air between your fingers" as you gesture, so your hands look relaxed. This will also help prevent you from wringing your hands if that is your tic. Another trick to release hand tension is to contract the hand muscles in a fist, then release the tension. Doing this "tense and release" technique moments before beginning the hearing can channel adrenaline and release the nerves building in that area. You can also use this tense and release exercise for your jaw and face by scrunching your facial muscles, then relaxing. (Best to do this in the courthouse bathroom away from opposing counsel and your client.)

If you think you are the only person with nervous tics, think again. Below are common vocal, body language, and other miscellaneous problems we have not yet talked about, with short-term and long-term advice about how to fix them.

14.2.1 Vocal Problems

- **Supersonic speed.** A common result of a case of nerves is breaking the sound barrier with the speed of your voice. If you are constantly being told to slow down your speech, be a slave to punctuation. As you speak, take a silent pause at all commas, periods, and transitional phrases. In the long term, use a metronome or metronome application such as Pro Metronome to regulate your speed to 155 beats per minute or 4:1 on the metronome setting.

- **Filler and qualifier words.** Filler and qualifier words are meaningless utterances that replace silence. "Um, er, like, so, you know, right, okay," and qualifiers such as "like, so, you know, sort of, kind of" sprinkled in our sentences steal the focus from the message and place it onto our verbal tics. Fillers and qualifiers reduce credibility. The first step to getting rid of these gremlins is to recognize them in your speech. Record yourself speaking. Replay and count the number and type of fillers or qualifiers you use. Or ask your friend or colleague to alert you each time you use a filler. Usually these throw-away words come into your speech in place of punctuation. Try pausing or taking a breath where the punctuation should be. Go back to grade school and write your favorite filler word in pen on your hand to remind you to cut it out of your speech. In the long term, train yourself to compress your thumb and forefinger on one hand every time you reach a punctuation mark. As you gently squeeze your finger, take a breath.

- **Loss of breath control.** If you find yourself running out of breath as you speak, before you stand up, tip your head down and yawn with your mouth closed to open up the throat muscles that control the voice box. When approaching the podium, use silent sighs to rush breath out. Between questions, take a short pause before answering. In the long run, train yourself to immediately speak after you inhale.

- **Quivering voice.** Practice breathing from your diaphragm. Practice tongue twisters. As you stand to deliver your argument, tip your chin and yawn with your mouth closed to stretch out your throat and release the tension in those muscles. When you hear yourself quiver, slightly lower your pitch and increase your volume.

- **Tightening of throat at the top of the neck and back of the mouth, causing a tense and strained tone to the voice.** Long term: Practice singing fast-paced songs with low-high skips and repeatedly stretch the back of the mouth and top of the throat with a closed mouth and a deep yawn. Short term: As you stand to deliver the argument, tip your chin and yawn with your mouth closed to stretch out your throat and release tension in those muscles. Start with a slightly lower pitch.

14.2.2 Body Language Problems

- **Posture collapse.** Pick a starting "home base" and practice your beginning at that home base every time you rehearse the argument. Practice strengthening your overall posture and stance so a habit of good alignment is formed.

- **Shaking hands.** Flex opposite muscle groups (if your hands begin to shake, flex muscles in your legs or buttocks). Start the hearing by holding a prop (pen or eyeglasses). Choose a starting home base that rests your hands on either side of the podium. Do a finger-tension exercise.

- **Fidgeting (hair flipping, wardrobe adjustments, pen clicking, coin jingling).** Use a prop to focus your nervous energy. Plan specific gestures that you synchronize with prechosen words. Write these in the margins of your notes. Practice your argument using heavy hand gestures that are contained and move slowly. Control any physical distractions (long hair in face, pocket full of coins). Empty your pockets. Choose a hairstyle that reduces the temptation to fidget with your hair, and consider pinning back your hair to avoid being distracted by your own locks.

- **Eyes that drift/roll up and out.** Train yourself to look down (almost pretending to consult notes). Sweep eyes down to your page, capture a line of text, reconnect with the judge, and deliver the text. Do not speak to your notes.

14.2.3 *Other Problems*

- **Foggy brain and/or forgetfulness.** Memorize the first and last five lines cold, until you can do it in your sleep. Consider memorizing transitional lines between sections.

- **Nausea.** Eat a low-acidic meal and consult your doctor for anti-acid medications, if needed.

- **Sweating face.** In the morning before the hearing, apply a clear, mattifying, sweatproof primer makeup.

- **Racing heartbeat.** Long term: Practice breath regulation exercises and audible, deep "sighs." Short term: On the day of the hearing, slow down to a methodical, slow saunter using deep breaths. When nerves start, exhale on a loud, audible sigh (in private). As you stand to deliver the argument, sigh silently as you approach the podium, have a glass of water at the edge of counsel's table ready if needed, breathe regularly with easy inhalation (do not take huge, deep breaths). Take an extra moment to settle yourself and your notes at the podium.

- **Lack of smile.** Facial muscles can be trained, just like other muscles in the body. If you discover you have facial expression freeze as an aftershock of nerves, rehearsing your opening again and again and again, video-recording yourself and watching it back to correct, is essential. This comes down to good old-fashioned hard work.

- **Red face and neck.** Through repetition, you can lower nerves in the long term which sometimes, but not always, helps dermatological tells. If you know you flush, pick courtroom attire which will hide the areas which usually flush (e.g., a turtleneck, tie, or scarf) if your neck turns red.

14.3 Trustworthiness

Judges need to know that they can rely on what you tell them. If you are not to be believed, you cannot convince. Great lawyers know that their word is their bond. It takes a lifetime to develop a trustworthy reputation and one blunder to destroy it. Lawyers talk to one another and to judges. The word quickly gets around if you are not to be believed.

Your credibility will be judged by more than simply your courtroom behavior. As Oprah says, "Real integrity is doing the right thing, knowing that nobody's going to know whether you did it or not."[4] We could spend chapters talking about making and maintaining a good reputation. For purposes of this book, here are some courtroom-credibility busters:

- Do not quote a case out of context. When the judge or his clerk reads the case, and they will, your credibility takes a hit.

- Even if your opponent does not cite a case that really hurts your client, cite it and then distinguish it.

- Do not use hyperbole. Avoid words like "always, clearly, never, all."

- Do not exaggerate the facts of the case. Be precise. A prepared judge will immediately correct you, embarrassing you and wasting your precious argument time.

- Do not overstate, period. If you do or if you misspeak, own it. Even if time has elapsed, stop and address the mistake. "Your Honor, I misspoke earlier, I stated the tolling period was four years. I misspoke; I should have said two years."

- Do not talk about evidence that is not contained in the record.

14.4   Excellence: Do Your Homework

Oprah had it right when she said, "Even if you are flippin' fries at McDonalds, if you are excellent, everybody wants to be in your line."[5] Strive for excellence. Excellence takes preparation and practice. Be honest with yourself about the preparation and work you will need.

Every letter, brief, or motion you write reflects on you. When your documents contain misspellings, grammatical errors, or flawed arguments, judges know what to expect of you orally—not very much.

We spent several chapters on preparation and practice for good reason. The hard work of researching, developing your best, simplest, and most concise arguments, and practicing them, is how you get the judge to stand in your line.

---

4. Oprah Winfrey Quotes. BrainyQuote.com, BrainyMedia Inc, 2020. https://www.brainyquote.com/quotes/oprah_winfrey_386951, accessed November 17, 2020.
5. Oprah Winfrey Quotes. BrainyQuote.com, BrainyMedia Inc, 2020. https://www.brainyquote.com/quotes/oprah_winfrey_757307, accessed November 17, 2020.

14.5 Connection: Get Out of Your Own Head and Build Rapport

In the competitive legal arena, most attorneys have the legal acumen and proper level of experience to adequately, and perhaps superlatively, provide legal services. Yet clients gravitate to the attorney they connect with—those with a good "deskside" manner. The smartest attorney is not always the best attorney. Having brains does not mean you are a good communicator; being brilliant does not guarantee success. To be successful in an argument, attorneys need to connect with the judge. Judges like positive, honest, confident, generous attorneys. Civility does not just sound nice—it increases your overall rapport with the court. Once the judge connects with you, it is harder for her to rule against you. She may still rule against you, but you want to make her think twice about doing it.

Rapport begins with your greeting to the judge. Be warm and engaging. This does not mean you need to be oozing with friendliness or flattery. It means you look professional, energized, and grateful to have the time with the judge.

Connecting with the judge requires knowing your audience and using that knowledge to your advantage.[6] Empathize with the judge. Let the judge know that you realize that her decision is difficult. Phrases like, "I understand your concerns," or "I had the same initial thoughts" convey that you appreciate her quandary. Show her that you are a partner whose job is to assist her in the task. Use inclusive language—"we are here to . . ." or "our job today is . . ." Even so, remember that you are not an equal partner in the relationship. Show the judge respect. Follow her rules. Call her "Your Honor" or "Judge Diaz." Do not lecture to her as if you are her superior and she is your underling.

Avoid extreme conclusions or positions, as they are not even considered by the court. Of course, "too extreme" is determined according to the facts and law of each case. Should you realize your position is too extreme mid-hearing, with the preauthorization of your client, retreat to your fallback position.

Avoid smugness, conceit, or sarcasm. Acting like a snob, bragging about your greatness, and finding flaws in others rarely increases your connectivity. Likewise, be chivalrous with your opponent. The rules of engagement are: no interruptions, insults, sour facial expressions, scoffs, or verbal attacks. Judges know that attorneys who are forever critical of others will be critical of them outside their presence. Do not say, "Counsel is lying." A better choice is to say, "Your Honor, I do not think that is quite right . . . I would refer you to Exhibit 8, which shows that counsel did not respond until one year after the request." Facts are always more convincing.

To build rapport with the court, do not self-deprecate. Self-deprecation from an intelligent, successful attorney usually comes across as false humility. Instead, heartily laugh at yourself when you actually fall on your face. Mistakes are not always terrible.

---

6. All the lessons learned in Chapter Two: Know Your Audience: The Judge(s) apply here.

Honest stumbles sometimes provide you the chance to pause and restabilize, a chance to laugh at yourself, a chance to show the court that you are human, a chance to connect with the judge.

The number one piece of advice for developing rapport with the court is to watch and listen to the judge. You have prepared your key arguments making them logical and succinct. You have responses to the counterarguments. You have prepared useful and helpful notes to rescue you when you falter. You have done everything right. Do not beat yourself up because you could have spent more time doing this or that. There will never be enough time. During the argument, shut off the editor in your mind that criticizes your performance blow-by-blow. Instead, concentrate on the judge and her needs.

The argument is the time to enjoy the fruits of your labor. Remain in the moment. Watch for and listen to the judge's reactions. Notice how the judge relates to you. Notice if she is slightly leaning toward or away from you when you argue a point. Listen to the tone of her voice—is it warm or cold when you are speaking? Listen to the deeper concern implied in the judge's questions. When she talks about a case asking you to distinguish it, is she begging you for a plausible differentiation? Or is she not convinced with your explanation?

How is the judge responding to the opposing counsel? How is the court receiving his arguments? What subtle body language and facial reactions does the judge have when your opponent argues? Connect with the judge. Get out of your own head. When you see that a point is not landing, pivot. Trust yourself.

14.5.1 *Learn to Act*

Learning to act expands your ability to express the right emotion. The right dose of emotion can often win the day over a well-reasoned, but stiffly presented, argument. Where appropriate, your smart choice during a hearing could be an appeal to humanity, a gesture of friendship, an empathetic tone, a frustrated expression, a brusque challenge, or a combination of these emotions.

Before you weave the right emotions into a hearing, you need a firm foundation to support your credibility. For an attorney, this foundation is rapport with the judge. Any emotion you portray is built on that connection. If you fail to establish a certain rapport with the judge, you run the risk of being seen as a fake, a charlatan. Be perceptive enough to sense the emotional needs of the judge. You know the moment is right in your gut. Acting trains you to display the right emotion at the right time and to transition between emotions during the argument.

Emotions and attorneys are not always the best of friends—finding the right pathos is an afterthought for some attorneys. The fact is that attorneys who have a reputation for being "hard to work with" often lack the desire or skills needed to act. They do not play nice. They force their instinctive emotion on everyone around them instead of responding with reserved emotion or civility.

When actors perform on stage, they transmit emotions across a wide space in an auditorium to the audience. When an actor acts in a movie, the emotional changes are more subtle and understated because the camera is often at close range. An attorney delivering an argument should be in between—like a stage actor, large enough to be seen; like a film actor, showing emotional subtleties, not exaggerated emotional displays intended to reach the folks in the third balcony. You are hired to think reasonably. Your emotions must be reasonably displayed. Avoid the extremes—weakness, bossiness, abrasiveness, and hysterics.

When you try new emotions and inject acting techniques into your presentation, concentrate on the transitions from one emotion to another. Most attorneys fail to make smooth transitions to the next emotion (e.g., moving from the friendly greeting to the serious tone needed to deliver the theme in the next section). When you practice delivering your argument, rehearse the transitions. If you can smooth these out, the argument will flow with proper pathos. Use the words of your transitional phrase to change from one emotion to another by delivering the transitions with a matter-of-fact tone. Use the transition line as a blank slate between two differently toned sections.

14.6   Be Yourself

Most importantly, you must be genuine. This requires that you know your personality and transmit it sincerely to the judge. A judge can smell a fake from a mile away, so be yourself. Be true to who you are. Find your own authentic style by watching others, incorporating bits of their style into yours, and practicing. Oprah became Oprah by being and practicing Oprah.

CHAPTER FIFTEEN

PRACTICE YOUR ARGUMENT EARLY AND OFTEN

At the end of the 2011 NBA finals, the last shot Lebron James took was a hopeful, twenty-five-foot jumper from the edge of the right wing. It was an inefficient and low-percentage shot. He missed. They lost. The following summer, Lebron James spent three entire months perfecting one type of shot, an efficient shot that he felt would be the difference at the end of high-stake games. It was a post-up jumper down at the left block. He spent three months perfecting this shot that would marginally increase his team's chances of winning. Fast forward a year later, Lebron James is holding the 2012 NBA championship trophy along with a 2012 Finals MVP. The one shot made the difference. As his coach, Erik Spoelstra, confirmed: "I don't know if I've seen a player improve that much in a specific area in one off-season. His improvement in that area alone transformed our offense to a championship level in 2012."[1]

If you were to tell any NBA basketball player that, like Lebron James, they could increase their number of wins by 20 percent by adding just one shot to their toolbox, they would practice that shot endlessly in order to achieve mastery. So, when a self-poll of three Eighth Circuit Court judges revealed that oral arguments changed the mind of a judge in 20 percent of cases, the logical conclusion is to master the art of oral advocacy.[2] What do Lebron James and oral advocacy have in common? To put it concisely, proficiency in oral advocacy is the equivalent of Lebron James's post-up shot. Oral advocacy is the legal "jumper" you need to perfect to win your championship—your case.

---

1. https://grantland.com/features/how-lebron-james-transformed-game-become-highly-efficient-scoring-machine/ (March 29, 2013).
2. "[The] judges concluded that oral argument changed their mind in 31%, 17%, and 13% of the appeals, respectively. Similar anecdotal evidence from other federal judges indicates oral argument changed their preliminary views in about 20% of the cases." Jerry Madden, *In Defense of Oral Argument in the Federal Circuit Courts of Appeals* (Mar. 11, 2020). Available at https://www.themaddenlawgroup.com/in-defense-of-appellate-oral-argument-in-the-federal-circuit-courts-of-appeals (last visited February 2, 2021). We are mindful that lawyers and judges have long debated the question of how often oral arguments change the outcome of the case. That said, most judges opine that an argument clarifies their thinking and often changes the way they write their opinion. Although oral arguments may not alter the result in the majority of cases, if your client's case is in that universe where the oral argument matters, it behooves you to practice.

You will never improve without practice. There is no substitute for practicing your argument aloud. Neither thinking about nor writing your argument compares. You must get on your feet and rehearse. Every time you step into a courtroom, you will improve. Unfortunately, for many attorneys, courtroom work is sparse. To keep up your skills, let alone increase them, you must practice.

Find every opportunity to rehearse alone, with a friend, or in a formal moot. Watch expert advocates and read transcripts of their arguments. Incorporate the winning techniques that mesh with your style. Adjust, incorporate, and refine until you find your own unique style.

Break down the skills you wish to improve into bite-size pieces. Drill component parts of your argument. Mimic Lebron James, who repeatedly performed individual skills—his jumper, free throws, dribbling. Throughout the book, we have incorporated exercises designed to improve one skill at a time from simplifying the law to compressing your opening. We gather these exercises together in the appendix.

In this chapter, we layer on additional ideas for how best to practice. We recognize that some recommendations in this chapter may be overkill for the typical motion hearing, but as the complexity and significance of your case increases, you may find these approaches worth the time and money. To become the Lebron James of oral arguments, only high-quality practice will get you there.

15.1   Practice Early

As soon as you are assigned a case, practice saying aloud the name of your client, the other parties, and the names of the witnesses. Repeat tongue-twisting names until you can pronounce them with ease. Say them to your administrative assistant, your colleagues, or to yourself. Even if the case never ends up in a courtroom, a misspoken name could lose you the confidence of your client.

Do the same with case names and legal terms. Do not walk into a court uttering *vor dyer* when the accepted pronunciation in that court is *vwar deer*. Or *Daubear* instead of *Daubert*. Little mistakes pick away at your credibility.

15.2   Practice Alone

Practice alone. The exercises we suggest in the book are ideal for your individual practice.

Rehearse in front of a mirror. Watch your gestures. Try out new ones that support your points. As you watch your reflection in the mirror, notice your facial expressions. Put on your neutral, enthusiastic, or serious face. See how these expressions look and feel, and then practice matching your words and sections of the argument with an appropriately matched facial expression.

Utilize the tools available in the digital age. Bring out your cell phone or tablet and video-record yourself speaking your argument. Force yourself to listen and watch the recording. Doing so can be painful. Your natural inclination will be to avert your eyes and micro-criticize the sound of your recorded voice or a body part that bothers you on camera. Avoid this destructive cycle. Use watching yourself on video as an opportunity to identify things you can fix—and we do not mean dropping twenty pounds. Seeing your errors helps build self-awareness, and is the first step toward improving.

Practice your argument in the shower, in the car, or in your office. Put in your earbuds and pretend to be talking on the phone while rehearsing on the subway or walking down the sidewalk. No one will know the difference.

Practicing alone has advantages. No special arrangements need to be made. You will maintain your friends. However, you still need the valuable feedback from others to get better.

15.3   Practice with a Colleague, Partner, or Friend

You will never improve without a good dose of humility. Constantly ask for feedback and welcome critique. Search for friends and colleagues who will give you an honest, unvarnished appraisal of your performance—ideally, ones who are skilled at constructive criticism. Pick friends who know the exercise is about you and not them. Put on your thickest skin.

Your practice sessions can be informal. Pull your administrative assistant aside and ask him what he thinks about an idea you have. Ask a colleague to give you ten minutes to react to a snippet of your argument. Any time you can say a portion of your argument aloud, you will improve.

Formal practice sessions are even more productive. Set up an uninterrupted time for you to practice and for your colleague(s) to critique you. If you are practicing a motion hearing and more than one colleague can attend, assign one person to be the judge and ask questions. If you are preparing for an oral argument, try to collect a few colleagues together to replicate a multi-panel court, and encourage them all to ask questions. Present your argument as you would to a court, and do not slip out of character. Depending on the importance of the argument, allow sufficient time to first deliver your short script uninterrupted, hear critiques, then present again with questions. If you are with a team of colleagues working on the case, assign one of your co-counsel to portray opposing counsel and deliver their best arguments. You can provide a brief background to colleagues pretending to be the judge(s), but make sure one of the judges has not read or heard anything about the case to optimize the moot.

Afterwards, lead your friends in a structured download of the argument. Encourage them not to hold back on their comments. Accept criticism graciously, thanking them for their insights. Do not be defensive. Be appreciative even with the remarks you believe are unfair. With even the slightest hint of anger, sadness, or hostility from you, the discussion will end. Keep your emotions hidden. You will have time to reflect on their comments afterwards.

Ask about your theme—did it work? Does it convey the essence of your argument? Was it too corny? Too obscure? Invite discussion on your arguments. Have them repeat your two or three strongest arguments back to you. If there was a disconnect, why? What can you say to explain your points more clearly? Were there places in your argument where you lost their interest? Where? How did you do, answering their questions? Did your tone encourage or discourage questions? Were they satisfied with your answers? If not, why not? Ask them what relief you want. Were they able to tell you? Are they convinced that you should win? Why or why not?

Ask about the style of your delivery. How was your posture? Were there any movements you made that distracted them? What were those movements? Did you maintain eye contact? What gestures were effective? What gestures did not work? Could they hear you? Was your voice interesting? Did you talk too slow or too fast? Did you take pauses? Did you look confident? Were you conversational?

Sit back and listen to the feedback you receive. Recalibrate your argument considering the suggestions.

15.4 Visualize

Practicing by doing is necessary to improve your skills, and after you have sufficiently practiced, it is time to visualize the argument. Studies have found that all individuals can use visualization to improve performance and increase confidence. Elite athletes, musicians, and surgeons have long used this technique. Visualization is taking your mind to your future performance, imagining yourself in the concert hall flawlessly performing your violin solo, seeing yourself seamlessly winning your tennis match, or perfectly arguing your case. The better an individual's imagery ability, the more improvement in the performance.

To effectively visualize, you must see, hear, and feel yourself in the argument. Go to the courtroom. Look at the placement of the lectern. What material is it made of? What color is it? How high is it? How wide? What does the podium feel like? Is there a clock or timer? Where? How far is the lectern from the bench? What do the bench and its background look like? Will there be one judge or more for your argument? What order will they sit? Notice as much as you can about the courtroom. Get comfortable being there.

Watch an argument. Learn the judges' voices, mannerisms, and questioning styles. The more you notice and can re-create in your mind, the better the visualization will work for you.

After your field trip to the court, visualize your argument. Go to a quiet place and shut your eyes. See the judges on the bench, you at the podium, and your opponent at counsel's table. Picture what you will wear. Visualize your opening comments, the questions asked, your answers, and your closing. Try to conjure up the perfect presentation. When you falter, redo that portion of the argument. Envision your argument as many times as you can before the real one.

Visualization is especially valuable before sleep, as sleep hits the save button on your memory.[3] Continue your imagery until the morning of your argument. Your proficiency will escalate and your confidence soar.

15.5   The Moot Court

A moot court is a test drive before the actual argument. Counsel argues his case before a judge or panel of judges simulating the actual argument. We differentiate a moot from casually practicing before your friends and colleagues, as a moot is a more formal process using panelists not involved in the case, not related to you, and ideally, familiar with the judges before whom you will appear.

Mooting before an argument is a safeguard to ensure you are prepared. Pressure to be polished in front of colleagues motivates the procrastinator. For that reason, creating a mooting schedule will serve to properly prepare the litigant, especially for an oral argument which generally allows for a longer preparation runway. You need to set aside enough time to prepare and practice. Leading up to a moot, you should do the following:

- Time permitting and ideally, eight weeks before the moot, review all briefs and/or appeal papers. Identify the legal theory, factual theory, and theme for your argument. Seven weeks before the moot, create a long and short script, and boil the short script into bullet points.

- Six weeks before the moot, create a crib sheet of your cases, statutes, and regulations upon which you will rely in the argument or the other side is likely to raise.

- Five weeks before the moot, prepare a rebuttal checklist.

- Four weeks before the moot, anticipate questions and prepare responses.

- Three weeks before the moot, rehearse, being keenly aware of the time constraints.

This systematic preparation equips you with the tools you need to maximize the utility of the moot.

---

3. *See* MATTHEW WALKER PhD, WHY WE SLEEP: UNLOCKING THE POWER OF SLEEP AND DREAMS (Scribner, 2017).

The time and expense of a moot may be justified depending upon the importance of the issue or case. While moots are more common in appellate arguments, they are often used in complex motion hearings where significant money or jail time is at stake. Legal teams can use internal moot participants to play the judge(s), or they can hire professionals such as retired judges or consultants.

Moot courts provide an opportunity to practice your argument, receive constructive criticism, and refine your presentation. Moots may also lay bare the weaknesses in your case—weaknesses you had increasingly ignored as time solidified your passion and conviction for your case.

Choosing your moot judges may be the most important part of a moot court. Hire retired judges from the court who know the thinking patterns, ideology, and questioning habits of the judges who will hear your actual argument. If utilizing a retired judge is impossible, then choose disinterested lawyers (internal colleagues or externally hired) who are tough questioners, have experience with the judges who you will appear before, and have no stake in the outcome. Use at least one expert in the area of law you are arguing. The expert will ask deeper and more challenging questions and her presence allows you to practice the dolphining technique we highlighted in Chapter Six: The Law.

Before the moot, give the panelists both parties' briefs so they can develop the challenging questions you expect. Tell the panelist you wish them to ask difficult questions; one of the greatest benefits of a moot is to anticipate the questions asked. A good moot argument should anticipate all the questions from the panel except the occasional off-the-wall ones.

Hold the moot in a setting that closely approximates a courtroom. If your institution, department, or firm does not have a dedicated moot court room, then set up your own. Invest in a podium or table-lectern. Have the same number of panelists as you will have in court. Place the panelists in a position that replicates the position of the judges as closely as you can. Have the panelists each assume a role of one of the judges before whom you will argue.

Moots are most beneficial if they are held close to the argument, but not so close that the attorney does not have the time to modify the argument based upon the panel's suggestions. Depending on the importance of the hearing, several moots may be performed, with adjustments made each time, continually sharpening the substance and style. It is ideal to finish the final moot one week before the argument so that you have time to practice all you have gleaned from the constructive feedback.

You, your co-counsel, and the panelists should be present for the argument. You must decide whether to have your client there—the upside is that your client will learn the weaknesses of his case, and he will see you in action. The downside is that you will not be as polished as you will be for the real hearing, and the client will need to be warned that this is a work in progress.

Assign a colleague to play opposing counsel; ideally, pick someone who argues similarly to the lawyer who will be arguing against you in court. As the appellee, having an opposing counsel allows you to practice beginning your argument where the opponent left off and using the judges' questions as a trampoline into your strengths. Time and money may be the determinative factors.

At the moot, all parties must stay in role. Approximate the argument as much as possible. If you do not know the answer to a question, say you do not know. Afterwards you will have the time to plan the answer. The exercise is primarily about learning the tough questions so you can best answer them when it counts. Professionals who run moot courts and consultants who coach lawyers know when to stop the moot and fix something that cannot wait for the final discussion session.

The moot will last longer than the actual argument; often by many multiples. However, a panelist should let the attorney know when the argument would have ended. This gives the attorney the awareness of how short the real argument will be and the necessity of brevity.

Videotape the argument. Review it after the moot to incorporate your own feedback into your renovated argument.

Immediately after the mock hearing, debrief. Allow each panelist to critique your performance. Listen with openness. After all panelists have completed their comments, ask questions. Pick the panelists' brains. Learn how they think each judge will receive your arguments.

You may receive conflicting advice from the judges. Let the judges try to resolve their differences. If they cannot reconcile the disparate views, you should after the moot. Advocacy is an art, not a science. Often times, different reactions help you thread the needle on a multi-judge panel and sharpen your argument.

Integrate into your argument the feedback given. Make your answers more concise. Develop better transitions. Learn from the traps you fell into. Use the themes that emerged.

15.6   The Evaluation Form for Moots and Other Practices

Using these forms may stimulate discussion with your judges in your moot or your friends in a more informal practice session.

PREPARED SUBSTANCE CHECKLIST	
Delivered a memorable theme(s)	☐
Told judge(s) relief or action needed	☐
Tied the requested relief with the cause of action	☐
Provided a road map with two or three succinct arguments	☐
Concisely recounted only the necessary law and facts	☐
Presented public policy argument	☐
Knew the record	☐
Organizational structure was easy to follow; strongest argument first	☐
Welcomed questions	☐
Effectively answered questions	☐
Used questions to advantage	☐
Transitioned from answers to strong points	☐
Empathized with judge's concern	☐
Chose a pathway for explanations	☐
Appealed to the concerns of the court	☐

VOICE CHECKLIST	
Regulated breath	☐
Used good vocal quality	☐
Projected voice	☐
Articulated clearly	☐
Controlled inflection	☐
Used appropriate overall pace	☐
Varied speed for meaning	☐
Paused effectively	☐
Exhibited varied range	☐
Stressed operative words	☐
Monitored qualifier patterns	☐
Avoided fillers	☐

BODY LANGUAGE CHECKLIST	
Aligned posture	☐
Used confident home bases	☐
Gestured for emphasis	☐
Used substantive gestures	☐
Avoided repetitive gestures and fidgeting	☐
Began with warm and engaging facial expression	☐
Matched facial expressions with operative words and tone	☐
Varied facial expression	☐
Maintained appropriate eye contact with judge	☐
Referred to notes appropriately	☐
Managed listening posture	☐
Used room space effectively (podium, table)	☐

EMOTION CHECKLIST	
Appeared confident	☐
Controlled nerves	☐
Matched tone with themes	☐
Appeared likable	☐
Welcomed questions	☐
Listened to judge	☐
Engaged judge(s)	☐
Controlled reaction to judge	☐

15.7   Prepare and Practice a Simple Presentation in Five Minutes

We understand that not all hearing work requires the time and attention you devote to more complicated motions or appellate matters. If you only have five minutes to prepare your simple motion, such as a motion to continue, here is our recipe for how to spend your time.

FIVE-MINUTE PREP			
Prepare the Motion	**Voice and Speech Pattern**	**Body Language**	**Emotion**
One minute— • Set themes, facts, public policy **One minute—** • Outline the motion in bullet point format, write transition lines	**One minute—** • Practice the first thirty seconds of motion • Project voice and eliminate upward inflection	**One minute—** • Check appearance • Align posture • Choose commanding starting home base • Plan a few gestures	**One minute—** • Concentrate on confidence and persuasion • Pick the right tone

CHAPTER SIXTEEN

REMOTE ARGUMENTS: THE NEW NORMAL?

On May 4, 2020, after over 200 years of in-person argument, the U.S. Supreme Court held its first remote argument. The beginning of a new era started shakily. Justice Breyer's connection was iffy; Justice Sotomayor forgot to turn off her mute button; and a never-to-be-known justice flushed the toilet in the middle of one attorney's argument.

The 2020 COVID-19 pandemic necessitated teleconferencing and video conferencing just to keep the courts open. Many courts without experience holding remote hearings were forced to jump on board.

Attorneys discovered that in some ways, remote hearings were not ideal; many conversational aspects of an argument suffered. Eye contact, a major persuader, disappeared. Instead, attorneys and judges looked into pinpoint cameras to feign eye contact. Interruptions and over-talking were problematic. Attorneys and judges were deprived of the visual cues—subtle facial expressions or body language—used to read one another and appropriately respond.

However, there was a silver lining. Neither attorneys nor judges had to travel from their homes to the place of the argument, saving time and money. The National Center for State Courts reported that litigants were more likely to appear for their hearings when held remotely. Court officials cited the convenience as the reason for the higher appearance rates. "If litigants can appear from their cars or their kitchen tables, they're more likely to do so."[1]

As technology advances, government budgets tighten, and citizens demand greater access to the courts, remote hearings will become more common. *Science:* You must be prepared to use this new e-medium to your advantage. First, let's start with the basics that apply to both tele- and video conferencing.

16.1 Check the Court Rules

Every court has developed rules for remote hearings. Get a copy. Find out what program the court will be using to be certain your computer, or device, can accommodate

---

1. Email to state court judges from the National Center for State Courts, May 13, 2020.

it. Zoom, Webex, Microsoft Teams, BlueJeans, and Skype are popular applications, but by the time this book is published there will be others.

Typical rules require practice sessions with the court's clerk a day or sometimes days before the hearing and an early check-in on the day of the hearing to test audio and video functions. Courtroom attire is mandatory. So too are orders to limit distractions—no dogs barking, children screaming, or sirens blaring. Some courts require you to use the court's background as your virtual background during the hearing.

Court rules typically require you to mute your equipment if you are not talking and only unmute when you are ready to speak. Interruptions can be common during remote hearings, so many courts have developed rules about whose turn it is to speak. So that no attorney or judge dominates the conversation, agree with opposing counsel to speaking-order rules for the court without rules. Common rules designate who speaks first, second, or third. No interruptions are allowed when it is someone's turn to speak; many advocates agree to hold all objections until the end of the hearing without the fear of waiving them. Since remote hearings are court hearings and not jury trials, the court will hear the objectionable material anyway. If you cannot agree to hold objections on videoconferencing, you can agree to raise a hand to visually signal your objection per the court's rules.

16.2   Ensure Your Technology Works and You Know How to Use It

Science: Make certain your technology works. Have a backup plan if your technology fails. If you are videoconferencing and your internet connection has limited bandwidth or is unreliable, dial your audio feed by phone. If you lose your internet connection to the argument altogether, your audio feed will remain.

Participate in a test run with a colleague or friend at least one week before the court's dry run so you have time to fix any problems. Check the volume; if it is a video conference, also check the picture. Consider investing in a low-cost microphone to enhance the sound. Headsets and ear pods improve the sound quality, but some look silly on screen. Confirm that you have clear audio matched with the best visual picture of you with your microphone system. If you moot your argument beforehand, recreate the remote courtroom experience the best you can.

Familiarize yourself with the functions of the equipment or software, including the mute and video-off functions. Especially important is knowing the different view settings in a videoconferencing program. Most advocates prefer "gallery view" so they can see the judge(s). If you are videoconferencing, change the name you display with your picture to your formal name so the judges can easily identify you. To look your best, you may use the touch-up-your-appearance setting.

If something does go wrong with the technology during the argument, do not laugh and say you are not used to the technology. Judges may politely smile at you, but they have heard the same line at least a hundred times before. Instead, address the tech mistake, apologize quickly if necessary, and proceed.

16.3   Choose a Space with No or Minimal Distractions

If you are conducting your remote hearing from home, pick a place with limited distractions. Say goodbye to your kids and pets for a while. Shut your windows to reduce any environmental noise. Tape a note on your door indicating that you are in a hearing. Mute all the notification sounds from the apps on your devices and computer. Have a soft surface to place your water glass on so it does not clunk. Stay away from the bathroom and kitchen.

16.4   Decide Whether to Sit or Stand

If the argument is a formal argument, you may stand as you would in a court-room. Use your standing desk or create a makeshift lectern by placing a box on your desk or counter. Standing helps you to breathe freely and gives your voice strength and clarity. Even if the argument is conducted telephonically without a video-feed, standing will improve your vocal performance. If you are on a video-feed, standing also shows respect for the court and enables you to use your full body language to your advantage. We recommend standing—but if you tend to sway when standing, better to sit during a videoconference as swaying side to side looks ridiculous and distracts the judge in the tight frame of a video.

If you plan to be seated for whatever reason, including a disability or rules of the court,[2] sit up straight so you have the same vocal quality. Slumping interferes with your breath, which is the fuel for your voice. If you are in a videoconference, sit in a chair that does not swivel.

16.5   Prepare Your Notes

Well-thought-through notes are critical for remote arguments. Your notes must be organized, concise, and accessible. Remotely, you lose many of the visual cues of a live hearing, so you must laser focus on listening. The cues predominantly come from changes in a judge's tone, volume, pace, and pitch. Even during videoconferencing, visual clues are difficult to detect while you are arguing and trying to maintain faux eye contact with the judge by looking into the camera lens.

Science: Minimal notes with planned checklists are a must. Prepare a checklist of opposing counsel's arguments and a checklist of the judge's possible concerns, with prebaked responses, so you can easily tick off items on the list with little distraction. Since the message is dependent primarily on your words, carefully choose those words

---

2. Some state trial court and international arbitration hearings are conducted from a seated position.

beforehand so the judge does not misinterpret your message. Off-the-cuff comments are inadvisable. Your intent may not come through because you lack the in-person connection and physicality to make your tone crystal clear.

The camera frame imprisons you in a box. Every movement within and outside the box can produce a distraction, even when you are in listening mode. Therefore, arranging your notes strategically is important. *Art:* Decide how and where to place your notes on- and off-camera. You do not want to be shuffling around your papers or wildly searching for your notes during the hearing. If your notes are too far away from you, your image will leave or partially leave the camera frame when you retrieve them. Some advocates place each page of their notes on cardboard backing and attach them to the top of their computer monitor, others print their opening and closing remarks in bold, large font, and hang them behind and slightly above the device camera. The advantage of this method, in videoconferencing, is that when looking at her notes, the advocate appears to make eye contact with the judge. Placing your notes on your desk, lectern, or keyboard is also acceptable if you remember to stop speaking when glancing at your notes. Resume speaking after you look up to project your voice into the microphone and not into your notes.

Wherever you place your notes, avoid reading from them during the whole argument. Strive to have a discussion with the judge(s), not a monologue. Even if you place your written argument on your computer screen thinking this will help you to maintain eye contact with the court, the court will know you are reading. Reading in a videoconference is every bit as unpersuasive as reading to the court at an in-person argument.

16.6   Dress the Part

Wear the clothing you would wear to a courtroom even though you may never be seen by the court. The science of enclothed cognition tells us that what we wear impacts how we behave. Researchers Halo Adams and Adam Galinsky of Northwestern University determined that each of us attach symbolic meaning to the clothes we wear.[3] In their experiment, Adams and Galinsky discovered that wearing a lab coat was associated with carefulness and attention to detail. And when their subjects donned lab coats, they were more attentive and less likely to make mistakes. Similarly, the attorney's uniform puts you in the right frame of mind to argue your case, evoking a sense of formality, professionalism, and confidence.

Although the court may never know you have your pajama bottoms on (unless you suddenly reach for the record in a video conference), you will know. And that knowledge will hurt your performance. Dress the part.

---

3. Halo Adams & Adam Galinsky, *Enclothed Cognition,* Journal of Experimental Social Psychology 918 (July 2012) https://doi.org/10.1016/j.jesp.2012.02.008.

16.7   Be Early

Sign in early to your conference. While you wait for the court to connect you, check your camera frame, test and then keep your audio on "mute," review your notes, take deep, calming breaths, and practice your good posture. Avoid primping in the camera frame to avoid an embarrassing moment on video should the judge, clerk, or opposing counsel be able to view you before the hearing begins.

16.8   Teleconferences

Teleconferencing without a video feed is challenging—like making a cake without a bowl and mixer. You lose access to many of your persuasion tools such as your eyes, body language, gestures, and overall in-person connection with the judge. Your ears, the content of your message, and your voice must make up for what is lost. You must listen intently, understanding and communicating information through words and the nuance of voice.

16.8.1   *Listen Intently*

Listening is one of the skills you possess in a teleconference. Your environment should be distraction-free with no background noise interfering with your concentration. If there is background noise from another participant interfering with your focus, politely ask everyone to mute their device.

Art: Identify and remember the voice of the judge(s) on the conference. Recognize who is asking a question of you. Listen to the tone of each voice. Recognize the change in volume, speed, and inflection of the judge. Practice other-centeredness—stay attuned to what the judge is thinking. Is the judge receptive to your message or not buying it? Is the judge interested in certain arguments and not in others? What is the judge's major concern? Is the judge speeding up and cutting you off, indicating frustration with your position? Is the judge asking you open questions, indicating that he wants to hear more from you?

16.8.2   *Get to the Point Quickly and Concisely*

Recognize that while you may only be teleconferencing or videoconferencing for one hour, the judge may be watching a screen or listening to a phone for six to eight hours that day. Needless to say, that is brutal for the judge and his attention span. *Science:* If you want to be heard and remembered in remote advocacy, get to your point.

Have your two major affirmative points ready to go. If an argument is a mountain, get to the top quickly. Do not spend your time trudging along carrying the minutia at the lower elevations. Have a quick pathway to the top. Get to the point. Theme development and deployment is even more important in remote advocacy because a strong theme and synonymous themes allow you to stay laser focused and brief.

Boil down your points into digestible soundbites. Give memorable and brief takeaways. Think through clever phrases to retain the judge's attention. Use word pictures so the judge can see your point. Make every word count. Read poetry. With a few words, carefully sequenced, the poet captivates the reader. Many advocates find that for remote delivery, having a note system that is bullet-point driven (recall this system from Chapter Eleven on Structure and Preparation Systems) becomes assistive in creating the "get to the point" approach, which will keep the judge more engaged.

Exercise

Read one or two great poems. Notice the brevity, yet precision detail of the master wordsmith. Pay attention to the emotions evoked. If you are at a loss for a poem to read, try Maya Angelou's "I Know Why the Caged Bird Sings."[4]

16.8.3   Be Aware of Your Voice

The voice is a powerful instrument. It energizes, bores, or alarms a listener. It can project stress, fear, or confidence. Maximize the potential of your voice in a teleconference.

Test your volume ahead of the hearing to ensure you are clearly heard at a consistent decibel level. In most cases, you will need to increase your volume above what you use in an in-person hearing, where you often have the benefit of a microphone system to artificially amplify you. Hearing is difficult through technology, especially for the many judges who are not as young as they once were. Make sure your volume is high enough for the judge to hear every word you speak. Project your voice into the microphone system of your device. Turning your head away from the microphone is easy to do and inevitably muffles the sound.

 Art: Pump up your energy level. The phone and video will naturally downgrade the energy you convey. You will appear "flatter" than you do in person, coming across as not as interesting or animated. So, increase your intensity. If in person your energy level is a seven out of ten, bring it to a nine.

Slow down the speed of your voice. If you regularly speak at 160 words per minute slow it down to 155 words per minute. Pause more often and longer than normal to account for the technological transmission delay. You do not want to be talking over the judge, and technology will make this task even more difficult. In remote delivery, more than ever, the habitualized baseline pause will prove effective and critical.

---

4. Maya Angelou, I Know Why the Caged Bird Sings (Random House 1969). Text of the poem is available at https://www.poetryfoundation.org/poems/48989/caged-bird (last visited February 4, 2021).

Pause, also, to allow thoughts to sink into the judge and give the judge an opportunity to ask questions. Engaging the judge will prevent his thoughts from drifting off and give you clues to his thinking process. Your intentional moments of silence will prompt many judges to ask questions and engage.

Be aware of certain drivers of increased speed which you will need to fight against—chiefly, nerves. Since remote delivery is new to many, the event creates nerves not experienced by previously seasoned advocates. Nervousness often means a quicker rate of delivery, which causes more comprehension problems. Consciously slow down into a measured pace. Just slowing your pace may settle you down. If the hearing is an emergency rather than in the regular course of business, talk slow and low to showcase calmness and confidence.

Use pitch to communicate a new beginning to your argument and help maximize transitions. When using transition phrases like, "I would now like to turn to my second point," throw your voice slightly upward in pitch. The upward pitch will signal to the judge a new topic and bring about a renewed interest in your argument like starting a new chapter of a book.

Especially during your greeting to the court, keep a professional and warm tone to your voice. Give the court a sense of enthusiasm and desire to converse. Use the tone you would use talking to a friend about a movie you loved. Do not exude coldness or stress. No one can see you on a teleconference call but activating your facial expression will help vary the pitch and stress in the voice. So, smile while you are speaking. The judge will hear the smile in your voice.

In a teleconference, weaponize your voice to transmit your message more effectively. As discussed in Chapter Thirteen, varying the speed, volume, pitch, and tone of your voice during the argument is important in any engagement with the court, but even more important to master when you cannot utilize in-person connection with the judge, non-verbal communication tools, and eye contact. The vocal variety will keep the judge interested in what you have to say and connected to you. Remote delivery is no place for monotone presentations, which are dull, tedious, and insufferable for a judge.

16.8.4 *Eliminate Filler and Qualifier Words*

In a remote hearing, disruptive behavior is even more alarming, and is prompted by minor movements in the camera and seemingly innocuous vocal interruptions. Successful remote deliveries necessitate the virtual elimination of unnecessary words. The annoying meaningless sounds of fillers take the focus from the message. Especially when the sole source of input is auditory over a teleconference, the annoyance from these verbal fillers and qualifiers intensifies. Use the practice tips in Chapter Fourteen to shed these gremlins.

16.8.5 Enunciate Your Words

If you are asked to repeat yourself, crispen your pronunciation while increasing your volume. The difficulty in understanding you may be due to a lack of clearly enunciated consonants. Speak clearly so you can be understood by enunciating your words. Emphasize your consonants and vowels. Articulation is important in in-person arguments but even more so when teleconferencing.

Try recording yourself to test and determine if you muffle your vowels or consonants. If you do, talk slower and cleanly form your consonant and vowel sounds. Practice building up speed while keeping your articulation. The more defined your words, the easier for you to be understood. Warm up your mouth before the hearing with tongue twisters.

Exercise

Say some of these short tongue twisters. Begin saying them slowly and gradually increase the pace.

She sees cheese.

Truly rural.

Rarely leery, rarely Larry.

Fresh fried fish.

16.9 Video Conferences

During a video-conferenced argument, utilize all the above suggestions. Besides audio capabilities, you have the added advantage, or disadvantage (if not managed correctly), of your image on the judge's device. We say "disadvantage" because in this technological age, we are all conditioned to watch a professionally edited program, backed by a soundtrack, performed by professionally trained actors or journalists. With this in mind, learning the tricks of video conferencing is essential. First the set up.

16.9.1 The Setup

16.9.1.1 The Computer

Science: Place your computer on a sturdy surface. No wobbling. Prop up the computer on a stack of books so the camera is slightly above eye level and horizontal to you. You do not want to be craning your neck up or down to look into the eye of the camera. Situate your screen so it is perpendicular to the floor. If the screen is tilting back, the judge will be looking up your nostrils—not a good look. Some laptops have a stand built into their back to hold up the screen. You may have to place a small book under the stand to make the screen completely perpendicular to the floor. If your stack of books consists of large coffee table books, then the small book holding up the laptop cover will not cause the entire configuration to be unstable. Jenga is not the idea here.

Frame the camera with something that will remind you to look directly into the lens. Two sticky notes will do, but pictures of your kids or grandkids might make you appear more animated. Add a cardboard box behind the computer and place a clock directly above the camera. If your grandkids will not help you to look straight into the camera, the clock will. Some courts place a timer directly on the video screen, relieving you of the need to position a clock near yours.

Here are pictures of two computer setups—one sitting and one standing:

16.9.1.2 The Background

Some courts require lawyers to use a court-approved virtual background. If required, place a green screen behind you. The green screen avoids the danger of your body parts disappearing and reappearing with the frame. Cone-shaped heads and vanishing forms distract from your message.

There are hierarchies in the world of staged backgrounds. Try to create a background that is as high on the list as possible.

- Highest and best: a simple, plain background framed with a few legally related items or nonpersonal items to balance your image, which should be centered in front of the plain background. Ideally, there is a wall behind you with nothing hung, preferably a neutral color, and then bookshelves flanking you, a plant, or a nonpersonal picture.

National Institute for Trial Advocacy

- Good: A full bookshelf behind you can provide an interesting backdrop, but you will need to ensure that all the titles are not legible (camera is far enough away) and there are no offensive books on the shelf.

- Will do in a pinch: a plain wall with nothing framing you.

Check your visual beforehand. Make sure that it does not appear that a vase is coming out of your ear or a light shade is balancing on top of your head. And please, put your cats in another room.

16.9.1.3 The Lighting

Project natural and/or artificial light sources in front of you and above you, not behind you. Preferably set up your computer with a window behind it to give you natural light. If you cannot move your computer, place a shaded lamp with a daylight bulb or a halo light behind your monitor. The lamp should be slightly higher than your monitor and in the middle of the back of your screen to give you some soft yet symmetrical lighting.

Avoid having the lighting emanate from behind you. You will appear darker than the rest of the frame—you do not want to look like someone in a witness protection program. If you must position yourself with a window behind you, close the blinds and arrange lighting facing you and to both sides to counterbalance the sunlight through the blinds. If you wear eyeglasses that do not have a glare-free coating, then adjust placement of the light and the angle of your camera to reduce glare on the eyeglasses.

16.9.1.4 The Picture Frame

Position yourself at least three feet away from your camera. Keep far enough from your camera so you have, at a minimum, your body in bust view within the frame. Show from the top of your head to the top of your podium or desk. Make sure there is enough space on the top of the screen so that when you move, you do not chop off any part of your head from view. Ensure that you have space to your left and right to comfortably gesture without your hands leaving the video frame. Try to distance yourself at least an arm's length from your camera.

16.9.1.5 Your Dress

Do not wear stripes or prints; they give the illusion of motion on camera. Solid colors are best. Wear comfortable clothing so you are not tempted to tug at your straps, sleeves, or collar.

16.9.1.6 Makeup and Hair

A camera washes out your face. If you wear makeup, wear slightly more makeup than usual to have your online appearance match the intensity of your in-person appearance. If your lighting causes you to have a glare on your forehead, nose, or chin, consider using a colorless powder that deflects light.

16.10 Other Tips for Videoconferences

16.10.1 *Look into the Camera*

Eye contact is powerful; it displays credibility and confidence. In a joint study between the University of Wolverhampton and the University of Stirling, researchers found that eye contact, even over video, makes the message more memorable.[5]

Online eye contact is tricky. You are trying to make it look like you are looking the judge in the eye while trying to observe the judge's reactions. When you are talking, spend most of your time looking at the tiny pinpoint camera lens to give the impression of eye contact, then occasionally scan at the judge's thumbnail to check for nonverbal cues. Just as you would in person, look away from the camera at times. You do not want to look like you are constantly staring at the judge. Avoid the lure of looking at yourself on the screen. If the temptation to look at yourself is too great, most programs have a turn-off-self-view function. When you pause, use it as an opportunity to perform a "check" on the judge and look for cues that the judge has a question. This will avoid you restarting when a judge would have liked to ask a question, but is reluctant to interrupt during an online hearing. Your focus on the camera will look like eye contact to each judge, so you do not need to worry about changing focus from one judge to another, but when you check for reactions you will need to look at each thumbnail and evaluate whether you have everyone's attention or if anyone appears to have a question.

Even when it is your turn to speak, you can peek at the judge to gauge his reaction to your argument. Knowing the functions of the video program you are using is important. All programs have an assortment of views. Pick the view that allows you to best see the judge's reaction while appearing to maintain eye contact. The gallery view with pictures in a row at the top of your screen helps maintain the illusion of eye contact, but if the view is thumbnail you may see no facial reactions. If your view makes it necessary for you to avert your gaze, then do so occasionally to monitor the judge's reactions. Of course, if the judge appears to be looking down at his notes, watch away.

When opposing counsel presents, turn off your video feed and display your publicity photo. You are no longer "on stage" and can stare at the screen, observing the judge.

---

5. Chris Fullwood & Gwyneth Doherty-Sneddon, *Effect of Gazing at the Camera During a Video Link on Recall.* 37:2 APPL. ERGON. 167–75 (Mar. 2006). Available at https://doi:10.1016/j. apergo.2005.05.003 (last visited February 2, 2021).

16.10.2 Facial Expressions

Facial expressions command increased importance because of the full-screen view. Every moment your video is on, you are on stage. All eyes are focused on your face. Practice your listening expression when the judge is asking a question; you should appear interested in his words. Practice matching your facial expression with the words you speak: your greeting of the court section should look far different than when you are imploring the court to seek justice. And practice your reactive facial expression, most pronounced and dangerous with an advocate who appears offended when interrupted. Be poised and engaged. Do not grimace, roll your eyes, or slip into a deer-in-the-headlights look. Remember, you are performing.

Exercise

Rehearse in front of a mirror. Notice your facial expressions. Put on your neutral, enthusiastic, or serious face. See how these faces look and feel.

16.10.3 Gestures and Other Movement

Do not move your lower body. Do not rock, twist, or lift up your leg. Movement is distracting and even more so when it takes a part of you out of the camera view. Stay as still as you can from the waist down so you appear calm, confident, and in control.

Gesture slow and close enough to your body so that your hands stay visible in the camera frame. Keep your shoulders relaxed and your gestures to the side. The boundaries of your gestures should look like a shallow "U" when the viewer is looking straight at you with your hands no higher than your nose. Do not gesture toward the camera. Doing so makes your hands and arms appear larger than they are and will take up more of the screen than you want. Positioning yourself at least three feet away from the camera will help with this "hands of a giant" problem and keep the proportions of your body and gestures more in line with your in-person physicality.

16.10.4 Exhibits

The ease of using exhibits may be the only advantage to a video conference. With the share function, you can effortlessly display an exhibit to the judge and opposing counsel. Provide essential exhibits to the judge's staff and opposing counsel before the hearing. Exhibits may be a portion of the record, a pleading, a picture, a statute, or a portion of a case. Use exhibits to explain your points to the court and break up the monotony of looking at a television screen. But pick your best exhibits because less is more, especially on video. Make sure you rehearse sharing your screen and the exhibit with the court during the dry run with the clerk.

16.11 Additional Considerations in Multi-Judge Arguments

All the advice we have given in this chapter applies to multi-judge courts. But other phenomena occur with several judges participating at once in remote advocacy.

16.11.1 Regular Questioning

If the court does not alter its questioning from an in-person hearing, judges can ask any question when the mood strikes. Interruptions may be rampant. Overtalking becomes messy and robs valuable time from you. Because there is a broadcasting delay, two simultaneous voices garble. Usually there is a pause after the muddle as each speaker gives the other the floor. After the pause, both speakers resume their overtalking, which leads to yet another jumble. Do not jump into the mess. When one judge or multiple judges speak, quit talking. There may be a moment of garble because of the transmission delay but wait to continue until you hear a verbal signal from the judge.

16.11.2 Sequential Questioning

Following the U.S. Supreme Court's lead, some multi-judge courts sequentially question. The chief judge begins with his questions, followed by the other judges in order of their seniority. This makes for a very different oral argument experience.

To the advocate's advantage, a brief opening statement is generally allowed. Keep this opening succinct and powerful, including the essence of what you need the court to hear. You should be able to get through your road map before the questioning begins. Likewise, a brief uninterrupted closing is generally permitted. Your last points can bring your argument home. Since this system grants you the opportunity for these brief speeches, practice them for perfect delivery.

Another advantage of sequential questions is that the argument takes more time. A one-hour argument may last one hour and twenty minutes to allow all the judges' questions. With sequential questioning, the judge reticent to fight for question time in an in-person argument may suddenly ask questions. Justice Clarence Thomas, well-known for his silence in arguments, has found his voice remotely.

The disadvantage of sequential hearings is the hearing sounds like a congressional hearing. Speeches from the judges are common before coming to the question. Judges demand immediate answers. During the argument in *Trump v. Mazars USA,* Justice Breyer cautioned oralist Patrick Strawbridge to answer his first question yes or no because of time constraints. Justice Alito in the same argument interrupted Strawbridge saying, "So, I mean—I don't want to cut you off, but I have very limited time."[6]

---

6. Trump v. Mazars Oral Argument, May 12, 2020. Audio clip and transcript available at https://www.oyez.org/cases/2019/19-715 (last visited January 29, 2021).

Knowing their time is brief, judges are more likely to cut off lawyers, speak quicker, and demand short and concise explanations. The value of having scripted, brief answers cannot be overstated. Draft your brief answers beforehand but do not rush the delivery speed. Do not mirror the judge's hurried pace. Speak your succinct answers slowly and deliberately to be clearly understood. As advocates, we must learn to always answer first, and then briefly explain.

Sequential questioning also results in a disjointed argument. Since each judge has one time to inquire, jumping around from issue to issue is common. Now your notes we described in Chapter Eleven are essential.

Here is a checklist of needs for your remote argument:

Remote Hearing Checklist	
☐ Check the court rules	☐ Webinar platform?
	☐ Court-ordered background?
	☐ Rules on using mute and stop-video function?
	☐ Speaking order of attorneys/judges?
	☐ How to handle interruptions?
	☐ Pre-submitted exhibits?
☐ Sound system	☐ Need for headset, earbuds, or lavalier microphone?
	☐ Pillows or towels for better acoustics?
☐ Video	☐ Camera at slightly higher than eye level
	☐ Background interesting but not distracting
	☐ Natural or soft lighting behind computer
	☐ No backlighting
☐ Comfort with technology?	
☐ Courtroom and comfortable attire	
☐ Checklist of opposing counsel's arguments	
☐ Checklist of responses to questions	
☐ Mount notes and support systems necessary for smooth delivery.	
☐ Equipment checks	☐ One week before court
	☐ A few days before court with court staff
	☐ One hour before hearing

16.12   Conclusion

So much goes into an oral argument. Who would have thought we could devote so many pages to a one-hour session? As Robert Jackson said, "I used to say that, as Solicitor General, I made three arguments of every case. First came the one that I planned—as I thought, logical, coherent, complete. Second was the one actually presented—interrupted, incoherent, disjointed, disappointing. The third was the utterly devastating argument that I thought of after going to bed that night."[7]

You will never have the perfect argument, but we hope that this book will help you develop and deliver an argument with more than one point well made.

---

7. Robert H. Jackson, *Advocacy Before the United States Supreme Court*, 37 CORNELL L. REV. 1, 6 (1951).

APPENDICES

Appendix A

Select Tables and Graphics

Chapter Two: Know Your Audience: The Judge(s)

THE JUDGE

Concern for law	Concern for fairness and justice
Sensitive to reversal	Oblivious to reversal
Concerned with case load	Unconcerned with case load
Dispositive	Not dispositive
Formal courtroom	Informal courtroom
Time certain	Cattle call
Relies on law clerk	No law clerks
Active questions	Does not ask questions
Stickler for rules	Easygoing
Serious	Fun-loving
Prepared	Not prepared
Expert in area of law	Novice in area of law
Developed judicial philosphy in area of law	Neutral philosphy in area of law
Concerned about consistency	Unconcerned about consistency
Conservative	Liberal
Elected	Appointed
Close alignment with opposing attorneys	Not aligned with opposing attorneys

Chapter Three: Ready Set: Preparing for Your Argument

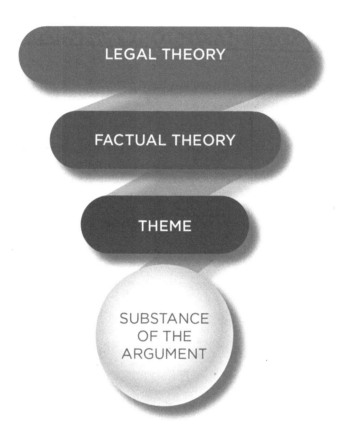

Motion Planning Worksheet

On the following page is the blank Motions Planning Worksheet. You can download a copy of this document for your individual use at

https://www.nita.org/motion-planning-worksheet

Password: PWM2.

MOTION PLANNING WORKSHEET	
Legal Elements	*Statute, Cases, Law*
Critical Good Facts	*Bad Facts*

Theme and Sub-Themes		
Time Allotted	*When*	*Where*
Witnesses	*Subpoenaed Date*	*Exhibits*
Questions		*Responses*

Strongest Argument
Argument 2
Argument 3
Opponent's Argument 1 and Response
Opponent's Argument 2 and Response

Fallback Position	*Client's Approval*

Chapter Four: Themes: The What, the Why, and the How

Good Themes

TECHNIQUE	DESCRIPTION	EXAMPLES
Headline	Create a headline for the newspaper about your case. What would the headline or bumper sticker read?	• Procedures aren't technical, they are foundational. • Procedures ensure fairness. • Hiding the ball prolongs litigation (discovery dispute). • It's time to put up or shut up (summary judgment).
Legal sayings	Legal maxims that have survived the test of time.	• Justice delayed is justice denied (laches motion). • Equity does not help those with unclean hands (defense of a restraining order). • Ignorance of the law is no excuse (prosecution of a contempt action). • No person is above the law (contempt).
Quotes from cases	Pick critical language that cannot be ignored and use it as your theme. Especially helpful to use with a judge who wants to be affirmed on appeal.	• We are here to get rid of the clutter.[1] • Reasonable suspicion to stop (motion to suppress).[2]
Other side's words	Turn the other side's words from their papers into your theme.	• We value judicial efficiency as much as the defendants (defending motion for interlocutory appeal or prosecution of a preliminary injunction).
Quotations or idioms	Quotes from books or on the internet.	• They are trying to make something out of nothing (summary judgment). • Much ado about nothing. • My client has never had a problem with drugs. He has had problems with the police (motion to suppress). • This is the second bite at the apple (claim/issue preclusion). • The plaintiff is opening up Pandora's box. • Some circumstantial evidence is very strong, as when you find a trout in the milk (summary judgment). • The defendant is acting like a tornado in a teapot (defending motion for sanctions).[3]

(Continued)

---

1. Heller Fin. v. Midwhey Powder Co., Inc., 883 F.2d 1286, 1294 (7th Cir. 1989).
2. Terry v. Ohio, 392 U.S. 1 (1967).
3. OKLAHOMA! (Magna Theater Corp. 1955).

TECHNIQUE	DESCRIPTION	EXAMPLES
Advertisements		• It's the real thing (patent infringement).[4] • Where's the beef? There is no scientific basis for this (excluding expert testimony).[5]
Songs or poems	Find songs of the judge's generation to make your point.	• You don't need a weatherman to know which way the wind blows. (Expert opinion is not helpful.)[6] • When you ain't got nothing, you have nothing to lose. (Plaintiffs have no standing to complain.)[7]
Rhetorical questions	Ask a question, but be sure to answer the question.	• Is there a material issue of fact? Yes, there are at least four of them (summary judgment). • Where are the safeguards? There are none (exclusion of evidence).
Metaphors	Comparing one thing to another simplifies complicated concepts.	• Fruit of the poisonous tree (motion to suppress). • Level the playing field. • Time is money.[8]
Rule of three	There is something magical about the rule of threes. (Father, son, and holy ghost. Beginning, middle, and end. See no evil, speak no evil, hear no evil. Never have so few given so much to so many.) They are memorable and can provide a structure to your argument.	• This case is about precedent, policy, and predictability. • They are asking too much, with too little value, at too high a cost (discovery dispute).
Clichés (+)	While clichés can be annoying ("This is a fishing expedition."), they often provide a quick way to brainstorm the right theme. Start with a tired cliché, and then dress it up or change it to be fresh and more unexpected.	• The plaintiff has cast its net too wide. • Alternative to "slippery slope": tsunami or avalanche, or "Slip sliding away."[9]

---

4. Coca-Cola Advertisement, 1969.

5. Wendy's Advertisement, 1969.

6. See Alex Long, *The Freewheelin' Judiciary: A Bob Dylan Anthology,* 38 FORDHAM URB. L.J. 1363 (2011), for an interesting discussion of opinions where judges cite song lyrics.

7. *Id.* (citing Chief Justice Roberts' majority opinion in Sprint Communication Co. v APCC Services, 555 U.S. 269 (2008)).

8. See George Lakoff and Mark Johnson, *Metaphors We Live By* (Chicago: University of Chicago Press, 2003), for an innovative look at how humans think in metaphors.

9. Paul Simon, *Slip Sliding Away,* on Greatest Hits, Etc. (Columbia Records 1977).

Bad Themes

TECHNIQUE	DESCRIPTION	EXAMPLE
Issue restatements	The judge knows this. You are wasting your time and the court's time. Say something the court doesn't know.	• We are here for the court to decide whether to grant summary judgment.
Name-calling	With the name-calling, the judge knows she is ready to watch a mud-slinging contest. Everyone gets dirty in the process.	• Counsel is being disingenuous. • There she goes again with the same faulty arguments. • She is misleading the court.
Hyperbole	Exaggeration damages your credibility immediately. Once lost, credibility is difficult to regain. If the case is so obvious or clear, the judge is asking why are you here.	• This is a simple case. • The other side is clearly wrong. • The answer is obvious.
Too cute by half	If the theme is too provocative, the theme becomes the subject of the discussion at the hearing.	• The defense is running against the wind[10] (motion to suppress on a fleeing charge). • If we can't regulate the sale of broccoli, then we can't regulate health care.
Clichés	The triteness does not inspire any judge and causes lost attention.	• Justice is blind.
Easy to turn	Don't use a theme the other side can turn to their use.	• Dependent on the case.
Over 3 or 4 sentences	The theme is a hook, not a dissertation.	• We have tried to negotiate with the other side, but they continue to throw roadblocks in our way. The defense will not budge on the dollar amount, and they won't consider a more creative settlement offer, blah, blah, blah…

---

10. Bob Seger, *Against the Wind*, on Nine Tonight (Capitol Records 1981).

Chapter Six: The Law

GOOD CASES		BAD CASES	
Same facts, same holding	Different facts, same holding	Different facts, different holding	Same facts, different holding
Quote the cases, weave into the theme.	Use carefully; show comparisons and admit distinctions before your opponent does.	Distinguish facts, show how if the facts in that case were the same as the present facts, the holding would have been different.	Distinguish holding or how it was applied, argue public policy.

Chapter Seven: The Questioning Formula

STEPS TO ANSWERING A QUESTION
Step 1: Listen to the end of the question.
Step 2: Pause before you answer.
Step 3: Ask clarifying questions, if necessary.
Step 4: Directly answer the question first.
Step 5: Explain your answer.
Step 6: Transition back to your argument and your strengths.

Chapter Eight: A Periodic Table of Questions

THE KICKOFF	
General	The initial question asked by a court. Be ready to leap right away.
Words	"Your Honor, I'm here to highlight issues and answer your concerns." "I can tell you facts that have developed since we wrote the papers." "Let me bring you up to speed since the last time we spoke, Your Honor."
Voice	Clear, projected
Body Language	Home base, calm gestures
Tone	Warm and engaging

THE BLANK-OUT RESPONSE	
General	The momentary lapse of memory.
Words	"Your Honor, may I have a moment?" "Just one second, please." "It's right here at my fingertips."
Voice	Clear, projected
Body Language	Home base, calm gestures
Tone	Warm and engaging

WAYS TO SAY "I DON'T KNOW"
"I had not considered that . . . ."
"I'm not sure, but I do know . . . ."
"I'm not familiar with that."
"I was not aware of that."
"That does not seem to be what we have here."
"I'm unclear on the details."
"That is not in the record."
"I'm not certain and do not want to tell you anything that is inaccurate."
"I do not have that at my fingertips. If you give me a moment, my colleague can provide that cite."
"That case does not appear in any of the papers filed."
"I'm not certain I can help you with this, but I will be happy later to provide the answer."

THE SOFTBALL QUESTION
"Absolutely, Your Honor."
"That's precisely why it matters."
"Yes, Your Honor."
"I absolutely agree."
"Yes, that's correct."
"Yes, we see this the same way."

THE GENUINE INQUIRY
"I'd be happy to, Your Honor."
"That brings us deeper into the issue of . . . ."
"I would be glad to elaborate."
Note: You can also use the judge's words to begin your answer.

HOSTILE QUESTIONS FROM AN INSISTENT JUDGE
"There is nothing more I can add to this discussion. May I move on?"
"Sadly, we must agree to disagree on this point, but we still win because . . . ."
"I'm disappointed we do not agree on this point, Judge. May I move to my next point?"
"It sounds to me like we will have to agree to disagree, but I am hoping you'll agree with me on . . . ."
"If I may turn the court's attention to another case on this issue . . . ."
"May I have some leeway here to better explain my point?"

THE HYPOTHETICAL QUESTION
"As I understand it . . . ."
"In your hypothetical, the facts are . . . ."
"Yes, under those circumstances, the court would dismiss the matter . . . ."
"It depends."
"No, Your Honor. That would not change the decision."
"It may, but one major difference with the scenario is . . . ."
"Your Honor, the court does not need to go that far. All we are asking for is . . . ."

THE RABBIT HOLE QUESTION
[Answer quickly and directly, then pivot to your point.] ". . . but that makes no difference here because . . . ."
"I share your concern with fairness, and right now, the issue that faces us *is* ultimately about fairness."
"That discussion sends us on a detour, which I'm happy to briefly discuss." [Answer quickly and pivot to your affirmative point.]
Answer the question briefly and pivot back to your strengths. The answer is, "Yes, Your Honor," and then pivot to your argument.

THE CONFUSED JUDGE
"Your Honor, today's argument focuses on . . . ."
"I understand your concern, but today we're here to . . . ."
"The point is . . . ."
"This case concerns . . . ."

THE MISINFORMED JUDGE
"Counsel is correct in this, but we win anyway because . . . ."
"The holding in *X* was not . . . but it does not make a difference because . . . ."
"Just to set the record straight, the facts here are . . . ."
"Perhaps I have not been clear."

"WHY HAVEN'T YOU SETTLED?"
"We have tried to find a solution and may still, but we are not there yet."
"We share your desire for resolution, and your decision on this motion will help to settle this case [or, if the motion is dispositive, will end the case]."
"A ruling will help move the parties in the right direction. Let me show you how."
"We need your guidance, Your Honor, and a ruling on this motion will give us the direction we need."

"LET'S MAKE A DEAL" (WHEN YOU CAN'T ACCEPT THE PROPOSAL)
"I cannot go as far as you want, but I can . . . ."
"I am having trouble with this one small aspect of your request . . . ."
"I need to consult with my client to get approval."
"I regret that we are too far down the road to accept this proposal."

WHEN YOU CAN CONCEDE
"Yes, Your Honor, my client can agree to that."
"We are happy to stipulate to that, and we ask the court to . . . ."
"That is correct, Your Honor, and it does not affect the ultimate result because . . . ."

WHEN YOU CANNOT CONCEDE
"I have to talk to my client before we can agree to that."
"Your Honor, that is not going to work in this situation."
"We cannot waive that, Your Honor."
"There are far greater consequences that prevent me from agreeing."
"We cannot concede that, and the reason is . . . ."

THE GUILLOTINE
"I would like to make the record clear that . . . ."
"Your Honor, I do need to make a record that . . . ."
"I understand the Court's position, although obviously I disagree for the reasons I have stated."
"I would ask the court to reconsider because [*new reasons*]."
"I do have one more argument I would ask the court to consider."

Chapter Nine: Questions from the Multi-Judge Court

	The Consistency Question	The Interrupting Judge	The Crossfire
General	Be prepared to answer questions about opinions written by a member of the panel on the issue presented. If the authoring judge asks the question, recognize him as the author.	If one judge interrupts another during questioning, answer the questions in the order asked. Or find a common thread between both questions.	When two judges are debating an issue, listen. Interject only if the conversation is going south for your client.
Words	As you know, Judge X, you wrote the opinion you ask about	As to the first question . . . , as to the second . . . . Both questions share the same concern which is	Let me remind the court that Client X did give the summons to the law firm before the default judgment was granted.
Voice	Raise pitch slightly and keep an even pace.	Extend baseline pause to avoid speaking over the interrupting judge, and stop speaking the moment you hear the judge's voice.	When you interject, slightly raise volume and pitch.

(*Continued*)

	The Consistency Question	**The Interrupting Judge**	**The Crossfire**
Body	Expand gesture box and use descriptive gestures to show connections.	Reduce gestures and remain relaxed and still.	Try stepping back from the podium slightly to allow the judges to discuss, then step forward to interject.
Emotion	Show enthusiasm.	Express no frustration when interrupted, and instead welcome the conversation.	Stay engaged during the judges' discussion, and show enthusiasm when interjecting.

	The Hostile Judge	**Concessions**	**"Let's Make a Deal"**
General	Hold your position. Explain it. When the judge will not budge, ask to be able to move on.	Concede if it will not hurt your client. Be careful conceding legal issues.	Negotiation seldom occurs in an appellate argument, but when the opportunity comes, only proceed if a clear majority of the judges are attracted to the deal.
Words	"We may have to agree to disagree, may I move on?" "I think I have not been clear; may I have some leeway in answering your question."	"We cannot concede that point. That question is for the jury to decide." "Yes, Your Honor, we concede that Person X could have . . ."	"Your Honor, I see your point."
Voice	Slow down your speech. Lower your volume.	Use an even vocal pace and tone.	Slightly lift the pitch of your voice if you can agree with the judge or find a way to negotiate.
Body	Take a step back. Have your palms upward. Look initially at the questioner and then send your eye contact to the other members of the panel.	Use descriptive hand gestures to showcase how you are trying to reach agreement.	Use descriptive hand gestures to showcase how you are trying to reach agreement.
Emotion	Do not argue back with the judge. Remain professional; if not, the other judges will side with their colleague.	Avoid appearing defeated, and instead showcase a grateful tone.	If you can agree, be pleased. If not, stay neutral.

(Continued)

	The Softball Question	The "I Don't Know" Question
General	Maintain eye contact with the judge asking the question, but then spend the majority of your time convincing the other judges of your position.	Pause. Attempt to find an answer. If an answer is not apparent, simply admit you do not know. Do not pretend to know. Faking it is not an option.
Words	"Yes, Your Honor, I agree. Ultimately, the question rests on whether . . . ." "I agree with that premise. Let me flesh out the reasoning behind . . . ."	"Your Honor, I am unclear on that point. I can come back to you with an answer at a later time, but right now I do not know."
Voice	Use an even vocal pace and tone.	Use an even vocal pace and tone.
Body	Stay consistent with your established body language.	Stay consistent with your established body language.
Emotion	Appear enthusiastic and seek agreement.	Avoid appearing defeated.

Chapter Eleven: Structure and Note Preparation Systems

Themes

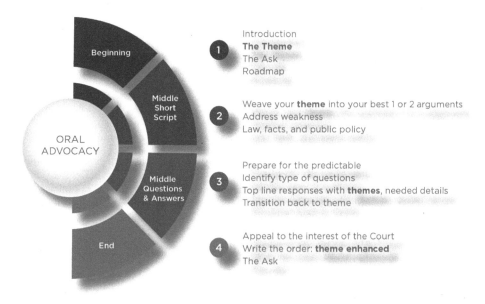

Dolphining

THEME

2-3 BEST ARGUMENTS

FACTS AND LAW

PREPARATION SYSTEMS		
System	**Advantages**	**Disadvantages**
Long script	Confidence building; clarifies thinking. Keeps an advocate who has trouble with wordsmithing (too long winded or not detailed enough) on the right track. Tends to calm nerves.	Tough to take to the podium with you. Risk that you will fall into reading to the judge. Less eye contact. Not able to connect with judge or watch his reactions. If memorized, the tendency is to be flustered when one word or phrase is missed. Bound by words on page. Stifles expression in body language and flattens vocal delivery. Tends to create overall fast or slow delivery. Quickly sounds stale. Not recommended.
Short script	Clarifies thinking to be concise and to the point. Simplifies difficult concepts. Develops magic phrases. Keeps attention of the court. Takes less time. Useful for rebuttal later. Easier to manipulate style changes than the long script. No fear of not making a record. Can be read for the disengaged judge.	If memorized, can be delivered flat with no connection to the court. Tendency to be flustered when one word or phrase is lost. Risk of the advocate knowing too much and starting the story in the middle.

(Continued)

National Institute for Trial Advocacy

PREPARATION SYSTEMS		
System	**Advantages**	**Disadvantages**
Bullet points (with or without transitions)	Security blanket for things you always forget. Helps with organization when law and facts are merged in deliveries. Easier to talk more conversationally off bullet points than full script. Transitions give you confidence. Magic phrases are front and center.	If too detailed, difficult to see and you cannot find your points quickly enough. You can get lost in the paper. May have to shuffle multiple pages. Usually flattens gesture pattern because hands are needed to keep place on outline and mark what has been covered.
Law driven	For the law-heavy case, the case law and statutes are at your fingertips. Use when the judge is an expert in an area and wants to get into specifics. Gives you confidence you will not forget the facts, holdings, or principles of multiple cases.	If judge is a big-picture person, then case-by-case analysis is too specific. If too detailed, difficult to use in the argument.

PREPARATION SYSTEMS		
System	**Advantages**	**Disadvantages**
Question driven	For those nervous with the prospect of answering questions. Plan transitions from questions back to your arguments or themes. Use with an active bench.	If the judge asks no questions, you will need a short script to preserve the record.
Point/ counter-point	Able to quickly respond to your opponent's arguments. Works well for rebuttal and respondent/appellee's arguments. During your opponent's argument, you can cross off those points not covered.	You have a danger of becoming too defensive and may not offensively argue your case.
Theme	Keeps you focused on your main arguments.	Lacks detail. You lose the specifics.

(Continued)

PREPARATION SYSTEMS		
System	**Advantages**	**Disadvantages**
The hand (three to five points, cued by words within a short phrase)	To be used when there is minimal preparation time. Allows for focused and simple directed delivery. Perfect for the spontaneous discussion with the judge. Easy to remember for you and the judge. This allows for the fullest expression of your vocal instrument and your body language because there are no notes. It fosters a relationship with the judge, as if you were discussing it outside the courtroom.	Lacks detail. You may forget something crucial for the motion. It is not right for an amateur in a complex case or the judge who wants to discuss the specifics.

Chapter Twelve: Rebuttals

REBUTTAL		
First	**Second**	**Third**
Respond directly to the judge's concern or opposing counsel's winning argument.	Make corrections, clear up misunderstandings in fact or law.	Go to the heart of the judge, write the order.

Chapter Thirteen: Now That I Know What to Say How Do I Say It?

STANDING HOME BASES	
Hands resting on either side of a podium	This is formal. Have no tension in hands—do not grip the podium. Avoid looking like you are holding on for balance.
Actor's neutral	Keep body aligned, arms at side, chest lifted. Good position to reach after you have incorporated yourself into the arguments.
Hand in pocket	Personality and body-frame driven. It is generally more useful for men because women's slacks rarely have pant pockets. This home base can purposely make you more approachable. Do not play with anything in your pocket, and use only one hand.

(Continued)

STANDING HOME BASES	
Hands clasped at mid-torso	Rest hands between belly button and belt. Do not clasp with tension. Keep arms relaxed.
Hand holding a prop	The prop can be a writing utensil or remote clicker/pointer. Be careful not to play with the prop or point it at the judge.
Standing to the side of a podium or table, with one hand resting on it	This is effective for a question-and-answer session, and/or to break up the monotony of a podium position. Some judges allow you to use this home base if you are passing documents or visuals to the bench and opposing counsel. Others allow this if you are close enough to touch the podium. Do not use this with judges who are sticklers for formality. Never use in an appellate court.

Chapter Fourteen: The "It Factor"

IDENTIFYING AND IMPROVING NERVOUS TELLS	
PROBLEM	**SOLUTION**
Tightening of throat at the top of the neck and back of the mouth	Long term: Practice singing fast-paced songs with low-high skips and repeatedly stretch the back of the mouth and top of the throat with a closed mouth and a deep yawn. Short term: As you stand to deliver the argument, tip your chin and yawn with your mouth closed to stretch out your throat and release tension in those muscles. Start with a slightly lower pitch.
Racing heartbeat	Long term: Practice breath regulation exercises and audible, deep "sighs." Short term: On the day of the hearing, slow down to a methodical, slow saunter using deep breaths. When nerves start, exhale on a loud, audible sigh (in private). As you stand to deliver the argument, sigh silently as you approach the podium, have a glass of water at the edge of counsel's table ready if needed, breathe regularly with easy inhalation (do not take huge, deep breaths). Take an extra moment to settle yourself and your notes at the podium.
Nausea	Eat a low-acidic meal and consult your doctor for anti-acid medications, if needed.
Posture collapse	Long term: Practice strengthening your overall posture and stance so a habit of good alignment is formed. Stand against a wall. Short term: Pick a starting "home base" beforehand and practice your beginning at that home base every time you rehearse the argument.

(Continued)

IDENTIFYING AND IMPROVING NERVOUS TELLS	
PROBLEM	**SOLUTION**
Upward inflection and increased filler pattern	Highlight the operative words in each phrase, but avoid choosing the last word in any sentence. Practice voice pitch inflection at each highlighted operative word. Audio-record the first minute of your presentation, checking for upward inflection. Re-record until the right amount of stress is put on the highlighted operative words.
Shaking hands	Flex opposite muscle groups (if your hands begin to shake, flex muscles in your legs or buttocks). Start the hearing by holding a prop (pen or eyeglasses). Choose a starting home base that rests your hands on either side of the podium. Do a finger-tension exercise (stretch fingers out and hold tension, then quickly release; repeat).
Quivering voice	If you hear the quiver, slightly lower pitch and increase volume. As you stand to deliver your argument, tip your chin and yawn with your mouth closed to stretch out throat and release tension in those muscles.
Sweating face	In the morning before the hearing, apply a clear, mattifying, sweatproof primer makeup.
Foggy brain and/or forgetfulness	Memorize the first and last five lines cold, until you can do it in your sleep. Consider memorizing transitional lines between sections.
Loss of breath control	Before you stand up, tip your head down and yawn with your mouth closed to open the throat muscles that control the voice box. When approaching the podium, use silent sighs to rush breath out. Between questions, take a short pause before answering. Effortlessly inhale before answering any question. Train yourself to inhale and immediately speak instead of holding breath at the top of the phrase.
Supersonic speed	Long term: Use a metronome or a metronome application on a smartphone (such as Pro Metronome) to regulate your rehearsal vocal speed at 155 beats per minute (allegrissimo, at 4:1 on the metronome setting). Short term: Be a slave to punctuation. At all commas and periods, take a silent pause.
Filler words (um, ah, er, and, so)	Long term: Train yourself to compress your thumb and forefinger on one hand every time you reach a punctuation mark. As you gently squeeze your fingers, it should cue you to take a breath that replaces the filler. Through repetition, you create a physical cue to link the inhalation with the pause at the punctuation. Short term: Be a slave to punctuation. At all commas and periods, take a silent pause.

(Continued)

National Institute for Trial Advocacy

IDENTIFYING AND IMPROVING NERVOUS TELLS	
PROBLEM	**SOLUTION**
Unnecessary movement	If you rock back and forth, place feet slightly "pigeon toed." If you sway side to side, place one foot slightly in front of the other to prevent this frustrating movement.
Fidgeting (hair flipping, wardrobe adjustments, pen clicking, coin jingling)	Use a prop to focus your nervous energy. Plan specific gestures that you synchronize with pre-chosen words. Write these in the margins of your notes. Any physical distractions (long hair in face, pocket full of coins) should be controlled. Empty your pockets.
Eyes that drift/roll up and out	Train yourself to look down (almost pretending to consult notes). Sweep eyes down to your page, capture a line of text, reconnect with the judge, and deliver the text.
Red neck from nerves	Choose clothing that hides it, e.g., a turtleneck, tie, or scarf.

Chapter Fifteen: Practice Your Argument Early and Often

PREPARED SUBSTANCE CHECKLIST	
Delivered a memorable theme(s)	☐
Told judge(s) relief or action needed	☐
Tied the requested relief with the cause of action	☐
Provided a road map with two or three succinct arguments	☐
Concisely recounted only the necessary law and facts	☐
Presented public policy argument	☐
Knew the record	☐
Organizational structure was easy to follow; strongest argument first	☐
Welcomed questions	☐
Effectively answered questions	☐
Used questions to advantage	☐
Transitioned from answers to strong points	☐
Empathized with judge's concern	☐
Chose a pathway for explanations	☐
Appealed to the concerns of the court	☐

VOICE CHECKLIST	
Regulated breath	☐
Used good vocal quality	☐
Projected voice	☐
Articulated clearly	☐
Controlled inflection	☐
Used appropriate overall pace	☐
Varied speed for meaning	☐
Paused effectively	☐
Exhibited varied range	☐
Stressed operative words	☐
Monitored qualifier patterns	☐
Avoided fillers	☐

BODY LANGUAGE CHECKLIST	
Aligned posture	☐
Used confident home bases	☐
Gestured for emphasis	☐
Used substantive gestures	☐
Avoided repetitive gestures and fidgeting	☐
Began with warm and engaging facial expression	☐
Matched facial expressions with operative words and tone	☐
Varied facial expression	☐
Maintained appropriate eye contact with judge	☐
Referred to notes appropriately	☐
Managed listening posture	☐
Used room space effectively (podium, table)	☐

EMOTION CHECKLIST	
Appeared confident	☐
Controlled nerves	☐
Matched tone with themes	☐

(Continued)

EMOTION CHECKLIST	
Appeared likable	☐
Welcomed questions	☐
Listened to judge	☐
Engaged judge(s)	☐
Controlled reaction to judge	☐

Chapter Sixteen: Remote Arguments: The New Normal?

Remote Hearing Checklist	
☐ Check the court rules	☐ Webinar platform?
	☐ Court-ordered background?
	☐ Rules on using mute and stop-video function?
	☐ Speaking order of attorneys/judges?
	☐ How to handle interruptions?
	☐ Pre-submitted exhibits?
☐ Sound system	☐ Need for headset, earbuds, or lavalier microphone?
	☐ Pillows or towels for better acoustics?
	☐ Turn off all app notifications
☐ Video	☐ Camera at slightly higher than eye level
	☐ Background interesting but not distracting
	☐ Natural or soft lighting behind computer
	☐ No backlighting
☐ Comfort with technology?	
☐ Courtroom and comfortable attire	
☐ Checklist of opposing counsel's arguments	
☐ Checklist of responses to questions	
☐ Mount notes and support systems necessary for smooth delivery.	
☐ Equipment checks	☐ One week before court
	☐ A few days before court with court staff
	☐ One hour before hearing

APPENDIX B

COLLECTED EXERCISES

Chapter Three: Preparing for Your Argument

> **Exercise**
>
> Practice reducing a written argument into an oral argument. Pick a written motion or response you have authored. Choose the strongest argument for oral delivery. Boil down the argument into a simple, understandable form. Practice delivering this argument in ninety seconds. (*Hint*: A regularly paced delivery should be 160 words per minute.) Can you give the reasons why you win in sixty seconds? In thirty seconds? Take the same argument and change the wording or angle so it does not sound the same. This accordion exercise will force you to choose only the pivotal facts needed, and then allow you to add context and essential details, all in keeping with a tight time frame.

> **Exercise**
>
> Practice identifying inconsistent arguments. Take the following example and note at which step you think the original and strongest argument loses strength.
>
> STEP 1: There was no meeting of the minds for the contract.
>
> STEP 2: If you find there was a meeting of the minds, then there was no consideration.
>
> STEP 3: If you find there was consideration, then the contract is ambiguous.
>
> STEP 4: If you find the contract is not ambiguous, then it is void because of impossibility of performance.

Exercise

Before your next argument, argue aloud the other side's case. Say the arguments with conviction. Now, plan how you will respond to these arguments. Are they all worthy of a response? If not, which are? Build your counterarguments.

Chapter Five: Facts

Exercise

Read trial court or appellate court opinions. Begin with the facts. After reading the facts but before the analysis, try to decide who won. Consider what facts brought you to your conclusion, and then check to see if you guessed correctly.

Exercise

For every case, practice both zeroing in on the facts and staying broad. Do this once a month. To zero in on the facts, set a three-minute timer for yourself and describe the facts in detail. To stay broad, retell the same set of facts in thirty seconds and force yourself to select the key facts. Audio-record yourself and listen for ways you can eliminate extraneous facts and summarize others.

Exercise

Practice telling the plot of a movie or TV show in thirty seconds, then in three minutes. Plan where you will slow down your rate of speed for emphasis, and where you will speed up to show enthusiasm and conviction. Time your deliveries. Once satisfied with your ability to manipulate speed effectively, switch topics to the facts of one of your cases.

Chapter Six: The Law

Exercise

Take one legal theory from an argument and spontaneously deliver it out loud, trying the different organizational options set out in Chapter Six. Keep the deliveries crisp. Decide what style best fits the particular legal theory.

Exercise

Take one legal theory from a brief and draft three different ways to present the theory:

1) Complicated

2) Over-simplified

3) Simplified

Exercise

Choose a legal theory within your motion or reply brief. Read the legal argument out loud as you record the delivery. Re-record the argument a second time, describing the legal theory in a dramatically different and conversational tone—as if you were describing the theory to your best non-attorney friend. Limit this conversational delivery to two minutes. After you listen to yourself, ask, "How will the judge talk to a friend or spouse about the case? Her staff? Which version could she easily remember and replay in her head?"

If possible, call one colleague unfamiliar with your case. (A phone call will prevent non-verbal influences from changing your colleague's interpretation of the message.) Tell her you want her to listen to a legal argument and resist taking notes during your delivery. Read aloud the section of your papers that describes the legal theory you have chosen. Call a second colleague unfamiliar with the case. Ask him, too, to listen to a legal argument and resist taking notes during your delivery. Read your simple, conversational delivery—of no more than two minutes—to your second colleague. Wait a few hours and call both colleagues independently. Ask them how much they remember from the description delivered earlier in the day and write down their responses. Compare the difference in the remembered content.

Exercise

Audio-record yourself discussing the facts of a case, then discuss a legal theory of the case. If you detect a noticeable difference in your vocal delivery, identify the change and practice saying the facts and law until both are discussed with the same vocal style.

Now video-record yourself discussing the facts of the case, then discuss a legal theory of the case. If you detect a noticeable difference in your body language, then identify the change and practice delivering the facts and the law until the same body language is used for both.

Chapter Seven: The Questioning Formula

Exercise

In everyday conversations, practice a pause pattern before answering questions. During the two-second silent pause, ask and answer to yourself two key questions: *What are they asking? Where do I go after I directly answer?*

Friend: "Did you like the BBC version of Pride and Prejudice?"

[You, internally: Pause, and ask yourself, *What is he asking?* I know him well. He is interested in the quality of the acting. *Where do I go after I directly answer?* I'll discuss Colin Firth's performance.]

You, aloud: "Yes. It's my favorite version of Pride and Prejudice. Colin Firth is the perfect Darcy."

Exercise

Practice in front of a mirror the "I don't know" response.

- Is your posture confident?

- Are you slumping your shoulders?

- Have you practiced the words "I don't know" enough so you do not stumble over them?

- Are you maintaining the volume of your voice?

- Are you avoiding the upward inflection of your voice, so you do not sound like you are asking a question?

- Do you look and sound confident?

Practice this exercise until your responses are automatic and you look comfortable with saying you do not know.

Chapter Ten: Appeals to the Concern of the Judge

Exercise

Plan your next motion hearing. Fill out the spectrum graph and table. Decide how to tailor your argument to the judge.

Chapter Eleven: Structure and Note Preparation Systems

Exercise

Practice the beginning of your argument. Time yourself. Begin with a three-minute opening, gradually reducing it to ninety seconds then thirty seconds.

Exercise

Think about an upcoming hearing you have. Why is it fair for your client to win? Draft and deliver a one-minute argument on why the fair result is a ruling for your client.

Apply the same appealing to the court's interest to clean his docket. Why would a ruling for your client lead to a quicker resolution of the case?

Exercise

Take a case that you have argued, or will, and reduce it to a three- to five-word phrase. Practice arguing, using each word as a cue.

Chapter Twelve: Rebuttals

Exercise

Create a rebuttal checklist for your next hearing.

Exercise

Pick a current case. Take one of the main themes and develop a sports analogy to help a listener understand the theme.

Chapter Thirteen: "Now That I Know What to Say, How Do I Say It?"

Exercise

Before an argument, practice your opening out loud in a space that allows you to replicate the expected distance between you and the bench. If you struggle with projection, consider enlisting a colleague to sit in the judge's position, get their "live" feedback on volume, and adjust.

To increase volume safely, breathe with diaphragm support. When audiences cannot hear you, they will tune out. When you speak too loud, audiences will be annoyed or perceive that you are shouting at them.

Adjust volume using your diaphragm, controlling the inflow and exhale of breath that fuels your voice box. Make certain that you are using your diaphragm while breathing by placing your hand above your abdomen between your ribs. When you inhale, that area should expand; when you exhale, the area should return to normal. Practice changing and adjusting your volume; you will develop muscle memory and better regulate your volume based on the acoustical needs of the setting. Noticing when to adjust volume is critical. Watch for nonverbal cues from the court to help you know when to dial up or down. The table below outlines a few nonverbal cues to look for to know whether to turn up or down your volume. Watch for a combination of these context clues and pivot in the moment.

Exercise

Practice greeting the court with calm, warm confidence by finding your natural pitch.

"Good morning, Your Honors." First, say this sentence in an abnormally high pitch. Next, deliver the sentence in an abnormally low pitch. Finally, deliver it in the middle—the natural pitch of your voice.

Exercise

Say: "I would like to go to the grocery store today." Inflect on the word *like*. Now inflect on *grocery* or *store*. Notice the difference in your inflection pattern.

Exercise

Say the following sentence out loud: "Judge, Washington Bank will close the deal in October." Your voice determines the operative words in the sentence for the listener and depending on the word emphasized changes the meaning of the sentence. If timing is important, you would stress the word *October*. Say the sentence with that word stressed. If the finality of the deal is important, you could stress *close the deal*.

Exercise

To improve your posture, stand with your back to a wall. Align ears, shoulders, hips, knees, and ankles in one straight line. Balance your weight equally on each leg. Now move from the wall, keeping the same alignment.

Exercise

To find your seated home base, place both feet firmly on the floor forming a ninety-degree angle at the knees. Do not lean forward or back. Place your hands or your arms below the elbow on the table. Avoid tightly clasping your hands so there is no impediment to your gestures. Do not cross your arms at your chest.

Once you find solid home bases, both standing and seated, practice transitioning in and out of each home base, eventually gesturing in and between these positions. Moving from base to base prevents you from looking like a statue.

Exercise

Choose a comfortable stance and place a piece of paper under one foot during a moot or practice session. See if the lodged paper keeps you grounded in the chosen stance and avoids the pacing habit.

Exercise

Stand up in front of a mirror. Do all the bad habits listed in Chapter Thirteen, one at a time. Say goodbye to those positions. Now, find three comfortable home bases from the table provided, and practice moving in and out of all three.

Chapter Fourteen: The "It Factor"

Exercise

Watch the ten-minute YouTube video of Oprah Winfrey's acceptance speech for the Cecil B. DeMille award in 2018 in the middle of the *MeToo* movement.[11] Whether you believe in her cause or not, ask yourself, does she believe in it? What makes you think so? What does she do to convince you of that? Notice the strength she exudes with the lack of movement of her body. Notice that her facial expressions match the content of her message; at one time she was so touched that she looked like she was about to cry. See how she connects to her audience through eye contact and stories the audience can see. Watch when she puts her left hand in a fist. Listen for her pauses, and when she slows down her speech and speeds it back up. Listen for the changes in her volume. Is her enthusiasm contagious?

Now record yourself talking about a topic that you are passionate about. What techniques do you use to show your conviction? Use your insights gained with this exercise to develop your own style.

Chapter Sixteen: Remote Arguments: The New Normal?

Exercise

Read one or two great poems. Notice the brevity, yet precision detail of the master wordsmith. Pay attention to the emotions evoked. If you are at a loss for a poem to read, try Maya Angelou's "I Know Why the Caged Bird Sings."[12]

---

11. https://www.youtube.com/watch?v=TTyiq-JpM-0
12. Maya Angelou, I KNOW WHY THE CAGED BIRD SINGS (1969). Text of the poem is available at https://www.poetryfoundation.org/poems/48989/caged-bird (last visited February 4, 2021).

Exercise

Say some of these short tongue twisters. Begin saying them slowly and gradually increase the pace.

She sees cheese.

Truly rural.

Rarely leery, rarely Larry.

Fresh fried fish.

Exercise

Rehearse in front of a mirror. Notice your facial expressions. Put on your neutral, enthusiastic, or serious face. See how these faces look and feel.
